Fuzzy Logic
and NeuroFuzzy
Applications in
Business and Finance

Also by Constantin von Altrock:

Fuzzy Logic and NeuroFuzzy Applications Explained
Prentice Hall PTR, 1995
ISBN: 0-13-368465-2

Fuzzy Logic and NeuroFuzzy Applications in Business and Finance

Constantin von Altrock

To join a Prentice Hall PTR Internet mailing list, point to:

http://www.prenhall.com/register

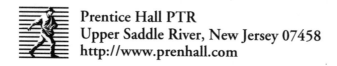

Prentice Hall PTR
Upper Saddle River, New Jersey 07458
http://www.prenhall.com

Library of Congress Cataloging-in-Publication Data

Von Altrock, Constantin.
    Fuzzy logic and neuroFuzzy applications in business and finance /
    Constantin von Altrock.
       p.   cm.
    Includes bibliographical references and index.
    ISBN 0-13-591512-0
    1. Business—Data processing. 2. Finance—Data processing.
    3. Fuzzy logic. 4. Neural networks (Computer science).   I. Title.
    HF5548.2.V66   1996
    650'.01'511322—dc20   96-26948
                                           CIP

Editorial/Production Supervision: Craig Little
Acquisitions Editor: Bernard M. Goodwin
Manufacturing Manager: Alexis R. Heydt
Cover Design: Lundgren Graphics
Cover Illustration: Andreas Schiebel
Cover Design Director: Jerry Votta
Interior "Fuzzy Logic Flag" Art: Gail Cocker-Bogusz

*fuzzy*TECH is a registered trademark of Inform Software Corporation. The *fuzzy*TECH Demo Edition is
under the copyright of Inform Software Corporation. The executable code of the software may not be
modified. Commercial use or any exhibition with other commercial software may only be made when
authorized by Inform Software Corporation.

MATLAB and SIMULINK are registered trademarks of The MathWorks, Inc., 24 Prime Park Way,
Natick, MA 01760, (508) 653-1415.

MS-Excel, MS-Access, MS-Visual Basic, MS-Windows, and MS-DOS are trademarks or registered
trademarks of Microsoft Corporation.

All other product names mentioned herein are trademarks of their respective owners.

The publisher offers discounts on this book when ordered in bulk quantities.
For more information, contact:

    Corporate Sales Department, Prentice Hall PTR, One Lake Street, Upper Saddle River, NJ 07458
    Phone: 800-382-3419, FAX: 201-236-7141, E-mail: corpsales@prenhall.com

Printed in the United States of America

10 9 8 7 6 5 4 3 2

ISBN 0-13-591512-0

Prentice-Hall International (UK) Limited, *London*
Prentice-Hall of Australia Pty. Limited, *Sydney*
Prentice-Hall Canada Inc., *Toronto*
Prentice-Hall Hispanoamericana, S.A., *Mexico*
Prentice-Hall of India Private Limited, *New Delhi*
Prentice-Hall of Japan, Inc., *Tokyo*
Simon & Schuster Asia Pte. Ltd., *Singapore*
Editora Prentice-Hall do Brasil, Ltda., *Rio de Janeiro*

Contents

4 Integration of Fuzzy Logic with Standard Software 203

5 Case Studies of Fuzzy Logic Applications 263

Preface

A crucial factor in competing in business in the 21st century will be clever use of information technology. Today's information technology systems are mostly data and communication tools for human workers. Tomorrow's information technology systems will be able to do more: automate decisions, intelligently analyze large amounts of data, and learn from their mistakes. Such systems need to have a better way of representing the logic and rationale behind human thinking. Central to this revolution will be finding a way to program a computer to express human-like decisions and evaluations in human language. For this you need fuzzy logic.

In this book, I take the practitioner's approach to fuzzy logic and NeuroFuzzy techniques. I will explain all elements of fuzzy logic system design using case studies of real-world applications—no formulas, no complex math, just everything you need for a hands-on start. Roll up your sleeves, and I will guide you step-by-step through fuzzy logic and NeuroFuzzy design on your PC. On the attached CD-ROM you will find a simulation-only version of a professional fuzzy logic design software and the source code of many real-world case studies I discuss. In just hours, these tools will get you design solutions without programming.

I would like to thank the "fathers" of fuzzy set theory, Lotfi Zadeh, Hans Zimmermann, and Enrique Ruspini, who introduced me to fuzzy logic in 1983, for their continuous support and encouragement of my work. I would also like to thank everyone at the Fuzzy Technology division of INFORM Software Corp. for their innovative and productive work on the *fuzzy*TECH software tools and customer application projects. In particular I would like to thank Adrian Weiler, who gave me the chance to build up the Fuzzy Technology division in 1990, and Bernhard Krause, who built up the business unit with me.

Constantin von Altrock
M.Sc.E.E., M.O.R.

Foreword

The past few years have witnessed a rapid growth in the number of books dealing with fuzzy logic, neurofuzzy systems, and their applications. But Constantin von Altrock's *Fuzzy Logic and NeuroFuzzy in Business and Finance*, or FLNBF for short, has the distinction of being the first in its field. Furthermore, like von Altrock's earlier book *Fuzzy Logic and NeuroFuzzy Applications Explained*, FLNBF is intended for computer-literate readers and is, in the main, an exposition of case studies, interspersed with insightful discussions of those basic concepts and techniques that are of direct relevance. I for one am highly impressed by von Altrock's expository skills, his keen understanding of both theory and practice, and his amazing ability to collect substantive data about systems whose detailed characteristics are hidden from view under the cloak of proprietary information.

FLNBF stresses the rule-based approach—an approach in which fuzzy logic is used as a quasi-programming language for manipulating fuzzy if-then rules and linguistic variables. As a branch of fuzzy logic, the rule-based approach is largely self-contained and easy to comprehend because it is close to human intuition. Furthermore, the rule-based approach is the fastest way of mastering those parts of fuzzy logic that are of direct relevance to applications in the realm of consumer products, industrial systems, and business and finance.

Applications of fuzzy logic and neurocomputing to business and finance have mushroomed during the past two years. The rationale for such applications is discussed with insight and authority in FLNBF. In what follows, I should like to add a few comments of my own.

The heart of the applications of quantitative methods to business and finance is decision analysis. Decision analysis as we know it today is rooted in the pioneering work of von Neumann, Morgenstern, Wald, Robbins, and others in the late '40s, '50s, and '60s. The pioneers were mathematicians and their premise was that it is possible to construct a theory of decision-making that has an axiomatic foundation and is prescriptive in spirit.

With the passage of time and accumulation of experience, it is becoming increasingly clear that real-world decision-making is much too complex, too uncertain, and too imprecise to lend itself to precise, prescriptive analysis. It is this realization that underlies the rapidly growing shift from conventional techniques of decision analysis to techniques based on fuzzy logic, neurocomputing, genetic computing and, more generally, on what I call "soft computing."

In essence, soft computing is a consortium of methodologies that are tolerant of imprecision, uncertainty, and partial truth. At this juncture, the principal constituents of soft computing are fuzzy logic, neurocomputing, genetic computing and probabilistic reasoning. The effectiveness of soft computing depends in large measure on the availability of software tools and hardware resources. This is the basic assumption that underlies the approach used by von Altrock in FLNBF.

A point that is of special importance is that the constituent methodologies in soft computing are for the most part complementary rather than competitive. As a consequence, it is frequently advantageous to employ the constituent methodologies in combination rather than singly, giving rise to so-called hybrid systems. Today, the most visible systems of this type are neurofuzzy systems. This is the reason why neurofuzzy systems play an important role in FLNBF.

Within soft computing, the principal contribution of fuzzy rests on fuzzification and granulation. Fuzzification—in a sense that is somewhat different from that employed in FLNBF—transforms a crisp set into a fuzzy set. Granulation, as its name suggests, approximates to a function or a relation by a collection of granules, that is, clumps of elements (fuzzy sets) that are drawn together by similarity or functionality. In fuzzy logic, fuzzification and granulation underlie the pivotal concepts of a linguistic variable and fuzzy if-then rule, and form the foundation for what might be called "computing with words."

Viewed in this perspective, Constantin von Altrock has succeeded to a high degree in presenting an authoritative, informative, and reader-friendly account of how fuzzy logic by itself and in combination with neurocomputing techniques can be applied in the realms of business and finance. Such applications are certain to grow rapidly in importance in the years ahead.

We owe to Constantin von Altrock our thanks and congratulations for authoring an innovative text that is leading the way. *Fuzzy Logic and NeuroFuzzy in Business and Finance* is must reading for anyone who has a serious interest in adding new tools to the armamentarium of decision analysis.

Lotfi A. Zadeh
Berkeley, California

Fuzzy Logic Primer

Fuzzy logic is a new and innovative technology, one that over the past few years has already revolutionized the development of technical control systems:

■ In appliances, fuzzy logic saves energy and provides ease-of-use.

■ In automotive systems, it provides user-adaptability, so that the performance of the car is optimized for a personal driving style.

■ In industrial control systems, fuzzy logic simplifies complex automation tasks.

For a comprehensive explanation of such technical applications of fuzzy logic, refer to [41].

Although, engineering applications of fuzzy logic have gained much more public interest in the past than business and financial applications, an even larger potential exists here. Fuzzy logic provides an easy and transparent method for incorporating common-sense type reasoning. By introducing a means of coping with "soft facts," "soft criteria," and "fuzzy data," you can implement human-like decision making in your applications.

Many other books deal with the theoretical implications of fuzzy logic. This book is different. It develops case studies to show the uses and benefits of fuzzy logic. You may follow some of these case studies on your own PC using the simulation version of *fuzzy*TECH for Business software provided on the enclosed CD-ROM.

What Are the Applications?

Specifically, this book covers applications of fuzzy logic in business and financial applications including:

Finance:

- Score Card Extension
- Balance Sheet Auditing
- Dynamic Portfolio Control
- Creditworthiness Evaluation
- Customer Profitability Analysis
- Cash Control
- Risk Assessment
- Company Rating
- Stock and Currency Exchange Forecasting
- Fraud and Forgery Detection

Business:

- Sales Forecasting
- Inventory Optimization
- Marketing Model Evaluation
- Insurance Claims Assessment
- Premium Rating
- Cost/Benefit Analysis
- Customer Profiling
- Product Matching
- Database Queries
- Supplier Evaluation
- Quality Control

1.1   The Fuzzy Logic Benefit

Since its introduction 50 years ago, progress in electronic data processing has been primarily driven by technological revolutions (Figure 1). With first batch processing systems, users had to wait a long time before they got the output of their computations. The introduction of time-sharing systems has given users the benefit of accessing their data in real time. The introduction of networks and client/server systems have given users the benefit of accessing their data from nearly anywhere. Fuzzy logic gives the benefit of enabling software to make human-like decisions.

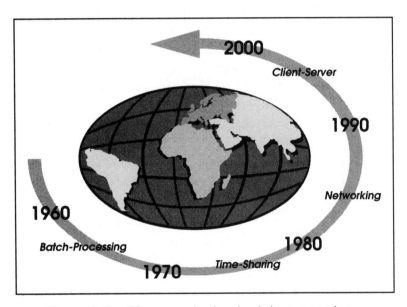

Figure 1: For 50 years, electronic data processing has been driven by technological revolutions

Why Must Software Make Decisions?

Enabling software to make human-like decisions yields many benefits:

■ For decisions that need to be made in large quantities, such as buy/sell decisions in a stock trading system, automation of decision making greatly expands capacity at a low cost.

■ Automation of decision making leads to a completely reproducible and consistent decision-making process.

■ Complex decision-making processes become transparent and can thus be explicitly evaluated and optimized.

■ The experiences of more than a single person can be agglomerated into one system.

Why Fuzzy Logic?

Conventional programming languages such as COBOL, C, or C++ are based on Boolean logic, the mathematical discipline computers stem from. Such programming languages are well suited to develop time-sharing, networking, and many other systems whose behavior can be well represented by mathematical models. However, to develop systems that mimic human-like decisions, mathematical models fall short. Human judgment and evaluation simply does not follow Boolean logic nor any other conventional mathematical discipline. Hence, conventional programming languages, being deeply tied to mathematical logic, are far from efficient when programming and are not sufficient for implementing human-like decision-making processes.

Fuzzy Logic's Underlying Principle

How can a logic which is "fuzzy" be useful? Professor Lotfi Zadeh, the founder of fuzzy logic, contends that a computer cannot solve problems as well as human experts unless it is able to think in the characteristic manner of a human being.

As humans, we often rely on imprecise expressions like "usually," "expensive," or "far." But the comprehension of a computer is limited to a black-white, everything-or-nothing, or true-false mode of thinking. In this context, Lotfi Zadeh emphasizes the fact that we easily let ourselves be dragged along by a desire to attain the highest possible precision without paying attention to the imprecise character of reality.

There are many subjects that do not fit into the precise categories of the conventional set theory: the sets "all triangles" or "all the guys named John" is easy to handle with conventional theory. Either somebody's name is John or its not. There is no other status in between. The set of "all intelligent researchers" or "all the people with an expensive car," however, is much more complicated and cannot be handled easily by a "digital" mode of thinking. This is because there is no way to define a precise threshold to represent a vague and blurry boundary. There are some obviously expensive cars, like the Rolls-Royce, but many other cars could easily fit into this category as well, depending on how much money you have, where you live, and how you feel!

Why fuzzyTECH for Business?

As previously mentioned, within conventional logic, terms can only be "true" or "false." Fuzzy logic allows for a generalization of conventional logic. It provides for terms between "true" and "false" like "almost true" or "partially false." Therefore, fuzzy logic cannot be processed directly on computers. It must be transformed by a special program called an "Inference Engine."

*fuzzy*TECH for Business provides such an Inference Engine, which can be either used alone or in an integrated form within other software packages (spreadsheets, databases, or application software on a PC, workstation, or mainframe). *fuzzy*TECH for Business features a complete graphical development environment by which an entire fuzzy logic system is developed without writing a single line of code. With *fuzzy*TECH for Business, you will be able to "draw" the system structure, all variables, and the rule sets just as you would draw with any other graphics program and your fuzzy logic system with all its components will be automatically created for you.

On the other hand, the subsequent tests and optimization procedures typically take more time and effort than the actual design of the fuzzy logic system. To make this step as efficient and comfortable as possible, *fuzzy*TECH for Business provides a complete set of visual tools. There are eight different debug modes to provide an optimum testing and simulation environment for all sorts of applications. In addition, there are also four graphical analyzer functions to support the verification of the rule sets through data.

You may use *fuzzy*TECH for Business stand-alone or in an integrated form in other software tools. If you use *fuzzy*TECH for Business stand-alone, you will be able to build complete systems by using the provided interfaces. But often fuzzy logic systems are integrated as subsystems. In that case, you can use *fuzzy*TECH for Business as a module in your own development environment, or you may wish to use one of the standard interfaces within Windows for software such as spreadsheets or databases. Section 4.1 explains this in further detail.

Within *fuzzy*TECH for Business, there is a "Fuzzy Design Wizard" that guides the developer step-by-step through building a system prototype. This allows a beginner to set up a fuzzy logic system without spending a lot of time getting to know the software. An experienced developer will be able to design the prototype of a complex system in just a few minutes.

Efficiency of the Fuzzy Inference Engine

*fuzzy*TECH for Business can process even large data sets in a very short amount of time. For instance, the code generator creates a fuzzy logic system with eight inputs and four outputs, each with seven terms and 500 weighted rules that can compute in just 0.4 milliseconds on a 486SX/33MHz PC. That means 2,500 decisions in just one second on a low-end PC.

1.1.1 Sample Applications

Three case studies are presented in this section as examples of how fuzzy logic can be applied in business and finance. These case studies are supplemented by the software and are treated in more detail in Section 4.

Case Study: Customer Profiling with MS-Access

In order to make direct marketing activities more efficient, it is necessary to have a clear definition of the target customers. For instance, if the target group is defined as *"fathers in their best years with an above average income,"* you must translate this into precisely defined selection criteria. These could be:

Selection Criteria of a Target Group:

Age: between 40 and 55

Children: at least one

Income: between $40,000 and $55,000

Unfortunately, such criteria are not plausible in some instances: a man of 38 years having 3 children and an income of $48,000 would belong to the target group but does not meet the selection criteria. Another man of 41 years having one child and an income of $41,500 will be selected by this database search even though he may not fit the target group as well as the first person.

To be sure that all the target persons are selected, one possibility is to make the selection criterion more liberal. However, the disadvantage of this solution lies in the fact that now there will be too many people selected who are not supposed to be in the original target group. In other words, if the conditions are too liberal, the selected group will be much bigger than desired, leading to wasteful marketing expenses. If the criteria are too strict, we will lose some target persons.

To resolve this conflict, a U.S. financial institution applied fuzzy logic in order to implement the target group selection process in the same way humans would make such decisions, that is, never by strict and fixed thresholds but by intuition and from past experiences. In this case, the fact that a person is 38 years old is not enough to prevent selection. Even though the other father at 41 years old fulfills the age condition, he may not be selected because he does not fit closely enough with the actual goal of *"fathers in their best years with an above average income."* Fuzzy criteria make such common-sense relationships between the conditions and the actual goal possible.

Combining Fuzzy Logic and a Database

The aforementioned expert uses *fuzzy*TECH in combination with a database server for profiling his customers. Three measures are used to classify the customers: personal background, financial background, and evaluation of residence location (a demographic indication of social status).

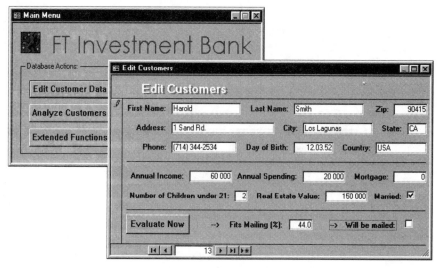

Figure 2: Database in combination with fuzzy logic: while collecting the data, you can select the button (Evaluate Now) and the system gives you the degree to which the customer fits into the desired group ("Fits Mailing"). It also makes the decision whether this degree is sufficient for a customer to be selected ("Will be mailed").

The first two measures include further criteria: the evaluation of personal data is based on details about age, number of children, and family status; and the evaluation of financial data is based on income, fixed expenses, real estate, and other properties.

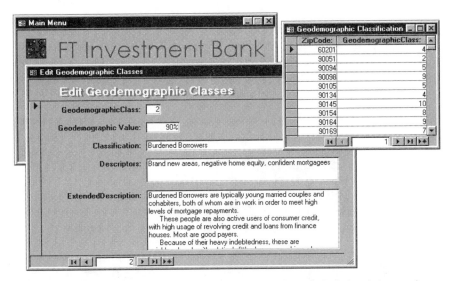

Figure 3: The demographic classification of social status is based on evaluation of a location and its typical inhabitants

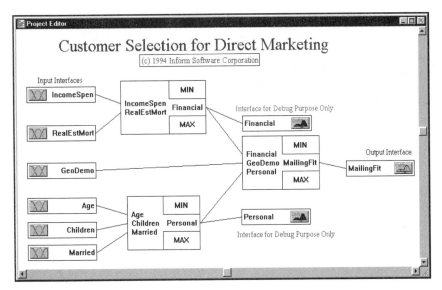

Figure 4: The structure of the customer profiling system. The function blocks on the right represent the six information inputs. The first two inputs show the prospect's financial status, the last three inputs the personal status. The output of the fuzzy logic system is the calculated degree ("MailingFit") to which a person belongs to the target group.

The fuzzy logic component of this system evaluates all of the social and financial inputs and computes the degree to which a customer belongs to a target group. According to a defined threshold for this degree, the system will select the desired group. Furthermore, there are also some analyzer functions with which you can, for example, calculate the number of persons selected relative to the value of the threshold.

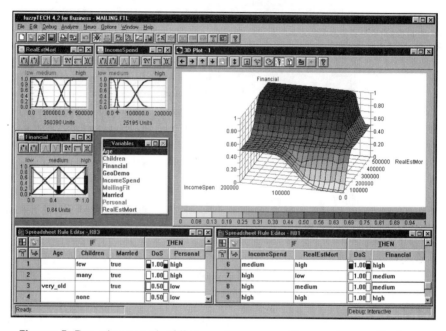

Figure 5: Development of the customer profiling system with *fuzzy*-TECH. The three small windows on the left side represent "fuzzy" criteria. The window underneath depicts some of the rules used in this project. The 3D plot shows one of the analyzing tools representing how the financial factor (vertical axis) depends on income and real estate properties (horizontal axis).

The developers required three man-months to design this fuzzy logic system and integrate it into their database on a mainframe. The system has been evaluated since November 1994. Thus far they estimate they have garnered a 10 percent improvement in the selection procedure. This means that up to 10 percent of the desired prospects would not have been selected by a conventional strategy, and also that up to 10 percent of the undesired ones would have been mistakenly selected without the fuzzy logic system.

Considering the expenses incurred for each single direct marketing activity, the fuzzy logic system amortizes after a short period of time. In the example of this case study, each direct marketing operation costs $300,000. Thus, $30,000 is saved with every direct marketing operation.

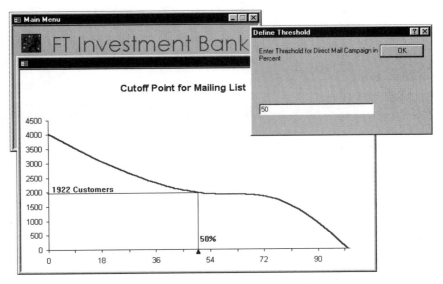

Figure 6: A statistical module visualizes how many customers are selected depending on the threshold.

Of course, there are numerous variations of this application possible. While there are excellent demographic databases available in the U.S., you might only rarely find an adequate one in Europe. In that case, you might consider evaluating the neighbors of the person as well, if your database is comprehensive enough.

Case Study: Evaluating Stocks Using MS-Excel

Decisions concerning stock activities are based on evaluation of incoming data that is time-dependent. Most profitable decisions are made by using recognizable trends. Successful business strategies benefit from solid and continuous trends with small losses through temporary ups and downs. The challenge of detecting continuous trends lies in distinguishing them from temporary ones in an automated form, since they are often not obviously distinct. The major goal of a decision support system is the detection of such trends.

There are various indicators and analyzing methods used to identify trends in different market situations. To have a useful system, it is not only important to merely detect the trends, but also that detection should occur early enough in order to take advantage of these trends. Only then will you be able to post a gain while a stock note shows a negative trend in general but is temporarily moving in a positive direction.

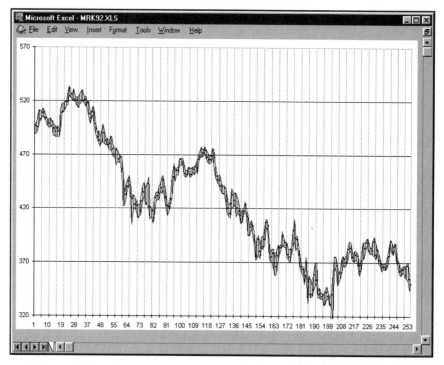

Figure 7: The course of the MRK stock is depicted as Low, High, Close, and Volume over a period of a year as displayed by Excel.

The available technical analyses are based on the assumption that a course prognosis can be determined by observing and analyzing the stock development. In spite of various efforts and the processing of countless observing methods, there is not yet confidence in the validity of this assumption.

The opposite method to the aforementioned is based on the "random-walk" theory, which understands a course development as a random progress. The backers of this theory assume that any course development depends on the previous position of the course but is independent of the bias of the progress. In other words, the best prognosis for tomorrow is the course of today. These ideas are not unknown within the strategy of technical analysis—a short-term prognosis can be included in medium- or long-term indicators—but this aggregation needs a flexible integration of the market and object-oriented strategies. These strategies are usually based on intuitive rules that are easily represented with natural linguistic rules. Fuzzy logic is the ideal way to accomplish this goal.

In the following case study, two indicators are chosen: the "Directional Movement Indicator" (DMI) from J. Welles Wilder, Jr. and the "Average Directional Movement" (ADX) indicator, which is derivable from the first one. These indicators, together with the trends of the day, will represent the parameters for the fuzzy logic system.

DMI assumes that a positive trend is indicated basically by the fact that the current "High" note for a specific stock is higher than it was the day before and a negative trend is indicated appropriately through the "Low" note. Medium-term prognoses about positive or negative trends are then computed by evaluating the normalization over all mean values of the ups and downs ("True Range") of the day.

ADX, on the other hand, provides an additional prognosis about the intensity of the current alternation by evaluating the normalized difference between the negative and the positive DMI.

The entire calculation of the indicators for this case study was performed within the Excel spreadsheet. Thus, it can be easily applied to concrete stock activities. Next we'll examine the integration of a fuzzy logic system for decision support that is based on these indicators. If the fuzzy logic system with its decision support is included in a Excel spreadsheet, it is possible to compare different strategies directly through an additional calculation. In this format, the comparison between different stocks and stock activities will also be easy to manage.

Microsoft Excel - MRK92.XLS

File Edit View Insert Format Tools Window Help

MRK	Date (d)	High (H)	Low (L)	Close (C)	Volume (V)	Marge 3	H(d)-H(d-1)	C(d)-C(d-1)	-DM	-DM	TR	Param -DM14	-DM
	01.07.1992	497.5	488.75	496.25	20753								
	02.07.1992	500	490	495	17225		2.5	1.25	2.5	0	10		
	06.07.1992	510	495	510	19157		10	5	10	0	15		
	07.07.1992	511.25	500	502.5	19690		1.25	5	1.25	0	11.25		
	08.07.1992	510	502.5	508.75	16317		-1.25	2.5	0	0	7.5		
	09.07.1992	512.5	506.25	508.75	16502		2.5	3.75	2.5	0	6.25		
	10.07.1992	511.25	503.75	503.75	9327		-1.25	-2.5	0	-2.5	7.5		
	13.07.1992	506.25	501.25	503.75	10781		-5	-2.5	0	-2.5	5		
	14.07.1992	502.5	496.25	500	13684		-3.75	-5	0	-5	6.25		
	15.07.1992	502.5	495	498.75	13042		0	-1.25	0	-1.25	7.5		
	16.07.1992	503.75	495	501.25	12869		1.25	0	1.25	0	8.75	1.75	-1.12
	17.07.1992	501.25	497.5	500	17374		-2.5	2.5	0	0	3.75	1.625	-1.04
	20.07.1992	498.75	487.5	493.75	16781		-2.5	-10	0	-10	11.25	1.5089	-1.68
	21.07.1992	497.5	487.5	491.25	16261		-1.25	0	0	0	10	1.4011	-1.56
	22.07.1992	495	486.25	493.75	12434		-2.5	-1.25	0	-1.25	8.75	1.3011	-1.54
	23.07.1992	496.25	487.5	491.25	8860		1.25	1.25	1.25	0	8.75	1.2974	-1.4
	24.07.1992	492.5	486.25	492.5	9388		-3.75	-1.25	0	-1.25	6.25	1.2047	-1.4
	27.07.1992	511.25	492.5	508.75	21820		18.75	6.25	18.75	0	18.75	2.458	-1.3
	28.07.1992	517.5	508.75	510	15622		6.25	16.25	6.25	0	8.75	2.7288	-1.22
	29.07.1992	517.5	510	512.5	17169		0	1.25	0	0	7.5	2.5339	-1.13
	30.07.1992	518.75	511.25	518.75	11433		1.25	1.25	1.25	0	7.5	2.4422	-1.05
	31.07.1992	518.75	515	518.75	8839		0	3.75	0	0	3.75	2.2678	-0.97
	03.08.1992	528.75	516.25	528.75	18217		10	1.25	10	0	12.5	2.8201	-0.90
	04.08.1992	533.75	526.25	531.25	18283		5	10	5	0	7.5	2.9758	-0.84
	05.08.1992	526.25	522.5	526.25	9081		-7.5	-3.75	0	-3.75	3.75	2.7632	-1.05
	06.08.1992	526.25	520	520	13145		0	-2.5	0	-2.5	6.25	2.5659	-1.1
	07.08.1992	531.25	520	521.25	15809		5	0	5	0	11.25	2.7397	-1.07
	10.08.1992	523.75	518.75	520	8790		-7.5	-1.25	0	-1.25	5	2.544	-1.06
	11.08.1992	522.5	515	520	11540		-1.25	-3.75	0	-3.75	7.5	2.3623	-1.27
	12.08.1992	523.75	513.75	513.75	11970		1.25	-1.25	1.25	-1.25	10	2.2829	-1.27
	13.08.1992	526.25	516.25	520	11375		2.5	2.5	2.5	0	12.5	2.2984	-1.18
	14.08.1992	528.75	518.75	528.75	9473		2.5	2.5	2.5	0	10	2.3128	-1.09

Figure 8: Trend indicators can easily be included in Excel tables.

Fuzzy Logic Integration in Excel

*fuzzy*TECH for Business provides for its integration into Excel via the "*fuzzy*TECH Assistant," through which all the necessary parameters for communication between the Excel tables and *fuzzy*TECH for Business can be set. Since the linkage is both for the input and the output of the fuzzy logic system, it can be viewed as an ordinary Excel function that combines cells the same way you would combine cells with mathematical operations.

The *fuzzy*TECH Assistant operates like the standard Excel Function Assistant. The allocation of the cells can be activated by simply clicking on the table. Once *fuzzy*TECH for Business is linked to the table, every change within the marked cells will automatically load the appropriate project and update the entries.

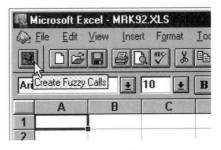

Figure 9: The *fuzzy*TECH Assistant integrates with Excel. It can be called by clicking on the *fuzzy*TECH icon or through the Excel menu.

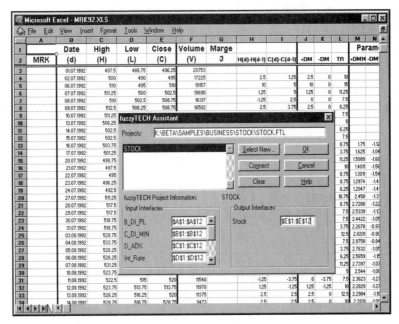

Figure 10: The *fuzzy*TECH Assistant links the cells of an Excel table directly with the variables of the fuzzy logic system.

The applied fuzzy logic system in this case study operates in two steps. First, the direction of the trend will be calculated from the two DMI values. Second, this direction will be combined with the indicator for the intensity of the current alternation (ADX) and the current trend. The computed linguistic variable "Stock" represents the actual decision. In the above example, the decision is made for "sell" with a firm gain prognosis.

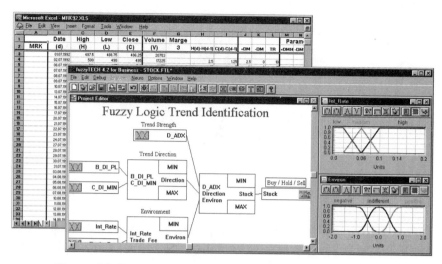

Figure 11: Trend identification by a fuzzy logic system.
All computations can be controlled by the analyzers
and visualization functions provided.

The temporary gains are correlated with the entire development of a specific stock. Even for extremely alternating stock developments, this fuzzy logic system has shown a good profit balance. For further literature on stock analysis and the trend factors used, refer to [42] and [6].

Case Study: Quality Control Using Visual Basic

In quality control applications, there are often various criteria to be combined for a single evaluation. It is also typical that these criteria cannot be put directly into mathematical relationships. In such cases, fuzzy logic usually offers fast and practical solutions.

In the following case study, a tire manufacturer has utilized *fuzzy*-TECH to optimize the properties of its tires. The fuzzy logic solution for this application comprises 17 input variables and 14 rule blocks for evaluating a tire. The output of this system, the actual evaluation, is just a single variable. The following represents only a portion of this fuzzy logic system showing the utility of this application.

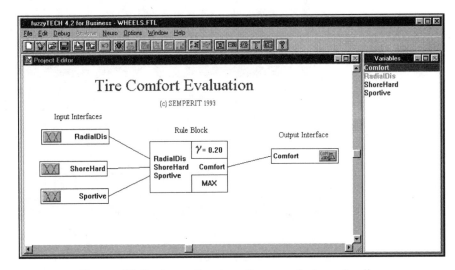

Figure 12: The MS-VisualBasic program reads the three input variables of the fuzzy logic system and invokes *fuzzy*TECH for Business to evaluate the tire quality.

Figure 13: System structure for comfort evaluation of the fuzzy logic quality control system.

For example, three variables are considered concerning comfort evaluation:

■ Radial displacement

■ Shore hardness

■ Sportiveness

Within this Visual Basic program, there is a function call that provides communication with *fuzzy*TECH for Business and controls the data exchange. Once the fuzzy logic project created in *fuzzy*TECH for Business is opened from the Visual Basic application, it can process data passed to it. For example, the Visual Basic application can let *fuzzy*TECH for Business calculate the comfort evaluation by passing the three input variables to the fuzzy logic system.

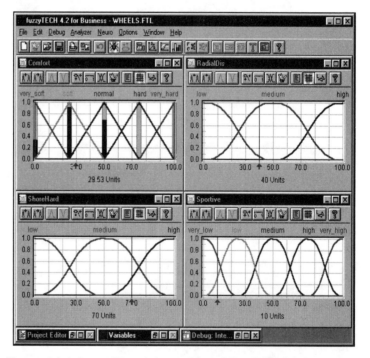

Figure 14: Interactive debugging of the fuzzy logic system via variable editors. The input values come either directly from Visual Basic or they can be entered manually by moving the small arrows below the appropriate variable editor.

The actual development of the fuzzy logic system takes place within *fuzzy*TECH for Business. In this case study, the four linguistic variables (three inputs, one output) are defined, followed by structuring of the fuzzy logic system via graphical editors. Finally, the rule blocks that connect the four linguistic variables can be defined. The actual strategy for comfort evaluation will be set through the rule bases.

*fuzzy*TECH for Business provides various analysis functions for optimizing and observing the decision behavior of the developed system. Once the desired fuzzy logic system is developed and optimized, *fuzzy*TECH for Business can run the fuzzy functions unnoticed by the end-user in background processing.

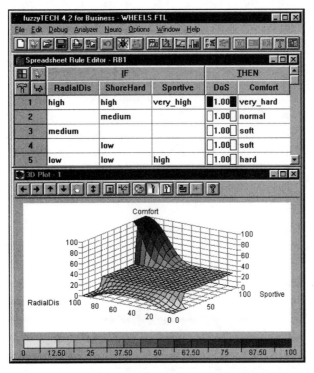

Figure 15: Interactive debugging of the fuzzy logic rules in table form and analysis of the decision behavior via 3D Plot.

As mentioned before, comfort evaluation is just a small portion of the entire fuzzy logic system for wheel quality control. Further details on this application are contained in [25].

All three case studies of this section are contained on the CD-ROM and treated in more detail in Section 4. In the following sections, the discussion involves the fundamentals of fuzzy logic and the methods necessary for building systems like those just described.

1.1.2 Types of Uncertainty

This section will introduce you to the basic principles of fuzzy logic. Reading this section is essential to understand how fuzzy logic systems work. Here, only the standard methods are introduced. Advanced fuzzy logic technologies are handled in Chapter 6.

Mathematical Principles of Uncertainty

Many mathematical disciplines deal with the description of uncertainties, for example, probability theory, information theory, and fuzzy set theory. It is most convenient to classify these disciplines by the type of uncertainty they treat. In this section, the discussion is confined to two types of uncertainty: stochastic and lexical. For a detailed treatise on different uncertainty theories, see [1, 26, 50].

Stochastic Uncertainty

Stochastic uncertainty deals with the uncertainty of the occurrence of a certain event. Consider Statement 1:

Statement 1
The probability of hitting the target is 0.8.

The event itself—hitting the target—is well defined. Close, but no cigar. The uncertainty in this statement is whether the target is hit or not. This uncertainty is quantified by a degree of probability. In the case of Statement 1, the probability is 0.8. Statements like this can be processed and combined with other statements using stochastic methods, such as Bayesian calculus of conditional probability.

Lexical Uncertainty

A different type of uncertainty lies in human languages, the so-called lexical uncertainty. This type of uncertainty deals with the imprecision that is inherent in most words humans use to evaluate concepts and derive conclusions. Consider terms such as "tall men," "hot days," or "stable currencies" that have no exact definitions underlying them. Whether a man is considered "tall" hinges on many factors. A child has a different concept of a "tall" man than an adult has. Also, the context and the background of a person making an evaluation play a role. Even for one single person, an exact definition on whether a man is considered "tall" does not exist. No law exists that determines the threshold above which a man is perceived as "tall." This would not make sense anyhow, since a law defining all men taller than 6' 2" (188 cm) to be "tall" would imply that a man with a height of 6' 1" (185.5 cm) is not tall at all.

The science that deals with the way humans evaluate concepts and derive decisions is psycho linguistics. It has been proven that humans use words as "subjective categories" to classify figures such as "height," "temperature," and "inflation." By using these subjective categories, things in the real world are evaluated by the degree to which they satisfy criteria.

Even though most of these concepts are not precisely defined, humans can use them for quite complex evaluations and decisions that are based on a variety of factors. By using abstraction and by thinking in analogies, a few sentences can describe complex contexts that would be very hard to model with mathematical precision. Consider Statement 2:

Statement 2
We will probably have a successful financial year.

At first glance, Statement 2 is very similar to Statement 1. However, there are significant differences. First, the event itself is not clearly defined. For some companies, a successful financial year means that they defer bankruptcy; for others it means to surpass last year's profit. Even for one company, no fixed threshold exists to define whether a fiscal year is considered successful or not. Hence, the concept of a "successful fiscal year" is a subjective category.

Another difference lies in the means of expressing probability. While in Statement 1 the probability is expressed in a mathematical sense, Statement 2 does not quantify a probability. If someone expresses that a certain type of airplane "probably" has problems, the mathematical probability can well be lower than 10 percent, which still justifies this judgment. If someone expresses that the food in a certain expensive restaurant is "probably" good, the mathematical probability can well be higher than 90 percent. Hence, the expression of probability in Statement 2 is a perceived probability rather than a mathematically defined probability such as that in Statement 1. In Statement 2, the expression of probability is just as subjective a category as "tall men."

Modeling Linguistic Uncertainty

Statements using subjective categories, such as Statement 2, play a major role in the decision-making process of humans. Even though these statements do not have quantitative contents, humans can use them successfully for complex evaluations. In many cases, the uncertainty that lies in the definition of the words we use adds a certain flexibility. For example, consider the annual wage increase negotiations between unions and industry representatives. Both sides want to achieve the same goal: an appropriate wage increase. The problem starts when they have to express in a percentage what they mean by "appropriate."

The flexibility that lies in the words and statements we employ is widely used in society. In most Western societies, the legal system consists of a certain number of laws, each of which describes a different situation. For example, one law could express that the theft of a car should be punished with two years in prison. Another law could define diminished responsibility. In one court case, the judge may have to decide the exact number of days in prison for a thief who stole a car while under the influence of a blood alcohol level of 0.1%, had a bad childhood, and was left by his spouse the day before. Since a specific law does not exist for each case, the judge has to combine all applicable laws to derive a fair decision. This is only possible due to the flexibility in the definition of the words and statements used in each law.

Fuzzy Logic as Human Logic

The basic idea is simple: in reality, you cannot define a rule for each possible situation. Exact rules (or laws) that cover the respective situation perfectly can only be defined for a few distinct situations. These rules are discrete points in the continuum of possible situations and humans approximate between them. Hence, in a given case, humans combine the rules that describe similar cases. This approximation is possible due to the flexibility in the definition of the words that constitute the rules. Likewise, abstraction and thinking in analogies is only rendered possible by the flexibility of "human logic."

To implement this human logic in system solutions, a mathematical model of human logic is required. Fuzzy logic has been developed as such a mathematical model. It allows the representation of human decision and evaluation processes in algorithmic form. There are limits to what fuzzy logic can do. The full scope of human thinking, fantasy, and creativity can not be mimicked with fuzzy logic. However, fuzzy logic can derive a solution for a given case out of rules that have been defined for similar cases. Thus, if you can describe in rules the desired decision context for certain distinct cases, fuzzy logic will effectively put this knowledge into a complete solution.

Fuzzy Logic vs. Probability Theory

People working extensively with probability theory have in particular denied the usefulness of fuzzy logic in applications. Even today, some claim conventional mathematical modeling techniques are sufficient to model human-like decision making. For example, author Jon Konieki wrote in *AI Expert* magazine in 1991:

> "...Fuzzy Logic is based on fuzzy thinking. It fails to distinguish between the issues specifically addressed by the traditional methods of logic, definition and statistical decision making...."

The founder of fuzzy logic, Lotfi Zadeh, attributes this criticism to the "hammer principle," which contends that if you have a hammer in your hand and it's your only tool, everything starts looking like a nail. The ensuing problem with this is that when you only want to put a frame on the wall, even a hammer and screw will work somehow. The danger then is that people develop more sophisticated and complicated hammers rather than looking for a more elegant and effective tool such as a screwdriver. Max Planck, who proclaimed his quantum theory in the year 1900 and won the Nobel price for his work, stated once:

> *"...A new scientific truth does not triumph by convincing its opponents and making them see the light, but rather because its opponents eventually die, and a new generation grows up that is familiar with it ...."*

Rather than continue this discussion here, I'll illustrate the difference between stochastic and linguistic uncertainty using Statement 3:

Statement 3

Patients suffering from hepatitis show in 60% of all cases high fever, in 45% of all cases a yellowish-colored skin, and in 30% of all cases nausea.

If you find such a statement in a medical textbook and you want to implement it in a system, it looks very easy at first glance. If you have a patient who suffers from high fever and nausea, but has normally colored, not yellowish skin, you can compute the probability for a hepatitis infection using Bayesian calculus.

Although this looks very easy, the problem begins when you have to define what a "high fever" is. If you read medical books or ask doctors, you will get an equivocal answer. Even if most doctors will agree that the threshold is about 102°F (39°C), this does not mean that a patient with a body temperature of 101.9°F does not at all have a high fever while another patient with one of 102°F does indeed have a high fever.

If such a sharp threshold is justified, the reverse must also exist. That is, that a very precisely measured body temperature will result in a very precise diagnosis. If this were true, you could measure your body temperature up to the fifth significant figure and expect a doctor to tell you, just from this very precise information, from what disease you suffer. That, however, is not the case. A doctor will get an accurate diagnosis not from the precision of a single parameter but rather from evaluating the parameters of many symptoms. Here, the precision of each parameter does not, for the most part, imply the quality of the result. If the doctor asks you whether you sweat at night, he is most likely not interested in the precise amount in ounces but rather in a tendency.

As Statement 3 illustrates, stochastic uncertainty and linguistic uncertainty are different. Stochastic uncertainty deals with the uncertainty of whether a specific event will take place, and probability theory lets you model this. In contrast, lexical uncertainty deals with the uncertainty of the definition of the event itself. Probability theory cannot be used to model this because the combination of subjective categories in human decision-making processes does not follow its axioms.

1.1.3 A "Fuzzy" Set

How can you model linguistic uncertainty adequately? If a doctor does not have a precise threshold in mind when evaluating whether a patient suffers from "high fever," how then does he work? Psycholinguistic research has shown that a doctor would compare the patient with two "prototypes." On one side, the "perfect" high-fever patient: pale, sweating, shivering. On the other side, the "perfect," balanced-temperature patient who does not show any signs of fever at all. Comparing with these two extremes, a doctor evaluates where his patient ranks in between the two.

How can this be modeled mathematically? Consider set theory, where you would first define the set of all patients with high fever. Then you define a mathematical function that indicates for each patient whether he is a member of this set or not. In conventional math, this indicator function has to uniquely identify each patient as either a member or non-member of the set. Figure 16 gives an example of the set of "patients with high fever" (black area), where the indicator function defines "high fever" as a temperature higher than 102°F.

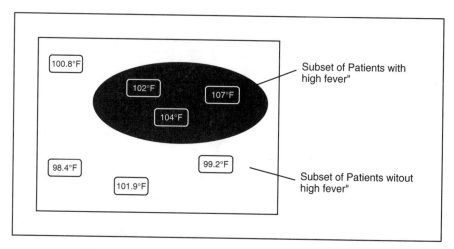

Figure 16: In conventional set theory, the set of "patients with high fever" is defined exactly by 102°F.

As pointed out before, instead of using this sort of rigid definition, a doctor evaluates the degree to which his patient matches the prototype of a high-fever patient. Figure 17 gives an example of a set where certain elements can also be "more-or-less" members. The "shade of gray" indicates the degree to which the body temperature belongs to the set of "high fever." This "shade of gray," which makes the black area in Figure 16 look "fuzzy," produced the name "fuzzy logic."

In Figure 17, each body temperature is associated with a certain degree to which it matches the prototype for "high fever." This degree is called the "degree of membership," $\mu_{HF}(x)$, of the element $x \in X$ to the set "high fever," HF. The body temperature is called a "base variable" x with the universe X. The range of μ is from 0 to 1, representing absolutely no membership to the set and complete membership to the set, respectively.

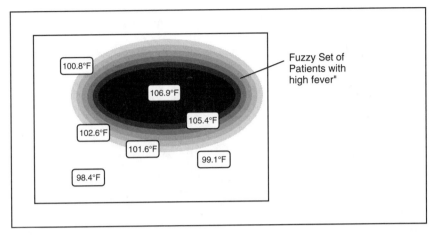

Figure 17: The "fuzzy" set of patients with a "high fever" also allows for elements that are "more-or-less" members of the set.

As a temperature of 94°F would have no membership at all, a temperature of 110°F would have complete membership to the fuzzy set HF. Temperatures in between are members of the set only to a certain degree. Example 1 shows a possible classification:

Example 1

$\mu_{HF}(94°F) = 0$	$\mu_{HF}(100°F) = 0.1$	$\mu_{HF}(106°F) = 0.9$
$\mu_{HF}(96°F) = 0$	$\mu_{HF}(102°F) = 0.35$	$\mu_{HF}(108°F) = 1$
$\mu_{HF}(98°F) = 0$	$\mu_{HF}(104°F) = 0.65$	$\mu_{HF}(110°F) = 1$

The degree of membership can also be represented by a continuous function. Figure 18 plots such a membership function. Note that a temperature of 102°F and a temperature of 101.9°F are evaluated differently, but just slightly and not as a threshold.

Note that fuzzy sets are a true generalization of conventional sets. The cases $\mu=0$ and $\mu=1$ for the conventional indicator function are just special cases of the fuzzy set. The use of fuzzy sets defined by membership functions in logical expressions is called "fuzzy logic." Here, the degree of membership in a set becomes the degree of truth of a statement. For example, the expression "the patient has a high fever" would be true to the degree of 0.65 for a temperature of 104°F.

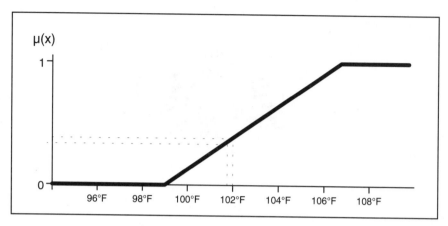

Figure 18: The degree, $\mu_{HF}(x)$, to which a temperature x
is considered to belong to the fuzzy set of "high fever," HF, can be
expressed as a continuous function.

The primary building block of any fuzzy logic system is the so-called linguistic variable. In a linguistic variable, multiple subjective categories are combined that describe the same context. In the case of fever, not only high fever but also raised temperature, normal temperature, and low temperature exist. These are called "linguistic terms" and represent the possible values of a linguistic variable "BodyTemperature." Figure 19 shows the membership functions for all terms of this linguistic variable plotted together.

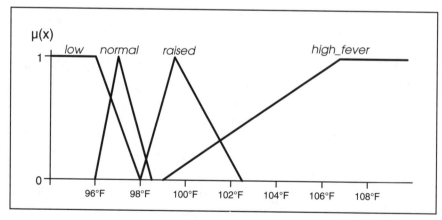

Figure 19: The linguistic variable "BodyTemperature"
translates real temperature values into linguistic values.

This linguistic variable now allows for the translation of a measured body temperature, given in degrees Fahrenheit, into its linguistic description. For example, a body temperature of 100°F would be evaluated as "significantly raised temperature, just slightly high fever." How to use this technology in system design is considered in the next section.

1.2 A Case Study on Fuzzy Logic Inference

In the past 30 years, a large number of methods using fuzzy sets have been developed. This book is restricted to the so-called "rule based" fuzzy logic technologies. Nearly all recent fuzzy logic applications are rule based. This section gives a brief introduction to the basic technology of rule-based fuzzy logic systems using as a case study the evaluation of financial liquidity of bank customers applying for loans. In Chapter 2, this case study is used to show you how you can design, test, and implement such systems using the enclosed software.

1.2.1 Financial Liquidity Evaluation Example

This case study is taken from an actual fuzzy logic system implemented in 1986 in Europe [19]. In the system, an evaluation of the creditworthiness of bank customers for consumer loans is derived from multiple financial and personal factors and used to decide whether a loan is granted or not. Figure 20 shows a simplified layout of the system's structure. A total of eight input variables are used for the evaluation. Note that the upper four input variables denote "hard facts," numbers that stem from inputs that are given numerically. The lower four input variables denote "soft facts," subjective evaluations of the applicant's personality and lifestyle.

The structure of the system is hierarchical; at each node, two elements are aggregated into a singular, new node. This makes three layers of abstraction. The first layer contains the elements Security, Liquidity, Potential, and Business Behavior, which each comprise the information of two input variables. Because information is condensed at each node, we speak of abstraction here. Similar to a human, who takes many input variables into account to come up with one abstract judgment, the aggregation hierarchy proceeds until the output node, Creditworthiness, is reached—the most abstract information in the hierarchy.

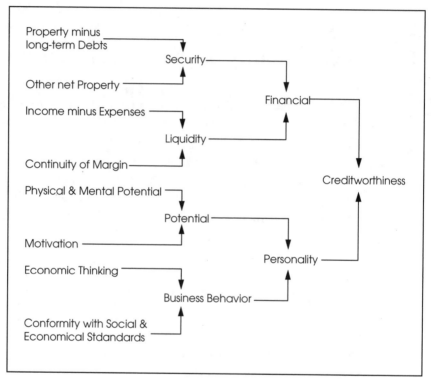

Figure 20: Aggregation hierarchy of a
fuzzy logic creditworthiness estimation.

In a way, such a hierarchical decision model "squeezes," step-by-step, the desired information on creditworthiness out of the raw data (the eight input variables).

While the design of such a decision hierarchy is relatively simple, it is difficult to decide how information should be combined at each node. For example, the node defining Liquidity uses the two inputs, Income minus Expenses and Continuity of Margin. Figure 21 magnifies the node. As stated in earlier sections, such an evaluation poses no problem for a human but is not easy to put into a mathematical model.

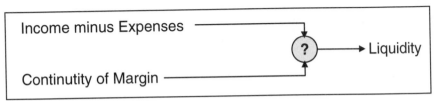

Figure 21: The Liquidity of a customer is evaluated
from Cash Flow Amount and its Continuity.

Table 1 shows four examples of customers. The Income minus Expenses is the annual value and the Continuity of Margin is a value
computed using statistical functions from the fluctuation of the Income
minus Expenses over past years. A continuity near 1 denotes a very
stable Income minus Expenses; a Continuity near 0 denotes a high
fluctuation.

Customer	Income minus Expenses	Continuity of Margin
DeMarco	$118,000	0.12
Pommerland	$45,700	0.71
Wang	$94,250	0.89
Beauchamps	$37,400	0.22

Table 1: Four sample customers.

1.2.2 Conventional Decision Support Techniques

For these types of decision models, a number of different techniques have been developed over the past few decades. This section presents the techniques that have gained most practical relevance.

Score Card Models

A common technique for mathematically modeling such types of decision-making systems is the score card technique. Here, each input variable gets assigned a number of points that quantify how much it adds to the value of the node. In a more complex score card scheme, many input variables are assigned a number of points depending on how much the respective input variable has a favorable value. Adding all numbers together yields a single number that expresses the overall evaluation.

In the example of the liquidity node shown in Figure 21, this technique verges on implausibility. For example, a customer that has no income and for whom this is a highly stable situation will score many points in continuity and none in income, resulting in a fair overall rating. This is an error that no human evaluator would commit and exemplifies one of the shortcomings of score card models. At a second glance, this is no surprise. How can one assume that the complexity of the human evaluation process can be mimicked by a scoring system that resembles that of a quiz show?

Using the example of Table 1, one could multiply the continuity value by 100 to get the continuity score and compute the score of the Income minus Expenses by the formula:

Income minus Expenses score :=
    (Income minus Expenses - $20,000) / $2,000

By doing so, the resulting scoring table is shown in Table 2. While at first glance the result looks plausible, there is one obvious problem: Customer Pommerland gets a pretty good ranking result even though his income is quite low. In contrast, a human credit expert would have ranked the liquidity of customer DeMarco higher, as his cash flow is much healthier than customer Pommerland's. Of course, one could reduce the impact of the continuity by giving it less weight in the decision process, but then one would lose discriminability. Also, once the score card model has grown to a certain size, fumbling at the weight factors of the scoring system tends to be more a "black art" than anything else.

Customer	Income minus Expenses Score	Continuity of Margin Score	Liquidity Score
DeMarco	49	12	61
Pommerland	13	71	84
Wang	37	89	126
Beauchamps	9	22	31

Table 2: Sample score card results.

In spite of the shortcomings of the score card model, it is widely used for various ranking applications ranging from real estate ranking, risk assessment, to company classification and many others. The reason for this is that all other conventional techniques for multi-criteria evaluations proved either too complex or too non-transparent for widespread commercial use. Fuzzy logic has the potential to change this situation. It eliminates the deficiencies of score card models while simultaneously delivering easy-to-handle transparent systems.

For more details on score card techniques, refer to [4].

Decision Tables

To overcome this scoring system problem, one can extend the system by including decision tables that provide an evaluation for certain combinations of input variables. Table 3 gives an example for such a decision table. The upper row represents possible intervals for the value of Continuity of Margin, the left column represents possible intervals for the value of Income minus Expenses. The values in the table fields then give the evaluation of Liquidity from any combination of Continuity and Income.

As can be found in Table 3, even the highest continuity will never result in being considered liquid if the income is below a certain line. On the other hand, even the highest income is only evaluated to medium liquidity, if it is highly non-continuous. Hence, such a decision table can represent human decision making quite accurately.

	0	0.1	0.2	0.3	0.4	0.5	0.6	0.7	0.8	0.9	1
-$20,000	0	0	0	0	0	0	0	0	0	0	0
$5,000	0	0	0	0	0	0	0	0	0	0	0
$30,000	0	0	0	0	0	1	1	1	2	2	2
$55,000	4	4	4	11	12	12	14	14	16	16	16
$80,000	12	12	12	17	27	30	45	48	48	48	48
$105,000	20	20	20	25	38	50	63	75	80	80	80
$130,000	32	32	32	39	50	62	73	83	88	88	88
$155,000	44	44	44	49	60	74	82	89	96	96	96
$180,000	50	50	50	55	68	80	88	97	100	100	100
$205,000	50	50	50	55	68	80	88	97	100	100	100
$230,000	50	50	50	55	68	80	88	97	100	100	100

Table 3: Decision table for Liquidity.

Thus, even a complex evaluation can be represented by a decision table, but this technique is impractical for other reasons. As a decision table enumerates all possible combinations of input variables in the intervals, it can get quite large. If, for example, you design a decision table with 5 input variables and 5 intervals each, the number of fields in this table is 5^5 or 3,125. Such a large table is impossible to create consistently and will be very hard to modify should the decision-making policy change. Even if one restricts the decision tables to two inputs for each node, the example shown by Figure 20 would require seven decision tables of the kind shown in Table 3.

Expert Systems

Before demonstrating how fuzzy logic can better handle modeling such an evaluation process, another technique that attempted in the past to provide solutions must be introduced: expert systems. Expert systems contain rules that can specifically address cases. For example, a customer with no or low cash flow is not considered liquid, no matter how continuos this financial situation is. Often, these rules are formulated in the "If-Then" format, such as:

(1) IF Income < $20,000 THEN Liquidity = 0.0

(2) IF $20,000 ≤ Income < $50,000 AND Continuity < 0.2 THEN Liquidity = 0.0

(3) IF $20,000 ≤ Income < $50,000 AND 0.2 ≤ Continuity < 0.4 THEN Liquidity = 0.2

(4) IF $20,000 ≤ Income < $50,000 AND 0.4 ≤ Continuity THEN Liquidity = 0.3

(5) IF $50,000 ≤ Income < $80,000 AND Continuity < 0.2 THEN Liquidity = 0.3

(6) …

The advantage of formulating rules rather than a table is that the intervals for the input variable values can be individually chosen for each rule. Hence, you need fewer rules than you would fields for a decision table. For example, rule (1) covers the 20 fields of the first two rows in the decision table shown in Table 3.

Even with this approach, some problems remain. First, the total number of rules necessary to design a system as complex as the one shown in Figure 20 would still be in the multiple hundreds. This is because each rule of an expert system can describe only one specific situation as identified by the condition intervals of the rule's premise. Hence, to have a smooth decision response, the discriminating factors chosen must evaluate the input domain with a high resolution, keeping the number of rules rather high. In contrast, humans do not use many rules designed for each and every situation, but rather they use rules that represent "tendencies" and "decisions in general." In these rules, no "hard" criteria such as "$20,000 ≤ Income < $50,000 AND 0.4 ≤ Continuity" exist. Rather, humans use "soft" criteria such as "medium income" or "high continuity," which can only be represented by fuzzy logic.

In expert systems, the criteria has to be hard because the rules are evaluated by a so-called inference engine that is based on Boolean logic. In Boolean logic, a statement can only be 100 percent true or 100 percent false, not "somewhat," "slightly," or "pretty much." The next section shows how the decision can be modeled by fuzzy logic rules.

For more details on expert systems and its fuzzy logic extensions, refer to [50].

1.2.3 Linguistic Decision Making

The last section showed that while "If-Then" rules are a transparent way to express human decision making, the hard facts stated by Boolean expressions in these rules make them inappropriate. Hence, most fuzzy logic applications make use "If-Then" rules but only in a way that is computed entirely differently from expert systems. Using fuzzy logic for this computation allows the use of "soft" facts. For example, a fuzzy logic rule could be:

(A) IF Income IS high AND Continuity IS medium THEN Liquidity IS high

At first glance, this rule (A) looks similar to rules (1) through (5) shown in Section 1.2.2. At second glance, they are very different. Just as Statements 1 and 2 of Section 1.1.2 look similar but convey an entirely different meaning, rules (1) through (5) represent a context that can well be described by conventional mathematics, while rule (A) cannot. Rule (A) uses words such as "high" or "medium" that are not as clearly defined as "$20,000 ≤ Income < $50,000." As discussed in Section 1.1.3, such concepts can be represented well as linguistic variables.

A linguistic variable translates a numerical value into a linguistic value. Just as the numerical description of a body temperature of 100°F (37.8°C) is translated into the linguistic description "significantly raised temperature, almost no high fever" by the linguistic variable shown in Figure 19, in the Liquidity assessment example, the numerical input variables Income and Continuity need to be translated into linguistic values. This step is called "fuzzification" since it uses fuzzy sets for this translation.

Figure 22 shows the complete structure of a fuzzy logic system. Once all input variable values are translated into respective linguistic variable values, the "fuzzy inference" step evaluates the set of "If-Then" rules that define the evaluation. The result of this is again a linguistic value for the linguistic variable Liquidity. For example, this linguistic result could be "a little less than medium." The so-called "defuzzification" step translates this linguistic result into a numerical value that represents the Liquidity as a number.

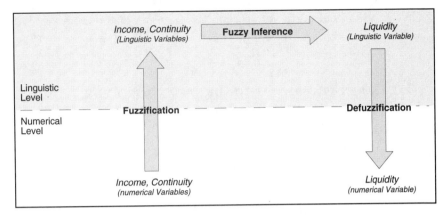

Figure 22: Structure of a fuzzy logic system for Liquidity Assessment.
The fuzzy logic computation consists of three steps:
Fuzzification, Fuzzy Inference, and Defuzzification.

The process is outlined in Figure 22. The decision process can better be described on a linguistic level using rules with soft facts, as rule (A) exemplifies. However, input information is given numerically and the output is required to be numerical, too. Thus, to compute the fuzzy logic rules, the two translation steps of fuzzification and defuzzification are required. These two translation steps are the cost involved in reaping the benefit of having rules that are computed in a human-like way. For both translation steps, a link between the numerical representation and the linguistic representation of a variable is needed. This link is the set of membership functions contained in each linguistic variable definition. Both fuzzification and defuzzification use the membership function definition to compute the translation step. The following sections illustrate how.

1.3   The Fuzzy Logic Algorithm

In a nutshell, fuzzy logic is a technology that translates natural language descriptions of decision policies into an algorithm using a mathematical model. This mathematical model consists of three major sections: fuzzification, inference, and defuzzification. These models and the underlying algorithms are discussed in the following three sections.

If you already understand the function of the fuzzy logic algorithm, you can skip the remainder of this chapter and move on to Chapter 2.

1.3.1 Fuzzification Using Linguistic Variables

Linguistic variables have to be defined for all variables used in the "If-Then" rules. As described in Section 1.1.3, possible values of a linguistic variable are called terms or labels. For the liquidity assessment example, the terms are:

Example 1

Linguistic Variable	Possible Values (Terms)
1. Income	∈ {low, medium, high}
2. Continuity	∈ {low, medium, high}
3. Liquidity	∈ {very_low, low, medium, high, very_high}

For every linguistic variable, each term is defined by its membership function. Figures 23 and 24 show possible definitions for the two input variables.

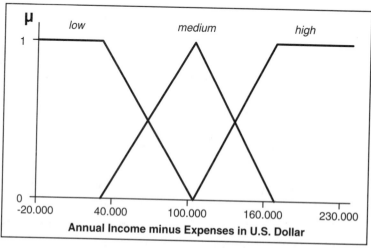

Figure 23: Linguistic variable "Income."

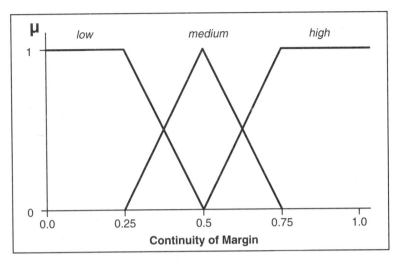

Figure 24: Linguistic variable "Continuity."

Consider the sample customers of Table 1. Table 4 shows how these numerical values could be translated into linguistic values.

Customer	Linguistic Value of Income minus Expenses	Linguistic Value of Continuity of Margin
DeMarco	{low=0, medium=0.85, high=0.15}	{low=1, medium=0, high=0}
Pommerland	{low=0.8, medium=0.2, high=0}	{low=0, medium=0.1, high=0.9}
Wang	{low=0.1, medium=0.9, high=0}	{low=0, medium=0, high=1}
Beauchamps	{low=1, medium=0, high=0}	{low=1, medium=0, high=0}

Table 4: Linguistic translation of the numerical customer data.

Note: the value of a linguistic variable can be expressed in two ways. One is as the vector of the degrees of membership to the fuzzy sets that define the terms of a linguistic variable. This is displayed in Table 4. Also, one can express this linguistic value using only words. The degrees of membership are then expressed by such words as "slightly," "almost," "little," "fairly," "rather," "very much," or "completely." Table 5 shows a possible linguistic interpretation of the values.

Customer	Linguistic Value of Income minus Expenses	Linguistic Value of Continuity of Margin
DeMarco	rather medium, little high	low
Pommerland	rather low, little medium	very much high, slightly medium
Wang	very much medium, slightly low	high
Beauchamps	low	low

Table 5: Linguistic interpretation of the values of Table 4.

Section 6.1 discusses how to design linguistic variables and their membership functions for a given application.

1.3.2 Fuzzy Logic Inference Using If-Then Rules

Now that all numeric input values have been converted to linguistic values, the fuzzy inference step can identify the rules that apply to the current situation and can compute the values of the output linguistic variables. As an illustration, Example 2 shows a subset of four rules:

Example 2

Rule α: IF Income = low THEN Liquidity = very_low

Rule β: IF Continuity = low AND Income = medium THEN Liquidity = low

Rule χ: IF Continuity = high AND Income = medium THEN Liquidity = high

Rule δ: IF Continuity = medium AND Income = high THEN Liquidity = medium

---

The computation of the fuzzy inference consists of two components:

■ Aggregation: computation of the IF part of the rules

■ Composition: computation of the THEN part of the rules

Aggregation

The IF part of rule χ combines the two conditions "Continuity = high" and "Income = medium." The IF part defines whether the rule is valid for the current case or not. In conventional logic, the combination of the two conditions can be computed by the Boolean AND, as shown in the following table:

A	B	A∧B
0	0	0
0	1	0
1	0	0
1	1	1

In the case of fuzzy logic, the Boolean AND cannot be used since it cannot cope with conditions that are "more-or-less" true. Hence, new operators have been defined for fuzzy logic to represent logical connectives such as AND, OR, and NOT. The first set of operators that has been proposed [47] are given below. These three operators are used in the majority of today's fuzzy logic applications:

AND: $\mu_{A \wedge B} = min\{ \mu_A, \mu_B \}$
OR: $\mu_{A \vee B} = max\{ \mu_A, \mu_B \}$
NOT: $\mu_{\neg A} = 1 - \mu_A$

Using the *min* operator to represent the logical AND, Example 3 shows how the IF parts of the rules of Example 2 would compute for Customer DeMarco.

Example 3

Rule α:	$min\{ 0.8 \} = 0.8$
Rule β:	$min\{ 0.0; 0.2 \} = 0.0$
Rule χ:	$min\{ 0.9; 0.2 \} = 0.2$
Rule δ:	$min\{ 0.1; 0.0 \} = 0.0$

These results are the degrees of truth of the IF parts and hence indicate how adequate for the current case each rule is.

Composition

Each rule defines the evaluation result for a certain prototypical case in the THEN part. The degree to which the evaluation result is valid is given by the adequacy of the rule for the current case. This adequacy is computed by the aggregation as the degree of truth of the IF part. Hence, rule α has the evaluation result "Liquidity = very_low" to the degree 0.8, and rule χ the result "Liquidity = high" to the degree 0.2.

Hence, the value of the linguistic variable "Liquidity" for customer DeMarco would be:

Liquidity = {very_low = 0.8, low = 0.0, medium = 0.0,
                        high = 0.2, very_high = 0.0}

A linguistic interpretation of this result could be "quite low, slightly high liquidity."

In some applications, a linguistic interpretation of the result is sufficient, for example, when the result is used to provide a verbal or qualitative answer. In other applications, a numerical value as output is required, for example, to rank cases or—as in the creditworthiness example—decide on acceptance or rejection of a credit application. In cases where a numerical output is required, a defuzzification step must follow the fuzzy logic inference. Defuzzification is discussed in the next section.

Fuzzy Associative Memories

A number of extensions of this simple fuzzy logic inference principle exist. Of these, only a few have gained practical relevance. The most common is the association of rules with a weight factor. Such a weight represents the importance of the rule in relevance to the other rules in the system. The use of weights is the most simple and transparent implementation of more general concepts such as Fuzzy Associative Memories [14] or the Compositional Rule of Inference [46]. In fuzzy logic inference, a weight in the interval [0; 1] is multiplied with the aggregation result in the composition step.

"Fuzzy" Rules

A possible interpretation of the weight factor is to consider rules themselves as "fuzzy." In the simple fuzzy logic inference principle, each rule either is a member of the set of valid rules or it is not. This is Boolean logic again; only truth degrees of 0 and 1 are allowed. If you extend these truth degrees to the continuous interval [0; 1], the set of valid rules becomes a fuzzy set and hence allows for the definition of "more-or-less" valid rules.

1.3.3 Defuzzification Using Linguistic Variables

At the end of the fuzzy logic inference, the result for Liquidity is given as a linguistic variable value. To use this value for comparisons or ranking, it has to be translated into a numerical value. This step is called defuzzification. The relation between linguistic values and corresponding real values is always defined using membership function definitions. Figure 25 plots the membership functions for the linguistic variable "Liquidity."

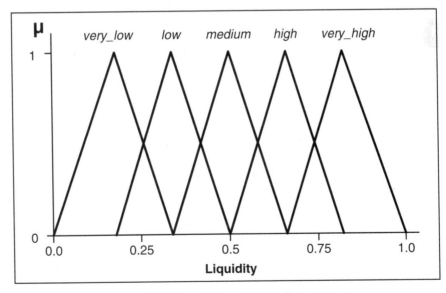

Figure 25: Linguistic variable "Liquidity."

The result of the fuzzy inference executed in Example 3 is both fuzzy and ambiguous because two different actions have non-zero truth degrees. How can two conflicting actions that are defined as fuzzy sets be combined to provide a numerical output for Liquidity? In Example 4, consider how humans might solve the problem of combining two fuzzy and conflicting actions:

Example 4

Consider yourself in an apartment house at 11pm. You would like to listen to some music, maybe Wagner or Guns 'n' Roses, music that requires some volume to be fun. On the other hand, your neighbors have already suffered quite a bit from your recent music sessions. Now, when you set the volume on your stereo, you have to combine these two conflicting and fuzzy goals into a crisp, exact value, as only such a value can be set at the volume knob of your stereo. To satisfy these two criteria, you turn on the music and adjust the volume until you have balanced out the two goals.

Since fuzzy logic mimics the human decision and evaluation process, a good defuzzification method should approximate this approach. Most defuzzification methods use a two-step approach for this. In the first step, a "typical" value is computed for each term in the linguistic variable. In the second step, the "best compromise" is determined by "balancing" out the results.

A) Compute the "Typical" Values

The most common approach to computing the typical values of each term is to find the maximum of the respective membership function. If the membership function has a maximizing interval, the median of the maximizing set is chosen. For the linguistic variable Liquidity shown in Figure 25, the computation of the typical values is illustrated in Figure 26. Here, the gray arrows point to the horizontal position of the typical values.

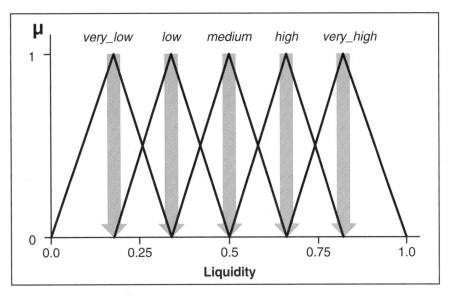

Figure 26: In the first step of defuzzification, the typical value for each term is computed as the maximum of the respective Membership Function.

B) Find the Best Compromise

In the second step, the best crisp compromising value for the linguistic result is computed. Figure 27 illustrates this step. At the horizontal position of the typical values, a "weight" is placed that has a size proportional to the degree to which the action is true. The weights are shown as the heights of the black arrows over the gray arrows. The exact compromising value is then determined by balancing the weights "on a point." In the example, the position that balances the fuzzy inference result is at the position of 0.27. This value is considered the best compromise for the Liquidity assessment.

This method of defuzzification is called "Center-of-Maximum" and is identical to the "Center-of-Gravity" method that uses singleton membership functions. These defuzzification methods are used in most fuzzy logic implementations. Other defuzzification methods are introduced and compared in Section 6.4.

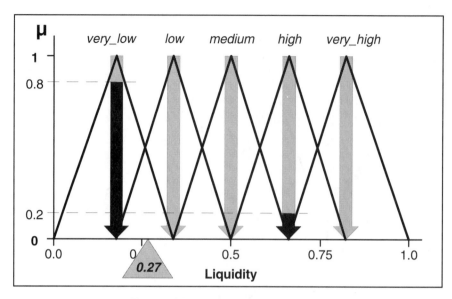

Figure 27: By balancing out the
conflicting results, a crisp result is found.

1.4   More Fuzzy Logic Theory

More than 30,000 scientific papers on fuzzy logic have appeared since 1965. The vast majority of these papers deal with the mathematical implications of relaxing classical logic to fuzzy logic. For an overview, refer to [51].

This book only treats the fuzzy logic theory to the extent necessary to understand and follow the attached software case studies. Also, this theoretical background is sufficient to start your own application work. However, if you embark on more extensive work in the field of fuzzy logic, you may want to learn more of the theoretical background, the history, and the engineering applications of fuzzy logic. For these topics, books that will give you a good start in these direction are listed below as additional literature.

Additional Literature:

■ For the background on fuzzy logic theory, refer to:

> *Fuzzy Set Theory—and Its Applications*
> by H.-J. Zimmermann (1991)
> ISBN 0-7923-9075-X, Kluwer Academic Publishers

■ For an easy-to-read book on the history of fuzzy logic, refer to:

> *Fuzzy Logic*
> by Paul Freiberger and David McNeill (1993)
> ISBN 0-671-73843-7, Simon and Schuster

■ For a comprehensive explanation of applications of fuzzy logic in engineering, refer to:

> *Fuzzy Logic and NeuroFuzzy Applications Explained*
> by Constantin von Altrock (1995)
> ISBN 0-13-368465-2, Prentice Hall

(A counterpart to this book, however it focuses entirely on engineering applications.)

Getting Started
with *fuzzy*TECH for Business

This Chapter helps you install and take the first steps with *fuzzy*-TECH for Business. You can follow all the steps in this Chapter with the software on your PC. Section 2.1 guides you through installation. Section 2.2 takes you through the first steps with *fuzzy*TECH as you design your first small fuzzy logic system. In Section 2.3, you will extend this system step-by-step to build a more complete system.

Notice: this Book does not cover all *fuzzy*TECH features. For a complete listing and reference, refer to the *fuzzy*TECH Reference Manual or the online help system of *fuzzy*TECH.

U.S. and Canada:

Inform Software Corporation
2001 Midwest Road
Oak Brook, IL 60521, U.S.A.

Phone: (630) 268-7550
Fax: (630) 268-7554

E-mail: fuzzy@informusa.com
WWW: www.inform-ac.com
FTP: ftp.inform-ac.com

Japan:

TOYO/Inform
26-9, Yushima 3-chome, Bukyo-ku
Tokyo 113, JAPAN

Phone: 03-5688-6900
Fax: 03-5688-6800

WWW: www.inform-ac.com
FTP: ftp.inform-ac.com

Europe and Elsewhere:

INFORM GmbH
Pascalstrasse 23
D-52076 Aachen, GERMANY

Phone: +49-2408-9456-80
Fax: +49-2408-9456-85

E-mail: hotline@inform-ac.com
WWW: www.inform-ac.com
FTP: ftp.inform-ac.com

2.1   Installation Guide

This section describes the installation of the enclosed software. If you do not want to install the software now, you can skip this section.

2.1.1 Installing *fuzzy*TECH and the Samples

Prerequisites

To install and run the attached software, you must meet the following minimum hardware requirements:

- 486 class PC

- VGA color graphics

- CD-ROM Drive

- 3½" floppy disk drive

- Hard disk drive with minimum 20 MB free space

- 8 MB RAM

- MS-Windows 3.1x, Windows 95, or Windows NT 4.0

This configuration is a minimum. For fast and convenient operation, we recommend:

- Pentium class PC or better

- 800x600 color graphics with 256 colors or better

- 16 MB RAM or better

- A mouse or similar pointing device

To connect *fuzzy*TECH to other software as described in Chapter 4, you also need:

- MS-Excel 5.0 or 7.0

- MS-Visual Basic 3.0 or 4.0

- MS-Access 2.0 or 7.0

If you use later versions of the listed software products, refer to the user's manuals of these applications for backward compatibility.

The release 4.2 of *fuzzy*TECH for Business software currently provided with this book's CD ROM is a 16-bit software, so that it runs both under Windows 3.1x as well as Windows 95 and Windows/NT. All interfaces to *fuzzy*TECH, such as the MS-Excel Assistant and the MS-VisualBasic interface are provided in their 32-bit as well as their 16-bit version. This allows the use of both 32-bit and 16-bit software with *fuzzy*TECH. The 32-bit version of *fuzzy*TECH is not provided with this book's CD ROM.

Starting the Installation Routine

Insert the CD ROM provided with this book into the CD drive of your PC. If you are using a newer version of MS-Windows, a splash screen appears as shown in Figure 28. If this screen does not open automatically, call AUTORUN.EXE directly from the root directory of the CD ROM.

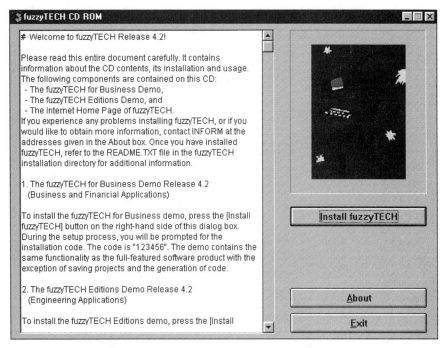

Figure 28: Splash Screen of the attached CD ROM.

The left window shows the contents of the file INFO.TXT located in the root directory of the CD ROM. This file contains detailed information on installation and latest information. Please read this file carefully before you install *fuzzy*TECH. Then press the [Install fuzzyTECH] on the right side of the splash screen to install the *fuzzy*TECH for Business Demo. The splash screen automatically starts the file SETUP.EXE located in the \DISK01\ directory of the CD ROM. The rest of the installation routine is menu-driven. If possible, use "C:\FT4BUIZ" as installation path because this path is referenced throughout this book. The installation routine is very similar to most other Windows-based software.

Deinstallation

To deinstall the software, erase the directory in which you installed *fuzzy*TECH and all of its subdirectories. The installation routine does not modify your AUTOEXEC.BAT and CONFIG.SYS file. However, the installation routine adds a [FTWIN] section to the WIN.INI file that contains the path of the current *fuzzy*TECH installation. This is necessary for the MS-Excel function assistant and the other interface software to locate *fuzzy*TECH on your PC. This entry can remain in the WIN.INI file since it has no negative effect if *fuzzy*TECH is erased from the hard disk.

Note: if you install another version of *fuzzy*TECH into a different directory, the installation routine will overwrite the previous path entry in the [FTWIN] section of the WIN.INI file. You can manually set the path in the [FTWIN] section of the WIN.INI to change the active *fuzzy*TECH installation.

2.1.2 Conventions

In this book, certain conventions are used that are explained below.

Typing Conventions

- File names are always capitalized, such as SETUP.EXE, CREDIT.FTL.

- Subdirectories are capitalized and delimited by the "\" character. For example, you could have installed *fuzzy*TECH in the \FT4BUIZ\ subdirectory.

- Menu options from the menu bar are delimited by the "\" character. For example, to open a file with *fuzzy*TECH, you click on the "File" entry in the menu bar and select the "Open..." option. This will be referred to as "selecting File\Open..." in this book.

- Buttons in the dialog boxes, such as the Help, OK, or Cancel buttons, will be referred to as [Help], [OK], and [Cancel] buttons, respectively. Buttons that do not display any text, such as toolbar buttons, are referred to by their function names.

Mouse Usage

- "Clicking" or "double-clicking" refers to the left mouse button, "clicking right" refers to the right mouse button. With *fuzzy*-TECH in general, clicking on an object highlights it, double-clicking on an object activates the object, and clicking right in a window area opens a properties menu that contains functions for the specific window in which you clicked. Double-clicking the right mouse button has no effect in *fuzzy*TECH.

- It is possible to access all the functions of *fuzzy*TECH through the keyboard alone. However, this book will only describe activation of functions by the mouse. To learn about hotkeys, select the Help\Shortkey Overview option from the menu bar.

Other Conventions

- In this book, it is assumed that you access the local function of each window by its toolbar. However, every function of the toolbars is accessible through menu functions as well. The functions of the main window toolbar are accessible from the menu bar. The functions of the other windows are accessible by their properties menu that you invoke by clicking right in the respective window.

- When you position the mouse pointer over a toolbar button, its name is displayed in a ToolTip window and a short description of that buttons is displayed in the left field of the status line at the bottom of the main window of *fuzzy*TECH (you do not need to click on the button).

2.1.3 First Steps

After having successfully installed *fuzzy*TECH, double-click on the *fuzzy*TECH for Business icon in the Program Manager's *fuzzy*TECH group. This causes the main window of *fuzzy*TECH to appear on the screen as shown in Figure 29.

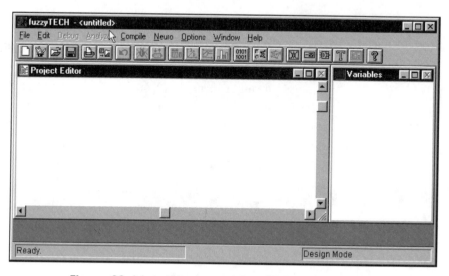

Figure 29: Main Window of *fuzzy*TECH for Business.

In the upper part of the main window, the toolbar provides direct access to the functions most often used by *fuzzy*TECH. Enabling and disabling of toolbars is described in Section 2.3.3. The client area of the main window always contains the two windows "Project Editor" and "Variables." The Project Editor window allows you to graphically design a system structure and the Variables window lists all linguistic variables of the current fuzzy logic system. Both of these windows can only be minimized, never closed. You cannot create additional Project Editor or Variables windows.

The lower part of the main window contains a status line, which displays various types of information. The left field of the status line displays the current basic operation of *fuzzy*TECH, such as opening, saving, or code generation. It also displays a quick description of every button of the toolbar. Move the mouse pointer, without pressing a button, over the buttons of the toolbar to see a quick description of the respective tool displayed in the left field of the status line. The right field of the status line displays the current debug mode, described further in Section 2.3.3. The middle field gives progress information on *fuzzy-*

TECH tasks that take longer, such as opening, saving, code generation, or drawing large plots.

Now that you are familiar with the features of the main window of *fuzzy*TECH, you can start with your first fuzzy logic system design in the following section.

2.2   Basic System Design Methodology

In this section, you will learn the basics steps for creating a fuzzy logic system. The simple example introduced in Section 1.2 guides you through the design steps.

2.2.1 Using the Fuzzy Design Wizard

The Fuzzy Design Wizard is a tool that guides you step-by-step though the design of a fuzzy logic system prototype. Through a sequence of dialog boxes, you will be asked a number of questions about the system you want to create. The Fuzzy Design Wizard uses this information to automatically set up the fuzzy logic system for you. The Fuzzy Design Wizard can do even more. If you have sample data representing the application for which you want to generate a fuzzy logic system, the Fuzzy Design Wizard can analyze this data and propose answers to the design questions for you.

Start the Fuzzy Design Wizard

Now, start the Fuzzy Design Wizard by clicking on the "Fuzzy Design Wizard" button of the toolbar. This is the second button from the left side of the main toolbar of *fuzzy*TECH, showing a rabbit-out-of-the-hat 🐰. Figure 30 shows the first dialog box of the Fuzzy Design Wizard. Here you can select whether the Fuzzy Design Wizard appends the new components generated for the current system or whether it creates a new system. By default, the "Create new system" option is selected. In the lower part of the dialog box, you can tell the Fuzzy Design Wizard to extract information about the system to be designed from a sample data file. Do not select this option and move to the next dialog box of the Fuzzy Design Wizard by pressing either the return key of the keyboard or clicking on the [Next>] button. The return key and the [Next>] button will always move you to the next dialog box of the Fuzzy Design Wizard.

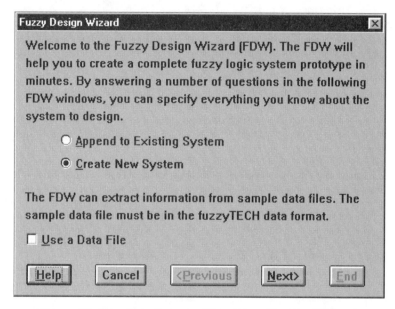

Figure 30: The first dialog of the Fuzzy Design Wizard.

Figure 31 shows the second dialog box of the Fuzzy Design Wizard. This dialog box lets you define the number of input, output, and intermediate linguistic variables of the fuzzy logic system. Also, you can set the number of terms for each type of variable. In later Fuzzy Design Wizard dialog boxes, you may revert back to this decision. The Fuzzy Design Wizard will generate input interfaces and fuzzification methods for each input variable and output interfaces and defuzzification methods for each output variable. Intermediate variables are linguistic variables that contain intermediate results of the fuzzy logic inference and are neither inputs into nor outputs from the fuzzy logic system. Intermediate variables are used to build more complex fuzzy logic systems. Their use is described in detail later.

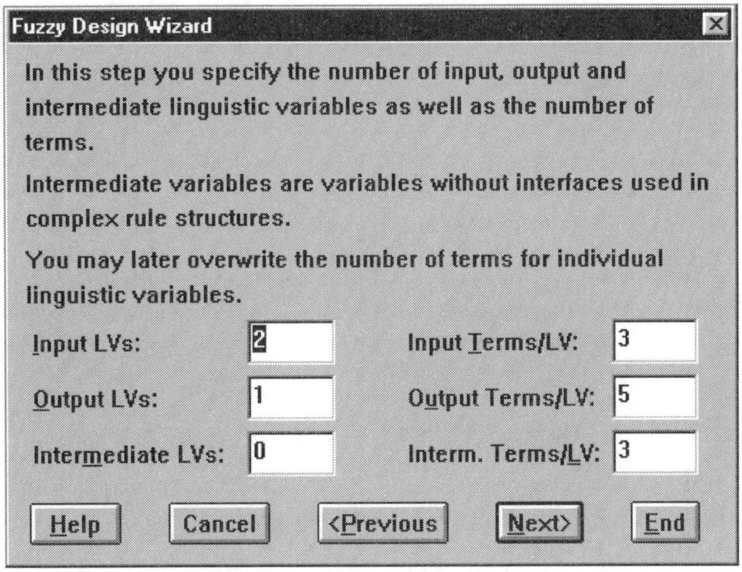

Figure 31: The second dialog lets you specify
input, output, and intermediate variables.

The Fuzzy Design Wizard suggests two input variables using three terms each, one output variable using five terms, and no intermediate variables. This is because this is about the smallest fuzzy logic system that makes sense. Since it is also the same size as the one given as the introductory sample in Section 1.2, you can leave all the values in the fields at the suggested values and press either the return key or the [Next] button to move to the next dialog box.

Specifying Linguistic Variable Details

You can always page back to the previous Fuzzy Design Wizard dialog boxes by clicking the [<Previous] button. Thus, you can change any earlier design decision later on. You can quit the Fuzzy Design Wizard any time by using the [Cancel] button or get more information about the Fuzzy Design Wizard by clicking the [Help] button to invoke the on-line help system. You may press the [End] button at any time to generate the fuzzy logic system with the specified parameters. Pressing [Next] or the return key on the last Fuzzy Design Wizard dialog box has the same effect.

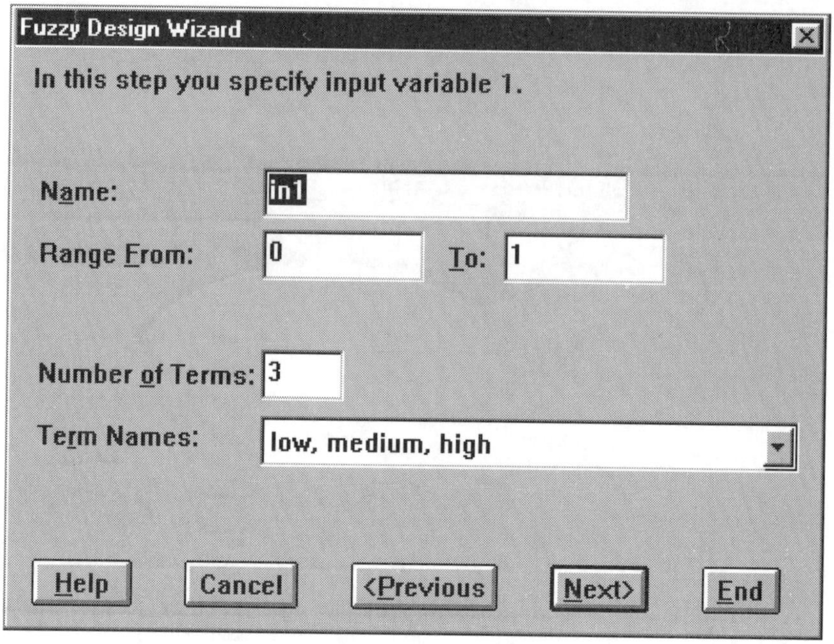

Figure 32: This dialog box specifies the
parameters for each linguistic variable.

Figure 32 shows the dialog box that the Fuzzy Design Wizard opens for every linguistic variable to be created. The caption of the dialog box is in the "Name:" field. Not knowing what kind of system you want to create, the Fuzzy Design Wizard proposes the name "in1." Overwrite this name with "Continuity."

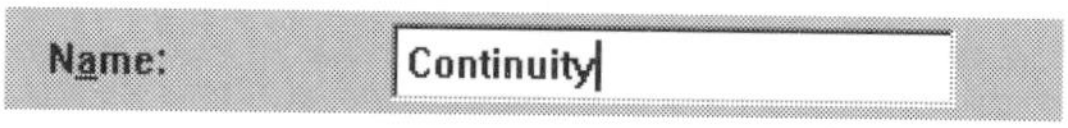

The "Range from:" and "to:" fields let you define the lower and upper bound of the linguistic variable. The field "Number of terms:" shows the number you specified in the Fuzzy Design Wizard dialog box shown in Figure 31. You may overwrite this number here if you want the input variables to have a differing numbers of terms. Use the tab key and shift-tab key combination to move in the fields. Depending on the number of terms specified in the field "Number of terms:," the drop list box "Term names:" proposes different sets of term names. Now press the ▼ button at the right side of the field to open the drop list box. For three terms, it suggests the following choices:

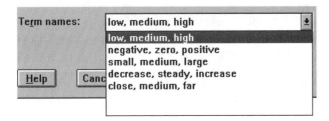

The {low, medium, high} term name set is appropriate for most variables that describe a qualitative evaluation such as risk, cash flow, or price. Thus, it is best to describe the linguistic variable "Continuity." Do not change the term name set {low, medium, high}. The {negative, zero, positive} term name set is appropriate for describing variables that are symmetric to zero, for instance, a variable that ranges from −100 to +100. The {small, medium, large} term name set is best for variables that describe a quantitative evaluation. The {decrease, steady, increase} term name set is best for variables that describe tendencies, while the {close, medium, far} term name set is best for variables describing distances. Note that for different term numbers, different term name sets will be proposed by the Fuzzy Design Wizard. Now, click on [Next] or press the return key to move to the next dialog box.

This dialog box is similar to the previous one because it lets you specify the second input variable. The "Name:" field proposes the name "in2." Overwrite this name with "Inc_Exp."

This second linguistic input variable describes the difference between annual net income and fixed annual expenses, such as mortgages and car loan payments. In the example, we have identified this linguistic variable to be in the bounds of the interval [−20,000; +230,000]. Move the cursor into the "Range from:" field to overwrite the "0" with the value "−20000" by using the tab key. Move the cursor into the "to:" field to overwrite the "1" with the value "230000."

Then press the [Next>] button or the return key to move to the next dialog box.

This dialog box is also similar to the previous one, letting you define the properties of the output variable. The "Name:" field proposes "out1" as the output name. Overwrite this name with "Liquidity."

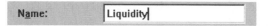

Leave all other values as the Fuzzy Design Wizard suggested them and press [Next] or the return key to move to the next Fuzzy Design Wizard dialog box. Figure 33 shows this dialog box, which determines the defuzzification method for each output variable from its characteristics. Since the evaluation of liquidity is a compromise of different aspects of a person's financial circumstances, the selection "Best compromise" is most appropriate for this fuzzy logic system. For more details on advanced defuzzification methods, see Section 6.4. Press [Next>] or the return key to move to the next dialog.

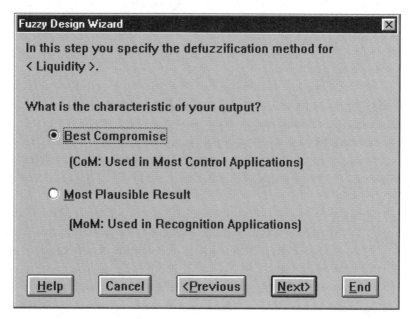

Figure 33: For each output variable, the characteristics of the variable determine the defuzzification method to be used.

Figure 34 shows the last dialog box of the Fuzzy Design Wizard. Here you can create rule blocks and rules. *fuzzy*TECH supports the design of multiple rule blocks within a fuzzy logic system, allowing complex systems to be structured transparently. Because the currently specified fuzzy logic system is rather simple, the Fuzzy Design Wizard suggests the generation of only one rule block. The Fuzzy Design Wizard also creates individual rules within a rule block if the "Create Rule Base" check box is enabled. Since you will manually enter the rules later, the Fuzzy Design Wizard does not need to generate the rules for you. However, leave the "Create Rule Base" check box enabled so that you can learn how to edit rules before you begin to generate your own. Now, press the [End] button to generate the fuzzy logic system with the current specifications. Pressing the [Next] button or the return key has the same effect as the [End] button because this is the last dialog box of the Fuzzy Design Wizard. Remember that you can always go back in the sequence of the dialog boxes and reverse design decisions by clicking the [<Previous] button.

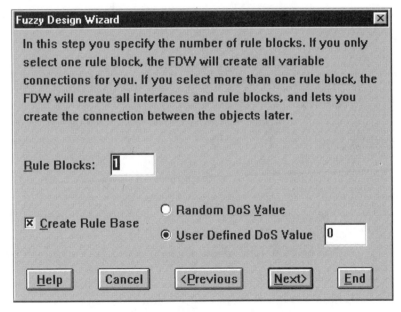

Figure 34: The last dialog box of the Fuzzy Design Wizard lets you create rule blocks and rules.

After you leave the Fuzzy Design Wizard, a dialog box like the one shown in Figure 35 asks you for confirmation. Click [Yes] to generate the fuzzy logic system.

Note that the system generated up to this point is stored as CREDIT1.FTL in the subdirectory \SAMPLES\BUSINESS\CREDIT\. If you want to start from here, just open this file by selecting File\Open... from the menu bar, pressing Ctrl-O, or clicking on the Open File button 🗁 of the main tool bar.

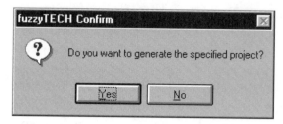

Figure 35: To generate the fuzzy logic system with the current parameters, click (Yes).

Working with the Generated System

Figure 36 shows *fuzzy*TECH with the generated system. The Project Editor window shows two input interfaces on the left side containing the input variables "Continuity" and "Inc_Exp." On the right side, one output interface contains the output variable "Liquidity." Input interfaces show the fuzzification icon 🔲 on the left side of the interface box, while output interfaces show the defuzzification icon 🔲 on the right side. You'll find the rule block linked by lines in between the input and output interfaces. Two small boxes showing the words "MIN" and "MAX" respectively are also displayed in the rule block box. These fields let you modify the fuzzy logic inference methods used. Refer to Section 6 for more details on advanced fuzzy logic design techniques.

You may freely rearrange the interface and rule block boxes in the Project Editor window. Just move the mouse pointer over the object, click and hold down, and then drag the object to the new position. Holding down the shift key before dragging objects locks the horizontal or vertical movement, depending on the direction you drag the object. You may access all these functions through the keyboard as well. Use the tab key to select, the cursor keys to move, and the return key to place objects.

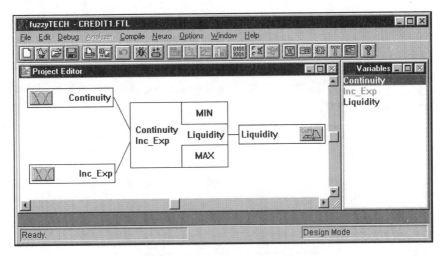

Figure 36: The fuzzy logic system as generated by the Fuzzy Design Wizard.

The Variables window shows a list of the three linguistic variables the Fuzzy Design Wizard generated. To generate new linguistic variables, you can either click on the "Create Variable" button of the main window toolbar, press Ctrl-C, select Edit\Create New Variable from the menu bar, or open the properties menu of the Variables window by clicking left in the Variables window area. If the new variable you want to create is similar or equal to one that is already listed in the Variables window, you can duplicate this variable. Just select the variable you want to duplicate in the Variables window and select Edit\Duplicate Variable from the menu bar. You may also press Ctrl-D or use the properties menu of the Variables window. To change the name of a linguistic variable, use the "Properties" option of the properties menu. For more details on creating and duplicating linguistic variables, refer to the on-line help system of *fuzzy*TECH.

Editing Linguistic Variables

The membership functions of linguistic variables in *fuzzy*TECH are created and edited graphically with the Linguistic Variable editors. You can open such an editor window for every variable of the system and work with them simultaneously. To open a Linguistic Variable editor window for the variable "Continuity," double-click on the name in the

Variables window. Figure 37 shows the editor's window with the membership function definitions created by the Fuzzy Design Wizard.

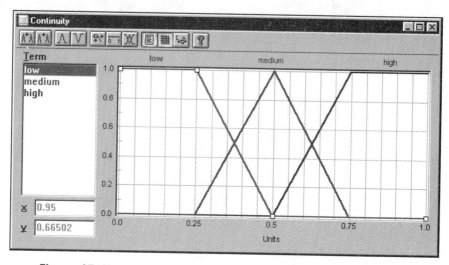

Figure 37: Linguistic Variable Editor window for "Continuity."

The main part of the window is a plot area for the membership functions. The left part of the window shows a list of all terms that are defined for the linguistic variable. The term names are also displayed above the plot area. To edit a membership function, you must either select the term name in the "Term:" list box or click on the term name printed above the plot area. Then the definition points of the membership function are marked by small squares:

You can select any point by a mouse click on the respective point, and you can move the selected point by dragging with the mouse. A selected definition point is indicated by a filled square. To create a new definition point, just double-click on the area where you want the new point to appear. To delete a definition point, select it and press the [Del] key.

Note: the left-most and right-most definition points can neither be moved horizontally nor be deleted.

Advanced Membership Function Editing

You may also move more than one definition point at a time. Try selecting the "medium" term in the "Term:" list box. Then select the second left-most definition point that is located by the coordinates (0.25; 0). Now, press and hold down the shift key and drag the second right definition point. This moves all definition points between the one first selected and the dragged one simultaneously. You cannot move the three points vertically because the interval of the degree of membership is limited to [0; 1]. To move only selected points, you may use the Ctrl key rather than the shift key. Select the second left-most definition point again and hold down the Ctrl key and drag the second right-most definition point. This moves only the two selected definition points.

A grid can be configured to assist with the definition of membership functions. Invoke the Grid dialog box by clicking on the "Grid" button ⊞ of the linguistic variable editor window toolbar. You can also select the option "Grid..." from the properties menu of the variable editor. Figure 38 shows the Grid dialog box. In the "Base Variable" field, enter the distance between two grid points as the dimension of the base variable. Since the base variable of "Continuity" is in the interval of [0; 1], a grid distance of "0.1" corresponds to 11 grid support points. Change the value in the field "Base Variable" to "0.02," which corresponds to 51 grid support points:

The check box "Show Raster" turns the fine gray lines in the plot area of the Linguistic Variable editor on and off. If the density of the grid points is low, the gray lines correspond to the grid intervals. With a higher density of grid points, the gray lines are only displayed at interval locations. The check box "Snap to Grid" forces definition points of the membership functions to lock to the defined grid. With this option disabled, the grid has no effect other than determining where the gray lines are plotted. Enable the check box "Snap to Grid" and press [OK] to return to the linguistic variable editor. If you try to move definition points now, you will see that you can only access points on the grid frame.

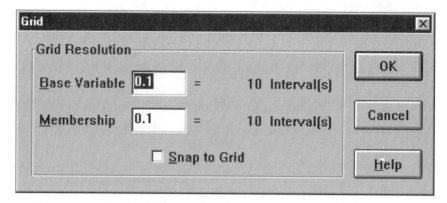

Figure 38: The Grid dialog lets you define
a grid for the membership functions.

Note: you can also turn the raster on and off from the linguistic variable editor. Use the Raster button ▦ of the toolbar of the linguistic variable editor window to toggle the display of the raster. **Note**: the two fields "x" and "y" located at the lower left of the Linguistic Variable Editor window show definition point coordinates and let you input them by the keyboard. As you move the mouse pointer in the plot area, the two fields show the current coordinates. When near a definition point, the two fields show the exact coordinates of this point. As an alternative to the mouse, you can also use the tab, return, and cursor keys to access all functions and move membership function definition points within the Linguistic Variable Editor.

Reversing Actions Using the UNDO Function

Before moving to the next steps, you have to restore the membership functions of "Continuity" to how they looked when the Fuzzy Design Wizard generated them. You can do this manually, but there is an easier way. *fuzzy*TECH has a multi-stage UNDO function that can reverse actions. You can access this function by selecting Edit\Undo from the menu bar, pressing [Alt]-[Backspace], or clicking on the UNDO button ↺ of the main toolbar. By pressing the button more than once, you can reverse the actions sequentially. **Note:** if you are changing parameters in many windows, the UNDO function reverses them in the exact reverse sequence in which they were carried out.

Defining Base Variables and Terms

Now, open an editor window for the linguistic variable "Inc_Exp" by double-clicking on the variable name in the Variables window. You do not need to close the editor for "Continuity" beforehand. Variable Editors are closed by a double-click on the system icon ⊠ of the title bar of the respective Variable Editor. The title bars of the variable editors show the name of the linguistic variable. Figure 39 shows the editor window for "Inc_Exp". The vertical axis of the plot area shows the degree of membership and the horizontal axis shows the base variable. To modify the base variable interval, open the Base Variable dialog box by clicking on the Base Variable button 🖅 of the toolbar of the variable editor, or by selecting the "Base Variable..." option from the properties menu of the Variable Editor.

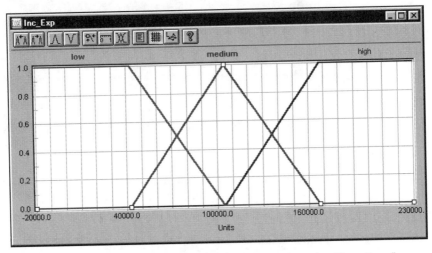

Figure 39: Linguistic Variable Editor window for "Inc_Exp."

Figure 40 shows the Base Variable dialog box that lets you define the range and the units of the base variable. The three fields on the upper-left-hand side, marked "Min:," "Max:," and "Default:," let you specify the lower and upper boundaries of "Inc_Exp." The default value is only required for variables that will be defuzzified, so you can ignore it for "Inc_Exp." The two upper right fields and the two buttons [Min] and [Max] are only relevant if integer code resolution is required for run-time code generated by a *fuzzy*TECH code generator.

Base Variable   ☒

Range

	Shell Values		Code Values	
Min:	-20000	**as**	0	Min
Max:	230000	**as**	65535	Max
Default:	105000			

☐ **Keep Definition Points**

Base Variable Unit

Units

Data Type: **Double Precision**

Fuzzification: **Compute MBF**

OK	Cancel	Help

Figure 40: The Base Variable dialog lets you
specify the range and unit of the base variable.

The field "Base Variable Unit" lets you input the unit of the base variable. For "Inc_Exp," the unit is the U.S. Dollar, so enter this in the field:

Base Variable Unit

US_Dollar

Then leave the dialog box by using the [OK] button. Now, the base variable unit is displayed under the horizontal axis back in the variable editor.

Converting to Standard Membership Functions

Now, open a Linguistic Variable Editor for "Liquidity" by double-clicking on the name in the Variables window. Figure 41 shows the window that opens for "Liquidity." For this variable, we want to change the typical values of the membership functions to the following values:

Term Name	Typical Value
very_low	0.0
low	0.2
medium	0.5
high	0.8
very_high	1.0

The first step is to move the $\mu = 1$ point (the maxima) of every term to the value given in the table. First, open the Grid dialog box and enable the "Snap to Grid" option. Then move the upper definition point of the term "very_low" to the base variable value 0.0 (to the maximum left). You may also erase the upper definition point and move the leftmost definition point from $\mu = 0$ to $\mu = 1$.

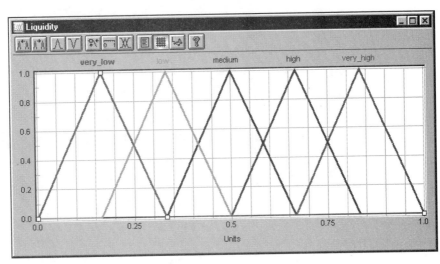

Figure 41: Linguistic Variable Editor window for "Liquidity."

To move the upper definition point of the term "low," select the term name in the "Term" list box such that the editor marks the definition points of "low" with small squares. Move the upper definition point to 0.2 and proceed in a similar manner with the other terms "medium," "high," and "very_high." Now, the membership functions are no longer overlapping Standard MBFs but rather look as shown in Figure 42.

Rather than moving the lower definition points accordingly, you can let
the Variable Editor do this for you. Click on the Standard MBF button
🗶 and confirm the operation in the dialog box to get *fuzzy*TECH to
convert the membership functions to those shown in Figure 43.

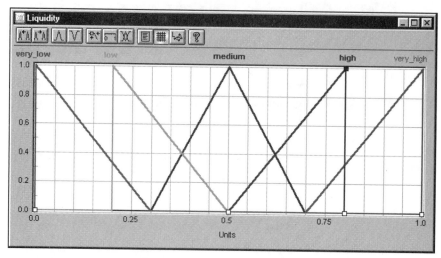

Figure 42: After moving the upper definition point, the membership
functions are no longer overlapping Standard MBFs.

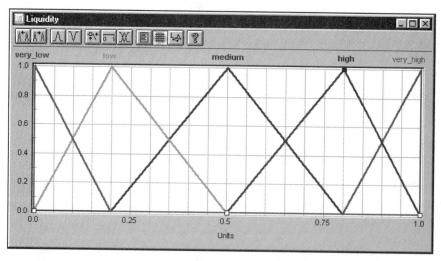

Figure 43: The "Standard MBF" Function converts any membership
function definition to overlapping standard membership functions.

The Linguistic Variable Wizard

The entire process of generating or editing linguistic variables and their membership functions can be expedited by the Linguistic Variable Wizard. The Linguistic Variable Wizard uses a series of dialogs for a stepwise definition of a linguistic variable. For an existing linguistic variable, the Linguistic Variable Wizard is invoked by the ⊞ button of the toolbar, and only allows for the definition of the membership functions. When creating a new variable, also the term and base variable definition are made by the Linguistic Variable Wizard. For a detailed description, refer to Section 2.3.1.

More Features of the Linguistic Variable Editor

If you have low video resolution on your PC or you want to display many Variable Editors on screen simultaneously, you can hide the "Term" list box. Click on List Box button ▤ of the variable editor's toolbar to show or hide the list box. To select a term when the list box is hidden, use the Select Next/Previous Term buttons ▣▣ of the toolbar or select the term name printed above the main area.

Note: all functions provided by the toolbar are also accessible via the properties menu of the Variable Editor window.

Creating, Editing, and Deleting Terms

You can create new terms by clicking the New Term / Inverse Term buttons ▣▣ of the toolbar. New Term will create a term with a Lambda type membership function where the upper definition point is in the middle of the base variable interval and the lower definition points are at the upper and lower bound of the base variable. If you want to create a term with an inverse meaning to an existing one, you can use the Inverse Term button. For example, if you want to create an inverse term to "very_high," select this term in the Term list box and press the Inverse Term button. This creates a new term with a membership function of $\mu_{new}=1-\mu_{selected}$. An alternative way to create a new term is to press the keyboard shortcut Ctrl-T.

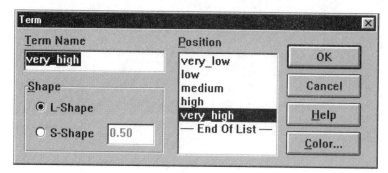

Figure 44: The Term dialog box lets you
name terms and change their sequence.

To edit the properties of an existing term, just double-click on the respective term name in the "Term" list box of the variable editor. The Term dialog box opens as shown in Figure 44 when you create or edit a term's attribute. The field "Term Name" lets you input the name for that term. The "Shape" group defines the membership function shape. For details, refer to Section 6.1.3. The list box "Position" lets you place the current term in the sequence of all terms. The button [Color...] lets you change the pre-assigned term color.

If you want to start development from here, open the file CREDIT2.FTL located in the subdirectory \SAMPLES\BUSINESS\-CREDIT\. It contains the fuzzy logic system with all the modifications made up to this point.

2.2.2 Creating a Rule Base

Now that you have used the Fuzzy Design Wizard to create an initial system and have learned how to edit the membership functions of linguistic variables, the next step is to define rules for the rule block that the Fuzzy Design Wizard has created. The rule block is the large box in the Project Editor window:

The input variables of a rule block are listed on the left side and the output variables on the right side. The two areas showing the words "MIN" and "MAX" display the aggregation and result aggregation operators employed. Sections 6.3.1 and 6.3.2 contain details on these operators. Click right on the rule block to open the properties menu of the options:

The option Properties lets you change the input and output variables of the rule block. You can also associate names to rule blocks that identify the rule block in the Analyzer tools if you have more than one rule block. By default, the first rule block was named "RB1." The options "Matrix Rule Editor..." and "Spreadsheet Rule Editor..." invoke different types of rule block editors. Select "Spreadsheet Rule Editor..." to open the Spreadsheet Rule Editor that looks similar to a business spreadsheet. As a shortcut, you can always open the Spreadsheet Rule Editor directly by double-clicking the rule block in the Project Editor window. The Spreadsheet Rule Editor should appear as shown in Figure 45. The rules are those that the Fuzzy Design Wizard has generated for you.

	IF		THEN	
	Continuity	Inc_Exp	DoS	Liquidity
1	low	low	0.00	very_low
2	low	low	0.00	low
3	low	low	0.00	medium
4	low	low	0.00	high
5	low	low	0.00	very_high
6	low	medium	0.00	very_low
7	low	medium	0.00	low

Figure 45: Spreadsheet Rule Editor window.

Each row corresponds to a single fuzzy logic rule. The left-most column numbers each rule (gray fields). Clicking on this field highlights the rule, clicking again de-highlights it. The next two columns comprise the "If-Part" of the rule. Above the columns are two buttons [Continuity] and [Inc_Exp], and above them the button [IF].

The two rightmost columns under the [THEN] button describe the "Then-Part" of the rules. The right one under the [Liquidity] button denotes the result term and the left one under the [DoS] button the individual weight of the rule. The weights (Degree-of-Support) are always in the range from zero to one.

Add and Modify Rules

To change a rule, simply click in the respective field. A list box shows all possible values for the field. To add a rule, use the last row of the table. Once you enter a new rule, another empty row appears at the end of the table. Incomplete rules, rules that either have no "If-part," no "Then-part," or no "DoS," will automatically be deleted when the Spreadsheet Rule Editor is closed. Empty fields in the "If-parts" are considered "don't care" conditions. A rule that contains an empty field is not influenced by the respective variable. Rules containing "don't care" conditions are not incomplete. In the list box that appears when you click on a field, the "don't care" condition is listed under the terms as "[...]."

Deleting Rules

To delete a rule, first highlight the rule by clicking the rule number at the left and then press the [Del] key. If you want to temporarily disable a rule, you can also set the DoS to zero. Such a rule has no effect on the system but is not considered incomplete.

Sorting Rules

To sort rules according to the sequence of the terms of a certain variable, just click on the respective button such as [Continuity],

[Inc_Exp], or [Liquidity]. You may also sort rules according to the sequence of their firing degree by pressing the [DoS] button.

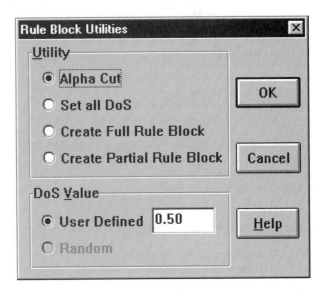

Figure 46: The Rule Block Utilities Dialog contains a number of different functions to manipulate an entire rule block.

Rule Block Utilities

Click on the Utilities button [T] to access the Rule Block Utilities dialog box shown in Figure 46. In the group "Utility," you can select the desired function.

■ "Alpha Cut" deletes all rules with a DoS lower than the value specified in the group "DoS Value."

■ "Set all DoS" forces the rule weights to the value specified in the group "DoS Value."

■ "Create Full Rule Block" deletes all existing rules and creates a rule for each combination of terms. For each possible combination of input variable terms for the rule block, a rule for each possible output variable term is generated. The weights of the generated rules are specified in the group "DoS Value."

- "Create Partial Rule Block" only creates a rule for each combination of input variables. You have to specify the output variable terms manually. The rules for which you do not specify an output term are incomplete and will be erased when closing the Spreadsheet Rule Editor. The weights of the generated rules are specified in the group "DoS Value."

Since we will now create a rule base for the Liquidity assessment example, erase all rules in the rule block at once by selecting "Alpha Cut" and pressing the [OK] button. This closes the Rule Block Utilities dialog box and deletes all rules in the Spreadsheet Rule Editor window.

Next enter the rules, as shown in Figure 47, in the Spreadsheet Rule Editor by clicking in the field you want to modify and selecting the term or DoS value from the menu that pops up. Adding a rule is easy since there is always an empty rule line at the end of the rule list.

	IF		THEN	
	Continuity	Inc_Exp	DoS	Liquidity
1		low	1.00	very_low
2	low	medium	1.00	low
3	medium	medium	1.00	medium
4	high	medium	1.00	high
5	low	high	1.00	medium
6	medium	high	1.00	high
7	high	high	1.00	very_high
8				

Figure 47: The rules for the liquidity assessment example.

More details on rules, fuzzy inference, and the use of the Matrix Rule Editor are contained in Section 6.3.3. The fuzzy logic system defined up to this point is stored as CREDIT3.FTL in the subdirectory \SAMPLES\BUSINESS\CREDIT\. If you are starting from here, open this file.

2.2.3 Interactive Debugging

In the last two sections, you have followed the basic steps of designing a fuzzy logic system. This section will show you how you can test the system's reaction to input data and view the entire inference process graphically.

Debug Modes

Experience shows that fuzzy logic designers spend most of their development time in debugging a system, that is, making it work the way it should. During debugging, you will test the system against sample cases and optimize its performance. *fuzzy*TECH features numerous debug modes to support this development step. All debug modes cooperate with the editors to expedite system verification. In this section, you will work with the Interactive debug mode.

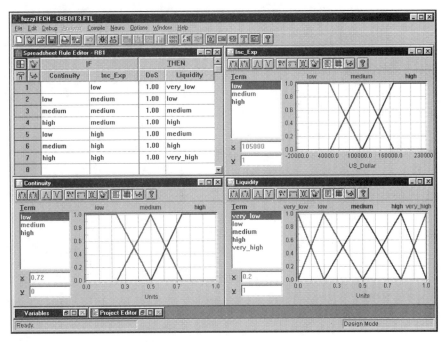

Figure 48: The fuzzy logic system CREDIT3.FTL..

When you switch from Design mode to any of the debug modes, the entire fuzzy logic system developed is simulated by *fuzzy*TECH. All editors become dynamic, that is, they display information flow, fuzzification, defuzzification, and rule inference graphically. However, most of the system components may still be edited during debugging.

Interactive Debug Mode

The Interactive debug mode shows the reaction of the system to input values set by yourself. All editors and analyzers of *fuzzy*TECH show the information flow graphically. When you modify any elements of the fuzzy logic system, you can see the effect instantly. This allows quick "If-Then" analyses. First, open the file CREDIT3.FTL, which contains the fuzzy logic system defined up to this point. Then open editors for the linguistic variables, open the Spreadsheet Rule Editor for the rule block, and arrange them as shown in Figure 48.

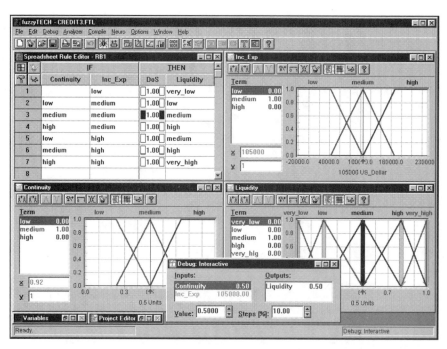

Figure 49: The main window of *fuzzy*TECH in Interactive debug mode.

Now, enable the Interactive debug mode in *fuzzy*TECH by either selecting Debug\Interactive from the menu bar or by clicking on the Interactive button 🔳 of the main toolbar. **Note:** the right field of the status line always shows the current debug mode.

Figure 49 shows the main window of *fuzzy*TECH immediately after the Interactive debug mode was enabled. A new window, the "Debug: Interactive" window, has opened. This window lists in the left list box "Inputs:," all input variables of the system, and in the right list box "Outputs:," all output variables with their current values. You can select a variable in the "Inputs:" list box and use the arrow buttons at the right side of the edit field "Value:" to change its value.

The field "Steps [%]:" lets you enter the stepwidth of the arrow buttons. Also, you can enter the value of the input variable directly in the "Value:" field.

Next enter the data for Customer DeMarco from the example shown in Table 1 into the Debug: Interactive window. Select "Continuity" in the left list box, enter the value "0.12" in the "Value:" field, and press the return key. Select "Inc_Exp" in the left list box, enter the value "118000" in the "Value:" field, and press the return key. The value of the output variable "Liquidity" is now displayed in the right list box as "0.26" (Figure 50).

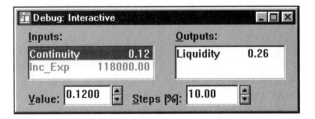

Figure 50: Data of customer DeMarco
in the Debug: Interactive window.

This decision, the ranking of customer DeMarco's liquidity as 0.26, is explained by all of the other windows in a fashion similar to that shown in Figure 49.

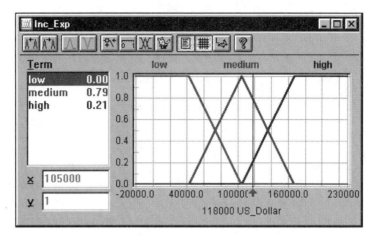

Figure 51: Linguistic Variable Editor
showing the fuzzification of "Inc_Exp."

Fuzzification Visualized

The editor windows of the input variables all visualize the fuzzification step. Figure 51 and Figure 52 show the editors visualizing the fuzzification of Inc_Exp and Continuity. The small red arrows under the horizontal axis of the associated membership function plot areas and the vertical lines at the same position denote the numerical input values. For Inc_Exp, this value is 118,000. **Note:** you may change this input value by dragging the red arrow to the left or right with the mouse. All other windows are updated automatically.

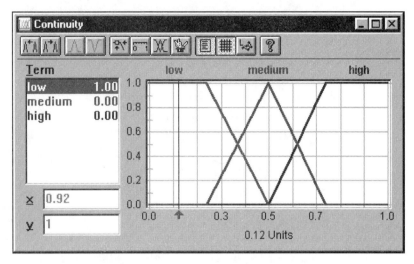

Figure 52: Linguistic Variable Editor
showing the fuzzification of "Continuity."

The vertical line shows how this numerical value maps into the membership functions. In the case of Inc_Exp, it cuts the membership function of the term "medium" at 0.79 and the membership function of the term "high" at a degree of 0.21. The "Term" list box at the left side of the variable editors shows these degrees of truth during any debug mode.

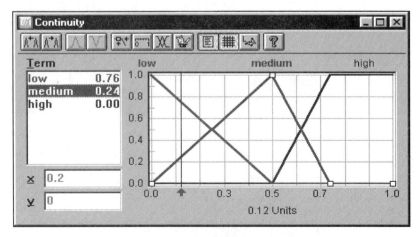

Figure 53: Editor for "Continuity"
after membership function modification.

Note: you can modify membership functions during debug mode. You may find that the membership function definition of the variable Continuity is not well reflected by the definition, as shown in Figure 52, because any value of Continuity lower than 0.25 is considered completely low. Modify the membership function definitions of Continuity as shown in Figure 53. First, drag the second definition point of the membership function of the term "low" to the left boundary. Now, select the term "medium" in the "Term" list box and also drag the second definition point of the membership function of the term "medium" to the left boundary.

Now, the vertical line cuts the membership functions of "low" and "medium" at degrees of 0.76 and 0.24 respectively. The "Term" list box also shows these degrees as well as all other windows of *fuzzy*TECH during debug mode. **Note:** the evaluation result for customer DeMarco has changed to a Liquidity assessment of 0.36. This is because of a more optimistic definition of the linguistic variable Continuity.

Rule Inference Visualized

Figure 54 shows the Spreadsheet Rule Editor in debug mode. Left and right of the DoS value, small bar gauges appear that give the firing degrees of the rules ▮1.00▮. The left bar gauge shows the validity of the "If-Part" of the rule, while the right gauge shows to what extent the "Then-Part" of the rule is valid. The "Then-Part" of the rule is valid to the degree the "If-Part" is valid, multiplied by the DoS. You may also change the value of the DoS during debugging. Simply click on the DoS value "1.00" of Rule 2 and select "0.5" in the list box that opens upon the click ▮0.50▮. With a DoS of 0.5, the "Then-Part" of Rule 2 only fires to a degree equal to half the validity of the "If-Part." While the bar gauges only give you coarse information about the rule firing degree, you can click directly on the gauge to open a properties window that lets you view the exact values:

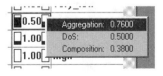

The degree of validity of the "If-Part" called "Aggregation" is 0.76. This results from the minimum for the degree of validity of "Continuity = low," (0.76), and the degree of validity of "Inc_Exp = medium," (0.79). Because the DoS is 0.5, the degree of validity of the "Then-Part" of the rule, that is "Liquidity = low," is evaluated to be valid to the degree 0.38. Change the DoS of Rule 2 back to "1.00" before you proceed.

	IF		THEN	
	Continuity	**Inc_Exp**	**DoS**	**Liquidity**
1		low	☐1.00☐	very_low
2	low	medium	■1.00■	low
3	medium	medium	☐1.00☐	medium
4	high	medium	☐1.00☐	high
5	low	high	☐1.00☐	medium
6	medium	high	☐1.00☐	high
7	high	high	☐1.00☐	very_high
8				

Figure 54: The Spreadsheet Rule Editor visualizes the rule inference.

As the bar gauges in Figure 54 show, Rules 2, 3, 5, and 6 do fire. **Note:** Rules 3 and 4 both have the same "Then-Part." Rule 3 concludes that "Liquidity = medium" with a degree of validity of 0.24. Rule 4 concludes the same result with a lower degree of validity, 0.21. The combination of these two rules is computed by the selected "result aggregation" method. Section 6.3.2 covers more details on this. The standard method is to use the maximum of the degrees of validity.

Defuzzification Visualized

Figure 55 shows the editor for the output variable Liquidity, a visual representation the defuzzification while in debug mode. The list box "Term" shows the results of the fuzzy logic rule inference:

Liquidity = {very_low = 0.00, low = 0.76, medium = 0.24, high = 0.21, very_high = 0.00}

The plot area of the variable editor shows gray arrows located at the maxima of each membership function. The degree to which a term is valid for the current linguistic value of Liquidity is indicated by the height to which the arrow is filled in black.

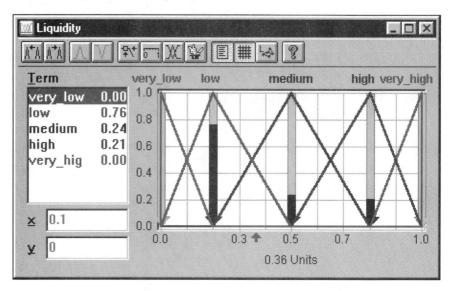

Figure 55: Linguistic Variable Editor
showing the defuzzification of "Liquidity."

The small red arrow under the horizontal axis shows the defuzzified numerical value of the variable. Because this value is the computation result of the fuzzy logic system, you cannot drag this red arrow. The numerical value is also displayed under the horizontal axis along with the base variable unit 0.36 Units .

You can also modify the membership functions of the output variable during debugging. For example, select the term "medium" in the "Term" list box, create a new definition point by double clicking on the term in the plot, and shape it such that it is similar to the one shown in Figure 56. Instantly, all open editors in _fuzzy_TECH reflect the effects of this modification.

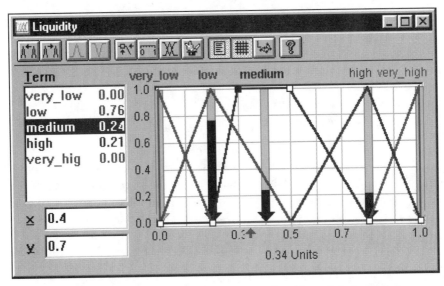

Figure 56: Defuzzification of the modified linguistic variable.

Debug Mode Modifications

You can change most parameters of a fuzzy logic system design while in a debug mode. These modifications include:

- adding, moving, and deleting membership function definition points

- adding, moving, and deleting the rules of the rule blocks

- changing any fuzzy logic operator

- changing the result aggregation

- changing the fuzzification or defuzzification method.

The effects of these changes are immediately reflected in all *fuzzy-*TECH editors.

Only structural modifications may not be made in debug mode. Structural modifications include the generation of terms, linguistic variables, rule blocks, and interfaces. Also, the UNDO function is disabled during debugging to ensure system consistency.

Other Debug Modes

To support all types of fuzzy logic applications, *fuzzy*TECH features a number of other debug modes. Here is an overview:

■ fT-Link

The fT-Link debug mode allows you to dynamically link *fuzzy*TECH to other software supporting the fT-Link interface. In contrast to using the *fuzzy*TECH DDE or DLL interface as a link between *fuzzy*TECH and other software, fT-Link provides a highly computation-efficient interface. If you have an application where massive amounts of data need to be exchanged between *fuzzy*TECH and the other software, you should use fT-Link.

■ Serial Link

The Serial Link debug mode allows *fuzzy*TECH to operate over the serial port. The settings for communication must be set in the Terminal dialog box, accessed via "Options\Terminal...." In Serial Link debug mode, *fuzzy*TECH acts as a slave to another computer that is connected at the serial port of your PC. After activation of Serial Debug mode, *fuzzy*TECH waits for the other computer to write all input values of the fuzzy logic system to the serial port. When all input values are received, *fuzzy*TECH computes the output values and writes them back to the serial port. Then, *fuzzy*TECH waits for the next input. The communication format is ASCII. ASC(31) is used as delimiter between values, and ASC(0) is used to indicate end of transmission. The Serial Link debug mode allows you to connect *fuzzy*TECH running on a PC with any other type of computer.

■ File Recorder

The File Recorder lets you use input data stored in files as input to the fuzzy logic system. These input data files may stem from databases, spreadsheet software, or the *fuzzy*TECH Pattern Generator.

■ Connection, Monitor, On-line

Once your final system is developed and you want to implement the fuzzy logic solution, you can use a *fuzzy*TECH code generator. These code generators generate source code in a programming language such as C, C++, or COBOL. If such code is implemented on another computer and you want to further debug this fuzzy logic system during operation, you can use these debug modes. They let you remotely, that is, over a serial port or a network, modify the fuzzy logic system on the other computer. These debug modes are only supported when the code generators are installed.

Using Debug Modes

You can switch between all debug modes without returning to design mode. Use the Debug pull-down menu of the menu bar to switch between modes. The currently active debug mode is displayed in the right field of the status line, the title bar of the Debug:<mode> window, and by check marks in the Debug pull-down menu. To return from any debug mode to design mode, either close the Debug:<mode> window by a double-click on the system icon ⊠ or select the currently active debug mode in the Debug pull-down menu again.

Note: you can save a project without leaving debug mode to make backup copies of your work and to document development progress.

2.2.4 File Debugging and Analyzers

This section introduces you to a different debug mode, the File debug mode, and to some of *fuzzy*TECH's analyzers that expedite the debugging step. First, open the file CREDIT3.FTL located in the subdirectory \SAMPLES\BUSINESS\CREDIT\, so that all modifications you have made in the previous Section are reversed.

The 3D Plot Analyzer

The benefit of fuzzy logic is that it elevates the level on which you model a decision from the numerical level to the linguistic level. This enables abstraction and generalization—features that are very hard to model mathematically. However, it is often useful to analyze the effects that a linguistic formulation of rules and membership functions has on the numerical level. To facilitate such an analysis, *fuzzy*TECH provides the 3D Plot analyzer.

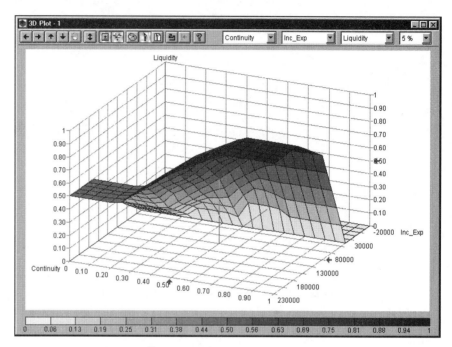

Figure 57: The 3D plot shows the numerical transfer characteristics of the system.

You can only open *fuzzy*TECH analyzers while you are in a debug mode. Thus, enable the Interactive debug mode now. Any active debug mode enables the Analyzer pull-down menu in the menu bar of *fuzzy*TECH and the analyzer buttons ▦▧▨▦ in the toolbar.

To open a 3D Plot, click on the 3D Plot button of the toolbar or select Analyzer\3D Plot... from the menu bar. This opens a window similar to Figure 57.

In the plot area of the window, the two input variables of the fuzzy logic system are displayed as horizontal axes and the output variable as the vertical axis. The height of the curve denoting the output variable value is also displayed, including a false coloring scheme.

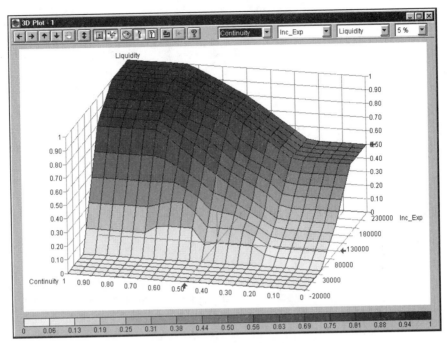

Figure 58: 3D plot after flip of horizontal axes.

The 3D Plot has its own toolbar that accesses functions local to the 3D Plot. You can also access all of these functions by invoking the properties menu with a right mouse click in the window. Since the curve is hard to see from the current viewpoint, invert the horizontal axis by clicking the Flip Horizontal Axis button 🔄 of the 3D Plot window's toolbar. This causes the 3D Plot to look as shown in Figure 58. The six fuzzy logic rules that you defined in earlier sections are computed by the fuzzy logic inference result in this transfer characteristic. From this plot, we determine that the area of low income, in light yellow (in the front of the plot), has been evaluated to have a value of very low liquidity. The higher the income, the better the liquidity evaluation. However, even the highest income with a poor continuity will not result in a liquidity assessment of higher than 0.5. On the other hand, high continuity only results in a fair liquidity assessment if the income is significant. Only if a customer has both a high income and a high continuity will they get an excellent liquidity assessment.

3D Plot Options

There are various tools that let you modify the 3D Plot to help you best visualize the three-dimensional curve. The five buttons on the left side of the toolbar of the 3D Plot ◄►▲▼◐ let you rotate the curve in any direction. If you click on one of the four arrow buttons, the plot moves a step in the direction of the arrow. To rotate, double-click on an arrow button. The rotation can be stopped by pressing the Stop Rotation button, indicated by a hand.

When you rotate the plot, it is refreshed, starting in the background and ending in the foreground of the 3D Space. This lets you "see" rear parts of a curve that would be otherwise hidden by the nearer parts of the curve.

If you do not want to see the rear parts of the curve, you can turn on the Background Paint option by clicking the Background button ▣ of the toolbar of the 3D Plot. Now, start rotation by double-clicking on one of the arrow buttons. With the background paint mode enabled, first the plot is completely computed and drawn in an invisible plot area, then displayed instantly upon completion. On fast PCs, the curve will rotate smoothly, allowing you to inspect it from any angle.

False Coloring

Because the height of a three-dimensional curve is hard to see, the 3D Plot uses false coloring. Every height—corresponding to a specific range of the output variable value—is associated with a specific color shade. The legend at the bottom of the 3D Plot window shows the mapping of output variable values to colors. You can change the color palette by clicking on the Change Color Palette button ▨ of the 3D Plot toolbar.

The three drop list boxes displaying variable names let you change the variables to be displayed. The drop list box displaying a percentage lets you select a resolution for the plot.

System Modifications in 3D Plot

As discussed before regarding the *fuzzy*TECH editors, system modifications made in any editor are reflected instantly in all other editor windows. In debug mode, this function is extended to all analyzers. If you learn during debugging that a low Continuity is not sufficiently compensated for by a very high Income as defined in Rule 5, you can click on the "Then-Part" field of Rule 5 in the Spreadsheet Rule Editor and change the entry from "medium" to "low." The 3D Plot instantly reflects the change in the transfer characteristics curve as shown in Figure 59.

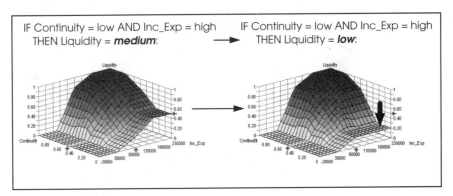

Figure 59: The effect of changing the "Then-Part" of Rule 5 from "medium" to "low" is shown instantly by the 3D Plot.

Note: the change in the curve is more obvious when the Background Paint option is enabled. Changes in the membership functions and other system parameters are immediately reflected by the analyzers as well.

Rule and Membership Function Tracing

The instant display of modifications in the 3D Plot can also be applied in reverse. For every point in the transfer characteristic, you can determine which rules and membership functions are contributing to a specific curve region. Simply drag the red arrows at the horizontal axes to the operating point in question. For example, drag the arrows to the middle of the horizontal space (Continuity = 0.5, Inc_Exp = 105,000).

The linguistic variable editors show the fuzzification and defuzzification, and the rule editors show the rule firing degrees that lead to the selected point of the transfer characteristic (Figure 60).

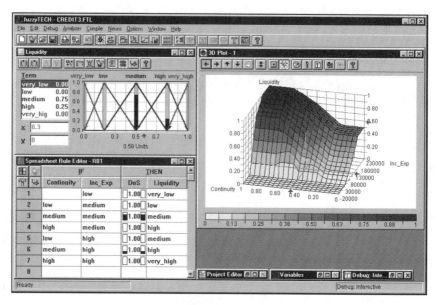

Figure 60: You can trace back every point of the transfer characteristic to the rules and membership functions leading to that behavior.

File Recorder Debug Mode

Often, fuzzy logic designers will test their systems with sample data. The sample data can be used with *fuzzy*TECH in many different ways. Integrated with *fuzzy*TECH is a File Recorder debug mode that can read ASCII formats of input data. In addition, a number of different interfaces with other software exist, such as those for DDE, DLL, OLE, Visual Basic, and Excel. Section 4 explains these interfaces in more detail.

The File Recorder debug mode can use row-and-column formatted ASCII files. The file formats are described in [21] and in the on-line help system. The sample customer list from Table 1 is contained in the file TEST1.IN located in the subdirectory \SAMPLES\BUSINESS\

CREDIT\. Select "File\View File…" from the menu bar, select the option "Input Data File (*.IN)" from the "Filetype" drop list box, select the file TEST1.IN from the "Files:" list box, and click [OK]. This opens an editor window for the file as shown in Figure 61. The first and third lines contain comments and the second line contains the input variable names. From Line 4 on, each line contains an input data record. The first column always contains the record name describing the record.

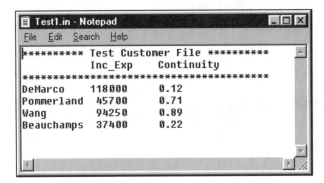

Figure 61: Test data file TEST1.FTL.

Close this editor window with a double-click on the system icon ⊠ and select "Debug\File Recorder" from the menu bar to open the "Read File Control Information From…" dialog box. Select the option "Input Data File (*.IN)" from the "Filetype" drop list box, select the file TEST1.IN from the "Files:" list box, and click [OK]. This opens the "File Control" dialog box as shown in Figure 62.

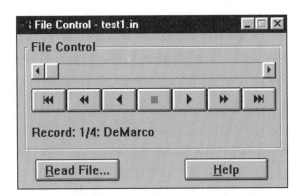

Figure 62: Navigate through sample date files from various sources.

The File Control dialog box always sits on top of all open windows to allow easy access to its controls. The group "File Information" in the upper part of the dialog box shows information about the sample data file and the current record. The current file TEST1.IN contains four records (Length: 4). The current record, named "DeMarco," is the first record (Number: 1). The group "Control" lets you browse through the data file. You may either use the scroll bar or the VCR-like control buttons. The leftmost and rightmost buttons ([|<<] and [>>|]) take you to the beginning and the end of the file respectively. The buttons with the single arrows ([<] and [>]) step one record back and ahead respectively. The double-arrow buttons ([<<] and [>>]) "play" the file in the respective direction.

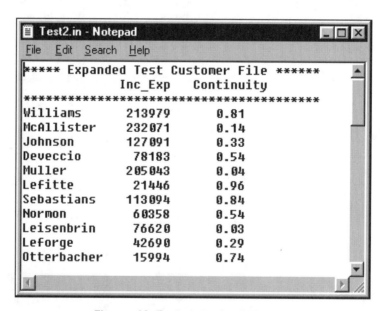

Figure 63: Test data file TEST2.IN.

Click on the right single arrow button [>] to step through the four examples. Similar to the Interactive debug mode, the fuzzy logic inference process—comprised of fuzzification, rule firing, and defuzzification—is shown in all editors and analyzers. The difference compared to the Interactive debug mode is that the input values are not set by the user manually, but rather come from the file opened by the File Recorder.

Data Tracing in the 3D Plot

In any debug mode, you can trace data in the 3D Plot analyzer. To enable the data tracing, enable the Trace button 📧 from the toolbar of the 3D Plot window. Rewind the sample data file in the File Control dialog box by clicking the leftmost button [|<<]. Press the right double-arrow button [>>] of the File Control dialog box to "play" through all four data records. The data points are traced in the 3D Plot analyzer as green dots. Press the [Read File...] button in the File Control dialog box and open the file TEST2.IN. This file contains sample data for 50 customers. Reset the trace in the plot by clicking the Reset button 📧 on the 3D Plot window toolbar. Then "play" the file TEST2.IN to trace the data points in the 3D Plot analyzer.

To see the data points more easily, click the Vertical button 📧. Figure 64 shows the 3D Plot Analyzer following these actions.

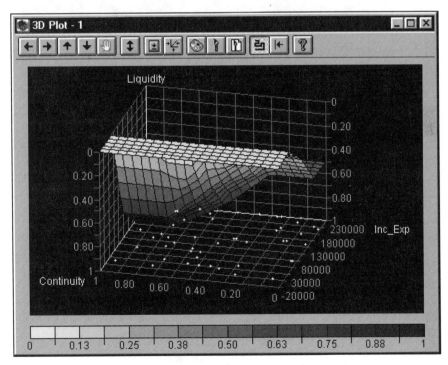

Figure 64: 3D Plot with Trace.

You can also view the 3D Plot in a "flat" perspective. Double-click on the Down button 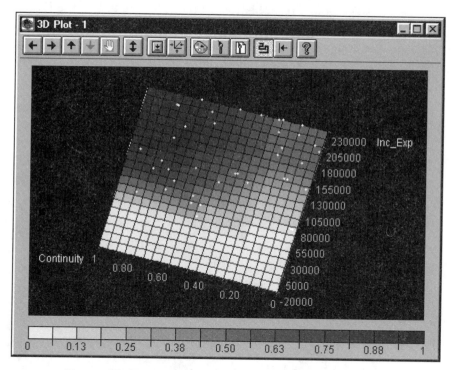 from the toolbar of the 3D Plot window. Open the file TEST3.IN, which contains a different set of 100 sample customer records, by clicking on the [Read File..] button of the File Control dialog box. Then, "play" the records by clicking the [>>] button of the File control dialog box. Figure 65 shows the 3D Plot after these actions.

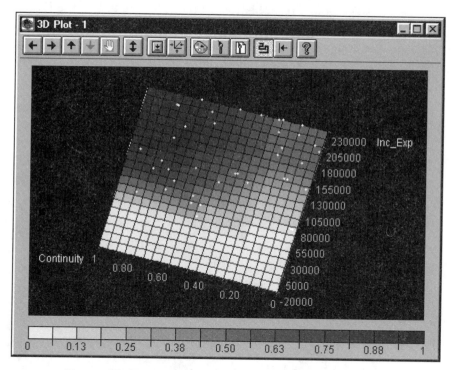

Figure 65: 3D Plot with trace and "flat" perspective.

You may open up to ten 3D Plots at the same time. Each 3D Plot may be configured differently and may display different variable combinations.

There is also another analyzer that is similar to the 3D Plot, but provides a different functionality: the Transfer Plot. The Transfer Plot is not discussed here; refer to the on-line help system or [22] on how to use the Transfer Plot.

The Statistics Analyzer

To optimize the rule base, it is useful to analyze how often and to what degree the rules of a rule base fire. The Statistics analyzer is a tool dedicated for this analysis. Simply select "Analyzer\Statistics" from the menu bar of *fuzzy*TECH or click on the Statistics button ▦ from the main window toolbar. Then open the Spreadsheet Rule editor that now displays another column titled [Statistics] as shown in Figure 66. The left bar gauge shows the minimum firing degree and the right bar gauge the maximum firing degree of each rule. The number in the middle counts how often the rule fires with a degree of larger than zero.

		IF		THEN		Statistics
		Continuity	Inc_Exp	DoS	Liquidity	min - # - max
1			low	1.00	very_low	0
2		low	medium	1.00	low	0
3		medium	medium	1.00	medium	0
4		high	medium	1.00	high	0
5		low	high	1.00	medium	0
6		medium	high	1.00	high	0
7		high	high	1.00	very_high	0
8						

Figure 66: Spreadsheet Rule Editor with Statistics column.

Now, "play" the file TEST3.IN with the File Recorder. While playing, the Statistics analyzer keeps track of the firing intensity and frequency. Figure 67 shows the results. From this information you can see that all rules have fired at least once with the sample customer data and that Rule 1 fires most often and Rule 4 least often.

You can reset the Statistics analyzer by clicking the [min-#-max] button. To configure the Statistics analyzer, click on the [Statistics] button. This opens the dialog box shown in Figure 68 that lets you switch the statistics display from absolute rule count to relative rule count and exit the Statistics analyzer.

Spreadsheet Rule Editor - RB1				
	IF		THEN		Statistics
	Continuity	Inc_Exp	DoS	Liquidity	min - # - max
1		low	▉1.00▉ very_low		74
2	low	medium	□1.00□ low		68
3	medium	medium	□1.00□ medium		54
4	high	medium	□1.00□ high		10
5	low	high	□1.00□ medium		14
6	medium	high	□1.00□ high		16
7	high	high	□1.00□ very_high		12
8					

Figure 67: Spreadsheet Rule Editor with Statistics column after processing the 100 customer records of TEST3.IN.

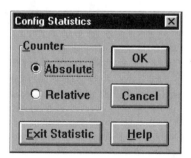

Figure 68: The Config Statistics dialog box.

The Time Plot Analyzer

If you have time-dependent data, you can use the Time Plot analyzer to plot variable values over time. The file TEST4.IN contains such time-dependent sample data. The file TEST1.IN is located in the subdirectory \SAMPLES\BUSINESS\CREDIT\. Select "File\View File…" from the menu bar, select the option "Input Data File (*.IN)" from the

"Filetype" drop list box, select the file TEST4.IN from the "Files:" list box, and click [OK]. This opens an editor window for the file as shown in Figure 69. From Line 4 on, each line contains an input data record describing Continuity and Inc_Exp of a customer for the years 1970 to 1995.

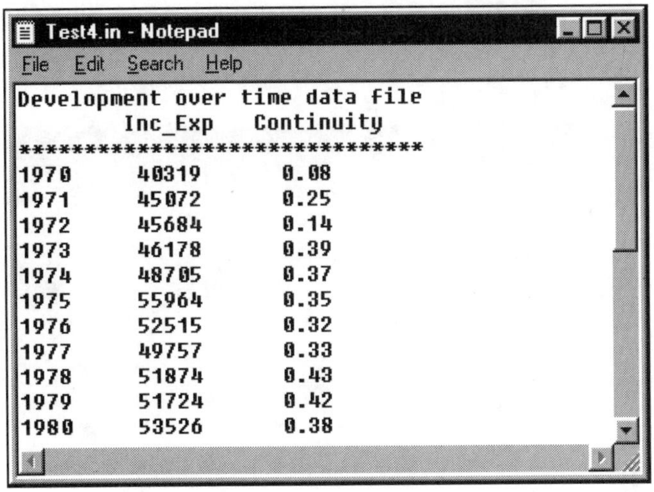

Figure 69: Test data file TEST4.IN.

Now close the Editor window and open the file TEST4.IN with the File Recorder by clicking on the [Read File...] button of the File Control dialog box. Select TEST4.IN in the Read File Control Information From... dialog box.

Configuring the Time Plot

To open a Time Plot, either select Analyzer\Time Plot from the menu bar or click on the Time Plot button 🖫 of the main window toolbar. This opens the Time Plot Configuration dialog box as shown in Figure 70. This dialog box lets you select the plot items for display. The currently selected plot items are listed in the "Plot Items:" list box at the right of the dialog box. The three other list boxes show possible items that can be selected for display. The list box "Variables:" lists the three linguistic variables of the current fuzzy logic system. The list box "Terms:" lists terms of linguistic variables that have no membership functions. Since the current fuzzy logic system does not contain any such variables, the list box is empty. The list box "Rule Block:" and the fields "Rule:" and "Out:" let you select individual rules for display. Next select the three linguistic variables for display. You can either select the variables with the mouse and then click on the [>>] button, or simply double-click on the linguistic variables. When all three linguistic variables are listed in the "Plot Items" list box, click the [OK] button to close the dialog box.

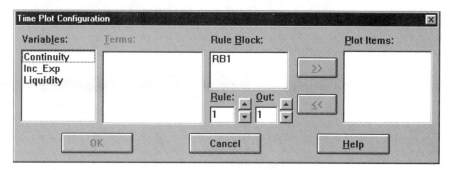

Figure 70: Time Plot Configuration dialog box.

This opens the Time Plot window as shown in Figure 71. The list box on the right shows the same plot item list as the Time Plot Configuration dialog box. Select a plot item in this list box to display its scale on the left side of the plot area.

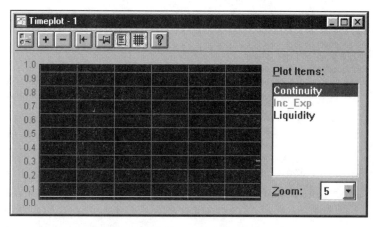

Figure 71: Time Plot window.

Now "play" the file TEST4.IN with the File Recorder by pressing the [>>] button of the File Control dialog box. Figure 72 shows how the Time Plot draws the contents of the file in the plot area. Over time, both the income and the continuity of the customer increased. As a result of this, the liquidity assessment increased as well. The "Zoom:" factor lets you stretch the horizontal axis of the plot. Set the zoom factor to "12" by clicking three times on the [+] button of the toolbar of the Time Plot, or by entering "12" in the "Zoom:" drop list box directly:

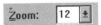

This stretches the display horizontally.

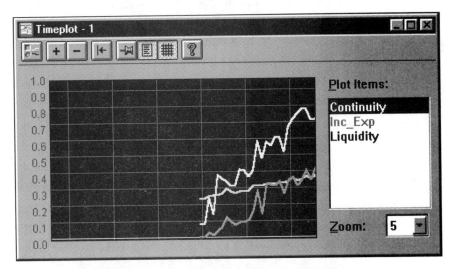

Figure 72: Time Plot window displaying the linguistic variable values of TEST4.IN.

Time Plot of Rule Firing Degrees

You may also display rule firing degrees over time intervals using the Time Plot analyzer. Just open a new Time Plot by selecting Analyzer\Time Plot from the menu bar or clicking on the Time Plot button [📊] of the main window toolbar. This again opens the Time Plot Configuration dialog box as shown in Figure 70. Now, select all rules of the system for display. Double-click on the "RB1" entry in the "Rule

Block:" list box to select the first rule of rule block "RB1." In the "Plot Items:" list box, this rule is listed as "RB1.1.1." This notation shows the rule block number, the rule number in the rule block, and the number of the output variable for the rule, separated by points. Since all rules of the rule block have only one output variable, the last value is always "1."

To select the second rule for display, click on the [^] button to the right of the field "Rule:", so that the field displays the value "2":

Then double-click on the "RB1" entry in the "Rule Block:" list box to select the second rule of rule block "RB1" for display. In the "Plot Items:" list box, this rule is listed as "RB1.2.1." Proceed with this until all seven rules of the rule block appear in the "Plot Items:" list box. Then click [OK] to close the Time Plot Configuration dialog box and to open the Time Plot window which shows the rule firing degrees. Also, set the zoom to "12" in this Time Plot window. "Play" the file TEST4.IN again to plot the rule firing degrees. The result is shown in Figure 73.

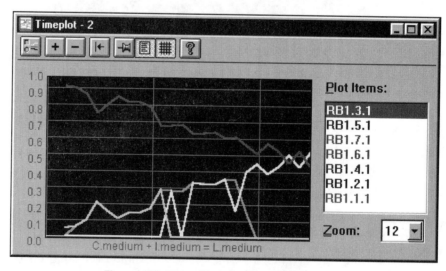

Figure 73: Time Plot window displaying
the rule firing degrees of TEST4.IN.

Note: when you select rules in the "Plot Items:" list box, a quick rule description appears under the plot area:

C.medium + l.medium = L.medium

The linguistic variable names here are abbreviated to their first letter. You can open up to ten Time Plot windows simultaneously. All ten Time Plots may be configured differently and may display different plot items. You can also mix rules with linguistic variables in the same Time Plot.

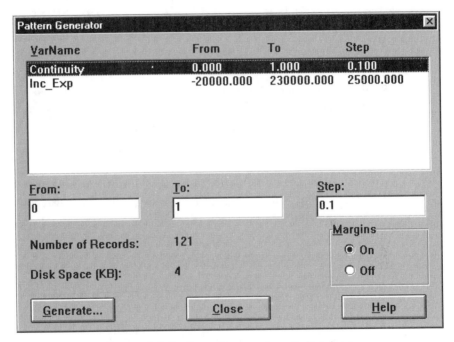

Figure 74: Pattern Generator dialog box.

Pattern Generator

Up until now, you have worked with prefabricated test data files. For consistency and completeness tests, you can also use the built-in pattern generator of *fuzzy*TECH. Select File\Pattern Generator... from the menu bar to open the Pattern Generator dialog box as shown in Figure 74. The Pattern Generator generates input data files that go through specified input variable combinations. For each input variable, the Pattern Generator lets you specify the interval and the step width of the values generated. To change the default settings, select the variable in the upper list box and change the values in the "From:," "To:," and "Step:" fields.

If you want to ensure that the "To:" values are always included in the patterns, even when they would not show up as a step, set "Margins" to "On." The Pattern Generator always shows you how many records will be generated with the current settings as well as how much disk space this will take. Accept the default settings and click the [Generate...] button. Accept the file name "CREDIT3.PTN" suggested by the Pattern Generator by clicking [OK] in the "Generate Pattern To..." dialog box. Click [Yes] to view the generated file in the "fuzzyTECH Confirm" dialog box, which opens after the file is generated. This opens a text editor window that lets you view the file contents. You can go ahead and close the editor window.

Batch Debug Mode

The generated file contains only input variable values. You may "play" this file using the File Recorder. If you also want to store the output variable values in a file, you can use the Batch debug mode of *fuzzy*TECH. **Note:** you can use the Batch debug mode with any data file, not only those generated by the Pattern Generator.

To invoke the Batch debug mode, select Debug\Batch from the menu bar. Specify the file "CREDIT3.PTN" you just generated as the "Filename" in the "Read Input From..." dialog box and click [OK]. Accept the filename "CREDIT3.OUT" in the dialog box "Write Output To..." by clicking [OK]. Click on [OK] in the "fuzzyTECH Confirm" dialog box that opens after the file is generated. This opens a text editor window that lets you view the file contents as shown in Figure 75.

The Batch debug mode copied the columns of the input variables and added a column for each output variable that displays its corresponding value for each input record. An additional column labeled "_flags_" indicates whether any rules fired or not. A value of "0" indicates that at least one rule did fire.

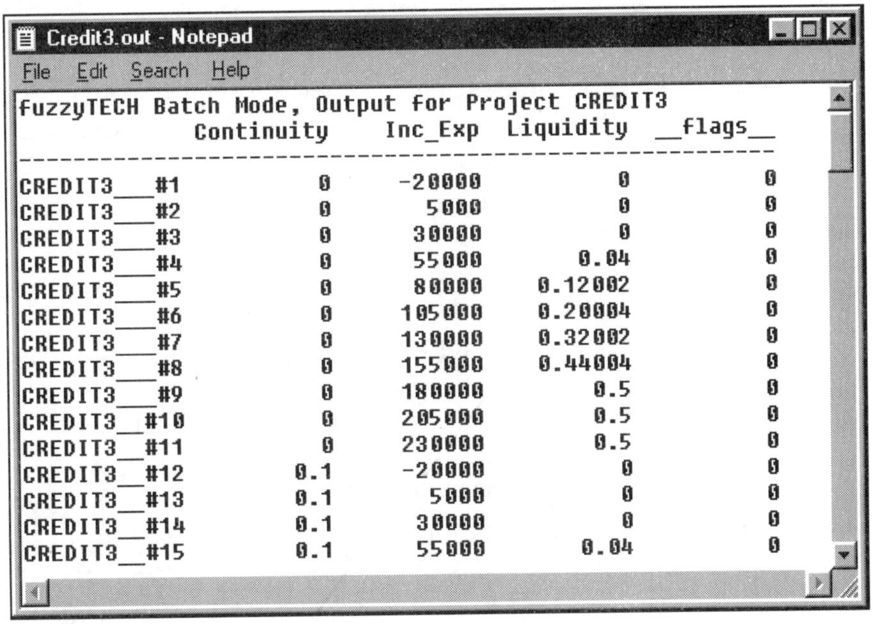

```
Credit3.out - Notepad                                    _ □ ✕
File  Edit  Search  Help
fuzzyTECH Batch Mode, Output for Project CREDIT3
             Continuity     Inc_Exp  Liquidity  __flags__
------------------------------------------------------------
CREDIT3___#1          0     -20000          0           0
CREDIT3___#2          0       5000          0           0
CREDIT3___#3          0      30000          0           0
CREDIT3___#4          0      55000       0.04           0
CREDIT3___#5          0      80000    0.12002           0
CREDIT3___#6          0     105000    0.20004           0
CREDIT3___#7          0     130000    0.32002           0
CREDIT3___#8          0     155000    0.44004           0
CREDIT3___#9          0     180000        0.5           0
CREDIT3__#10          0     205000        0.5           0
CREDIT3__#11          0     230000        0.5           0
CREDIT3__#12        0.1     -20000          0           0
CREDIT3__#13        0.1       5000          0           0
CREDIT3__#14        0.1      30000          0           0
CREDIT3__#15        0.1      55000       0.04           0
```

Figure 75: Edit window for the output of the Batch debug mode.

2.3   Extending the System

The last section introduced you to the basic functionality of *fuzzy-*TECH using a very simple two-input, one-output fuzzy logic system. In this section, you will expand the fuzzy logic system and explore more features of the *fuzzy*TECH design software.

2.3.1 Adding New Components

To reverse all changes you may have made to the current fuzzy logic system, open the file CREDIT3.FTL again now. In this Section, you will learn how to add objects, such as linguistic variables, rule blocks, interfaces, and remarks, to the system manually rather than using the Fuzzy Design Wizard.

Creating Remark Objects

Remarks are text objects that can be placed freely in the Project Editor window to illustrate and comment on the structure of the fuzzy logic system under design. To create a remark, you either select Edit\Create Remark from the menu bar, open the properties menu of the Project Editor window, or click on the Create Remark button 🗒 of the main window toolbar. This opens the Remark Properties dialog box as depicted in Figure 76. Enter the text "Creditworthiness Evaluation" in the "Text:" field, and press the button [Color]. This opens the Color dialog box that is shown in Figure 77.

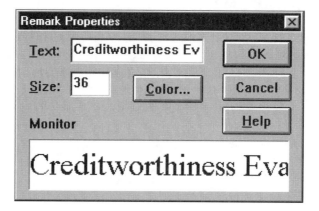

Figure 76: Remark Properties dialog box.

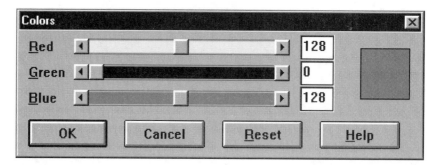

Figure 77: The Colors dialog box lets you define object coloring.

The Color dialog box lets you define the coloring of objects in *fuzzy*-TECH. Remarks can be colored to illustrate complex fuzzy logic system structures. For example, you can set the scroll bars as shown in Figure 77 to color the remark in a shade of purple. When you have selected the color, click [OK] to return to the Remark Properties dialog box. The "Monitor" field of this dialog box shows how the remark will look with the current font size and color. To change the font size, you can enter a different number in the "Size:" field.

Click [OK] to close the Remark Properties dialog box. Then position the remark object in the Project Editor window by mouse click similar to Figure 78. The frame around the text indicates that the object is highlighted. A double-click on the text will open the Remark Properties dialog box again.

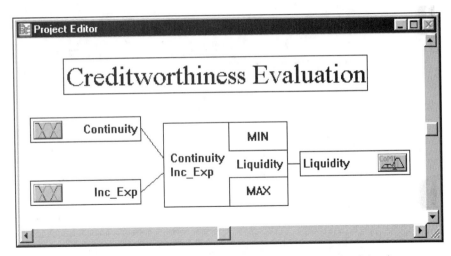

Figure 78: Project editor windows with remark object.

Creating Linguistic Variables

To expand the current fuzzy logic system, you will now create two new linguistic variables, Security and Financial. Security will be a new input variable that will be combined through a new rule block with the output of the first rule block, Liquidity, to result in the new output variable, Financial. New linguistic variables can be created by both the Fuzzy Design Wizard as well as directly using the Edit\Create New Variable function that invokes the Linguistic Variable Wizard.

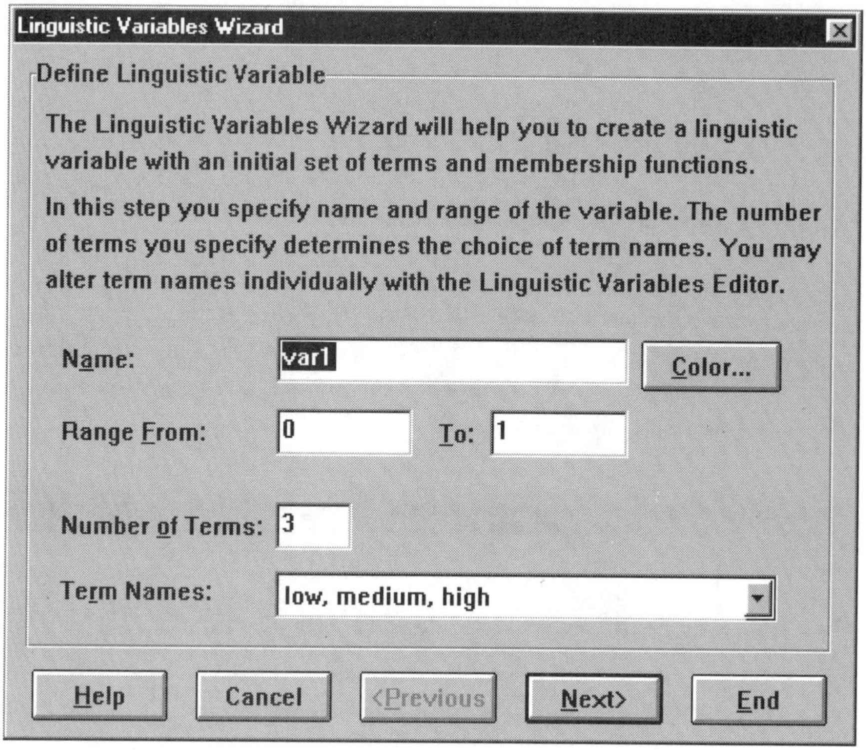

Linguistic Variables Wizard   ⊠

Define Linguistic Variable

The Linguistic Variables Wizard will help you to create a linguistic
variable with an initial set of terms and membership functions.

In this step you specify name and range of the variable. The number
of terms you specify determines the choice of term names. You may
alter term names individually with the Linguistic Variables Editor.

Name:	var1	Color...
Range From:	0 To: 1	
Number of Terms:	3	
Term Names:	low, medium, high	

Help	Cancel	<Previous	Next>	End

Figure 79: Name, Range, and Term definition
with the Linguistic Variables Wizard.

To create a new linguistic variable, either select Edit\Create New
Variable from the main menu bar, open the properties menu of the
Variables window and select the Create Variable option, or click on the
Variable button ▣ of the main window toolbar. Each action opens the
first window of the Linguistic Variables Wizard which is depicted in
Figure 79. Enter the text "Security" in the "Name:" field

Name:	Security

the range [-1; 1]

Range From:	-1 To: 1

the term number "7"

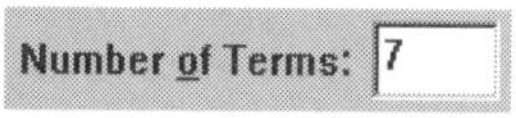

Number of Terms:	7

and click the [Next>] button. This moves you to the second window of the Linguistic Variables Wizard as shown in Figure 80. In this window you can define a complete set of membership functions in one single step.

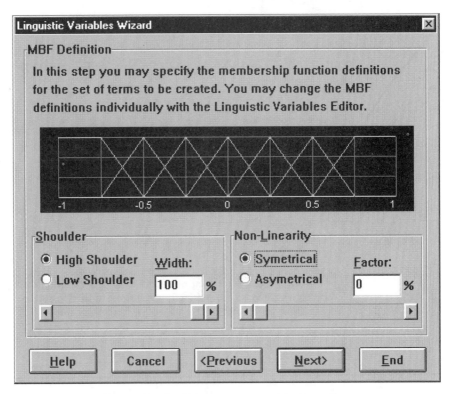

Figure 80: Defining membership functions
with the Linguistic Variables Wizard.

The group "Shoulder" lets you define width and value of limit for the membership functions. "High Shoulder" is used for most input variables, "Low Shoulder" for most output variables. The "Width" of the shoulder can be set with relative respect to the distance of the membership functions. The group "Non-Linearity" lets you modify the relative distance of the membership functions in a "Symmetrical" or "Asymmetrical" fashion. The amount of non-linearity is expressed by a relative "Factor".

Try out the different options and parameter settings to see the effect to the membership function definition in the small plot area of the Linguistic Variables Wizard. Then set the options as shown in Figure 80, and press the [Next>] button to open the third window of the Linguistic Variables Wizard which is shown in Figure 81.

In this window you verbally describe the variable for later documentation. You can always view and edit this text by selecting the "Comments.." option from the properties menu of the variable in the Variables window.

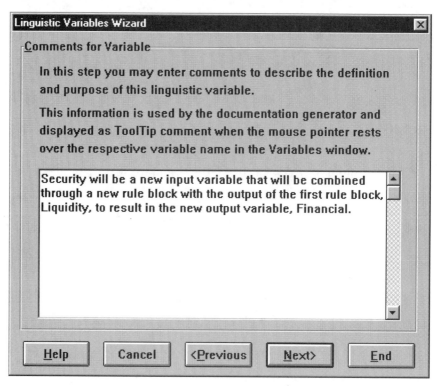

Figure 81: Entering Comments for the new
variable with the Linguistic Variables Wizard.

Press the [Next>] button to generate the specified variable and confirm the dialog that appears. This creates the new variable Security and opens a variable editor window for it at the same time. Figure 82 shows this variable editor window.

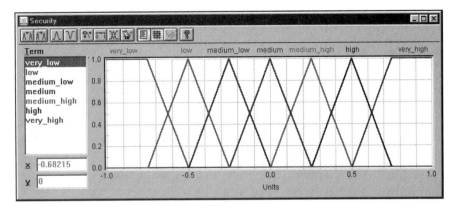

Figure 82: Variable Editor window for Security.

Editing Terms

Because the linguistic variable Security only requires three terms, erase the terms "very_low", "medium_low", "medium_high", and "very_high" by selecting them in the Term list box and pressing the [Del] key. Alternatively you may use the Delete option of the properties menu of the term. Press the Standard MBF ▨ button of the toolbar to convert the membership functions to Standard MBFs. Your set of membership function should now look as shown in Figure 83.

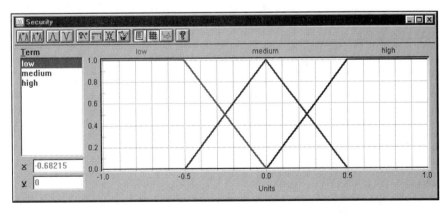

Figure 83: Variable Editor window for Security.

To edit term names and properties, just double-click on the term name in the "Term" list box. Double-click on "low" to open the Term dialog box as shown in Figure 84. This dialog box lets you change the name of a term in the "Term Name" field, select a membership function shape in the "Shape" group, and define the position of the current term in the sequence of terms in the "Position" list box. You can also change the color in which the term is plotted by clicking the [Color...] button.

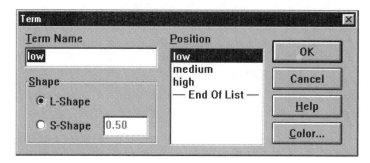

Figure 84: Term dialog box for "term1."

Now enter the text "bad" in the "Term Name" field

and click the [OK] button. Then, double-click on "medium" in the "Term" list box to open a Term dialog box for the second term. Change the name of the term to "fair". Repeat the operation once more for "high" to change the name of the this term to "excellent".

To change the base variable interval, click on the Base Variable button  of the toolbar of the variable editor for Security. Set the base variable interval to [-1; 2] by entering "-1" in the "Min:" field and "2" in the "Max:" field

| Min: | -1 |
| Max: | 2 |

of the Base Variable dialog box. Click [OK] to leave the Base Variable dialog box.

You may also use the Fuzzy Design Wizard for adding system components. For example, use the Fuzzy Design Wizard to generate the second new linguistic variable Financial.

Adding System Components with the Fuzzy Design Wizard

Invoke the Fuzzy Design Wizard by clicking the respective button ![icon] of the main toolbar. In the first Fuzzy Design Wizard dialog box, select "Append to existing system"

> ◉ **Append to existing system**

and press the return key or click the [Next>] button. In the next dialog box of the Fuzzy Design Wizard, enter "0" in the "Input LVs" field, "1" in the "Output LVs" field,

> **Input LVs:**   `0`
>
> **Output LVs:**   `1`

and either press the return key or click the [Next>] button to move to the next dialog box. Here, overwrite the "Name:" field with the text "Financial"

> **Name:**   `Financial`

and either press the return key or click the [Next>] button. Accept the defuzzification method selection in the next dialog box by pressing the return key or clicking the [Next>] button. In the next dialog box, enter "0" in the "Rule Blocks:" field because you will generate the new rule block manually:

> **Rule Blocks:**   `0`

Press the return key or click the [Next>] button to confirm and click [Yes] in the confirmation dialog box to close the Fuzzy Design Wizard and append the defined components, i.e., the new linguistic variable, to the current fuzzy logic system under design.

As a result of this, the Fuzzy Design Wizard has created both the linguistic variable Financial as well as an interface

in the Project Editor window. Open a linguistic variable editor window for Financial by double-clicking on "Financial" in the Variables window. Now, move the membership functions for very_low and very_high so they appear as depicted in Figure 85 because the most typical values for these terms are zero and one respectively.

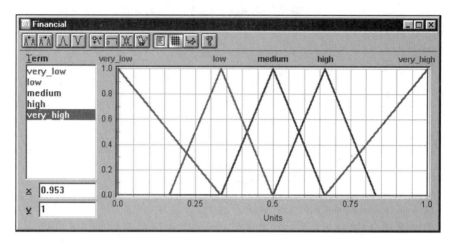

Figure 85: Linguistic Variable Editor window for Financial.

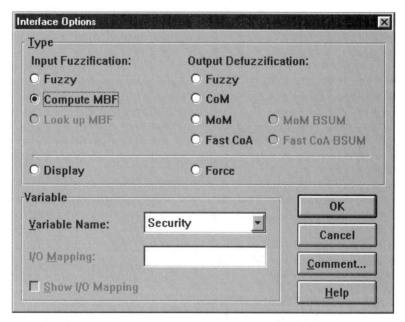

Figure 86: The Interface Options dialog box lets you specify fuzzification and defuzzification methods to be applied for the interface variable.

Adding an Interface

While the Fuzzy Design Wizard has automatically created an interface for the system structure in the Project Editor window, the variable Security which was created manually does not have an interface yet. Thus, either select Edit\Create Interface from the menu bar, open the properties menu of the Project Editor window, or click the Interface button ▣ of the main toolbar. This opens the Interface Options dialog box that is depicted in Figure 86. In this dialog box you select the method of fuzzification or defuzzification to be applied in the interface. The method you select here implies whether the interface is created as input or output interface. For more details in fuzzification and defuzzification methods, see Section 6.

The variable for which the interface shall be generated is selected in the "Interface Variable" group. Because currently only one variable in the system exists for which no interface has yet been defined, the list contains only "Security" as an option. You can leave all the selections of the Interface Options dialog box at the values suggested. Click on [OK] to leave the dialog box and create the interface. This causes the interface block for Security to appear in the Project Editor window:

Creation of a Rule Block

Now that two new variables and two new interfaces are generated, you need a new rule block to compute Financial out of Security and Liquidity. To create a new rule block, either select Edit\Create Rule Block from the menu bar, open the properties menu of the Project Editor window, or click on the Rule Block button ▣ of the main toolbar. This opens the Rule Block Wizard as shown in Figure 87. The list box "Variables" lists all linguistic variables available to the rule block. To select variables, first highlight the variable name in the list box, then click the [>Input>] or [>Output>] button for the selection. To reverse a selection, first highlight the variable name, then click the [<Remove<] button. Select Liquidity and Security as input variables and Financial as an output variable.

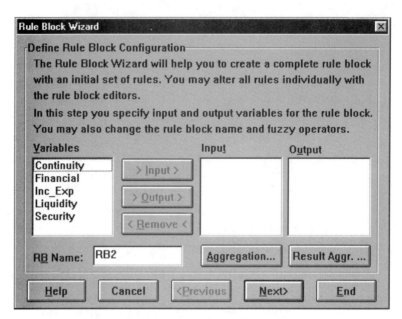

Figure 87: Select the input and output variables
of a rule block in the Rule Block Wizard.

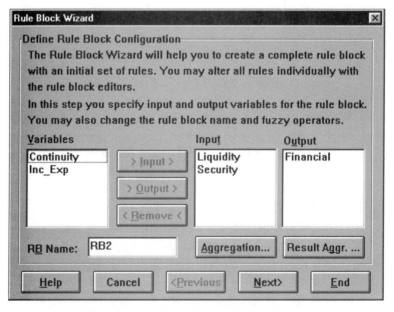

Figure 88: Select Liquidity and Security as input
variables and Financial as an output variable.

To distinguish rule blocks and the rules therein, you can give each rule block a name in the field "RB Name:". Enter "Second_RB" in this field. When you have made all selections as shown by Figure 88, click on [Next>] to move to the next window of the Rule Block Wizard shown by Figure 89.

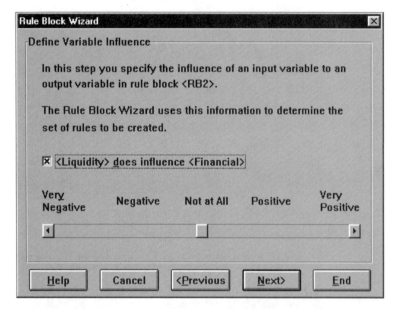

Figure 89: By specifying the influence of each input variable to each output variable, the Rule Block Wizard automatically generates rules.

This and its subsequent windows can automatically generate an initial set of rules for the rule block if you specify whether, in what direction, and to what extend each output variable is affected by each input variable of a rule block. Because in this example, the rules will be entered later manually, disable the check box:

☐ <Liquidity> does influence <Financial>

to indicate that the Rule Block Wizard shall generate no rules for the variable Liquidity's influence on Financial. Click [Next>] to move to the next window of the Rule Block Wizard shown by Figure 90. This window defines variable Security's influence on Liquidity. Also, disable this check box and click [Next>] to move to the next window of the Rule Block Wizard shown by Figure 91.

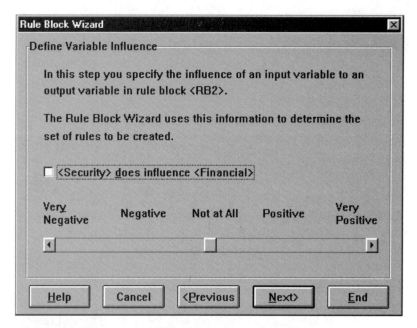

Figure 90: Disable the check box to suppress rule generation.

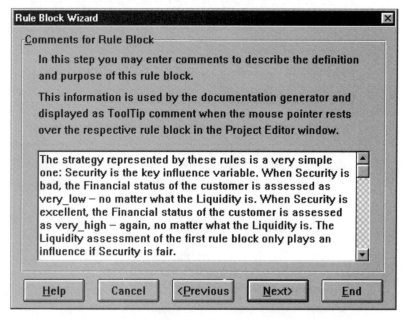

Figure 91: Entering Comments for the new
rule block with the Rule Block Wizard.

In this window you verbally describe the rule block for later documentation. You can always view and edit this text by selecting the "Comments.." option from the properties menu of the rule block in the Project Editor window. Press the [Next>] button to generate the specified rule block and confirm the dialog that appears. This creates the new rule block in the Project Editor.

The new rule block is depicted by a larger box showing the respective input and output variables:

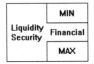

Arrange all the objects in the Project Editor window so their positions are similar to Figure 92 by dragging them with the mouse. **Note:** you can also move highlighted objects with the cursor keys. You may also add remarks to help explain the structure of the fuzzy logic system.

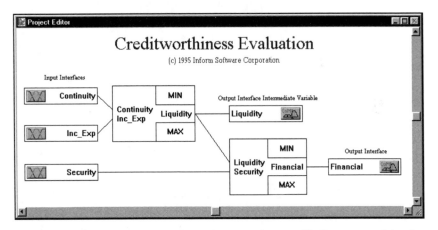

Figure 92: Structure of the fuzzy logic system with the new objects.

Defining Rules for Second_RB

The only step left to complete the expanded system is the definition of rules for the new rule block Second_RB. Open the Spreadsheet Rule Editor for the new rule block by double-clicking on the rule block box in the Project Editor window. Now, enter the rules as shown in Figure 93.

Spreadsheet Rule Editor - Second_RB				
	IF		**THEN**	
	Liquidity	Security	DoS	Financial
1		bad	1.00	very_low
2		excellent	1.00	very_high
3	very_low	fair	1.00	very_low
4	low	fair	1.00	low
5	medium	fair	1.00	medium
6	high	fair	1.00	high
7	very_high	fair	1.00	very_high
8				

Figure 93: Rules for the new rule block.

The strategy represented by these rules is a very simple one: Security is the key influence variable. When Security is bad, the Financial status of the customer is assessed as very_low – no matter what the Liquidity is. When Security is excellent, the Financial status of the customer is assessed as very_high – again, no matter what the Liquidity is. The Liquidity assessment of the first rule block only plays an influence if Security is considered to be fair. **Note:** this is no reasonable assumption at all; the rules in this example shall only serve for illustration on how to design and analyze fuzzy logic systems.

2.3.2 Interactive Debugging of Complex Projects

If you start work here, open the file CREDIT4.FTL that is located in the subdirectory \SAMPLES\BUSINESS\CREDIT\. It contains the fuzzy logic system as designed up to this point. In this Section, you will debug the expanded fuzzy logic system and learn about some more advanced debugging techniques.

To debug the system, either select Debug\Interactive from the menu bar or click the Interactive button [■] on the main toolbar. Open a 3D Plot analyzer by either selecting Analyzer/3D Plot from the menu bar or by clicking the 3D Plot button [■] of the main toolbar. In contrast to what happened when you clicked this button with the smaller system that you designed in Section 2.2, now a 3D Plot Configuration dialog box opens. Figure 94 shows this dialog box. Double-click on the variables Inc_Exp and Security to make them appear in the list box "3D Plot Input:". Double-click on the variable Financial to make it appear in the list box "3D Plot Output:". Alternatively, you can first highlight a variable in a list, and then click one of the buttons in the middle of the list boxes. Now, click [OK] to close the 3D Plot Configuration dialog box and open the 3D Plot analyzer window.

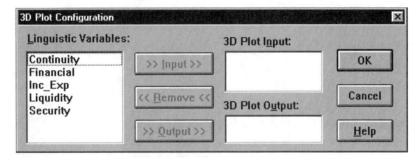

Figure 94: In fuzzy logic systems with more than 2 inputs and 1 output, the 3D Plot Configuration dialog box specifies variables for display.

For better viewing, rotate the 3D Plot window as shown in Figure 95. Also, activate the background paint mode of the 3D Plot by selecting the Background 🔳 button of the toolbar of the 3D Plot window. Open editors for all linguistic variables, hide their term list boxes, and configure their window sizes such that they are as small as possible. Arrange all windows in a manner similar to that shown in Figure 95.

The upper three variable editors show the three inputs of the system. You can set any combination of input variables by dragging the small red arrows. The two lower variable editors show the output variable Financial and the intermediate variable Liquidity. In an actual implementation, the interface of Liquidity can be erased if only the result Financial is required.

Of the three input variables, only two—Inc_Exp and Security—are displayed as input variables in the 3D Plot analyzer. This is because the 3D Plot analyzer can only plot three dimensions: two inputs and one output. To show the effect of input variables of the fuzzy logic system that are not displayed as input variables in the 3D Plot analyzer, the 3D Plot is computed dynamically when the repaint option is on (default setting). Try it: move the red arrow in the variable editor for Continuity—the input variable not displayed in the 3D Plot—to the left and to the right. This causes the surface of the curve in the 3D Plot analyzer to change. If you have high CPU and video performance on your PC, this will appear as a smooth movement.

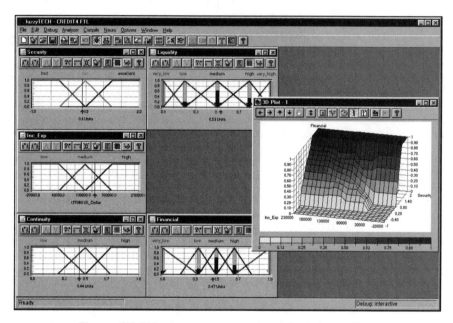

Figure 95: Windows arrangement for interactive debugging of the expanded system.

Figure 96 shows the effect of the variable Continuity on the transfer curve. These curves can be interpreted as follows: for Security = high, Financial = very_high; for Security = low, Financial = very_low. This is what you expect with a rule set as defined in Figure 93. For Security = medium, the evaluation of Financial depends on the assessment of Liquidity. Liquidity depends on Inc_Exp and Continuity. Inc_Exp is a plotted variable while Continuity is not. Any change of the value of Continuity is thus reflected in the shape of the curve. If Continuity = high (right curve in Figure 96), a high Inc_Exp will result in Financial = very_high, compensating for the fact that Security is only medium. In the case of a low Continuity (left curve in Figure 96), a high Inc_Exp will not compensate for Security = medium.

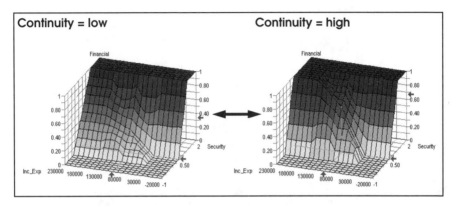

Figure 96: The evaluation of financial from the inputs Inc_Exp on the value of continuity as visualized by the changing surface of the transfer curve.

Analyzing the curves is one way to understand the conclusion a fuzzy logic system reaches. Another way is to look at fuzzy logic inference on a linguistic level, that is, at the rule inference level. Consider the example records shown in Table 6. You can either enter the values in the Debug:Interactive window or use the File Recorder and load the file TEST5.IN that contains these records. Table 7 shows the fuzzy logic evaluation results. You can use the Batch debug mode to generate these results in file format from the file TEST5.IN.

Record	Inc_Exp	Continuity	Security
rec_1	25,500	0.30	1.1
rec_2	100,000	0.84	1.1
rec_3	100,000	0.84	0.4
rec_4	100,000	0.50	0.4
rec_5	100,000	0.35	0.4
rec_6	175,000	0.35	0.4

Table 6: Example records for the extended system (TEST5.IN).

For rec_1, Figure 97 shows the inference flow. During the fuzzification step, this customer is evaluated to have a low Inc_Exp; a very low, somewhat medium Continuity; and a pretty much excellent, just slightly fair Security:

Inc_Exp	=	{ low = 1.0; medium = 0.0; high = 0.0 }
Continuity	=	{ low = 0.77; medium = 0.23; high = 0.0 }
Security	=	{ bad = 0.0; fair= 0.2; excellent = 0.8 }

Record	Inc_Exp	Continuity	Security	Financial	Liquidity
rec_1	25,500	0.3	1.1	0.80	0.00
rec_2	100,000	0.84	1.1	0.86	0.73
rec_3	100,000	0.84	0.4	0.58	0.73
rec_4	100,000	0.5	0.4	0.43	0.46
rec_5	100,000	0.35	0.4	0.35	0.30
rec_6	175,000	0.35	0.4	0.50	0.62

Table 7: Evaluation results for the example records of Table 6.

This fires only one rule in the first rule block "RB1":

If Continuity = low THEN Liquidity = very_low (firing degree = 1.0)

Thus, Liquidity is assessed as very_low. In the second rule block "Second_RB", the following rules fire:

If Security = excellent THEN Financial = very_high (firing degree = 0.8)
If Liquidity = very_low AND Security = fair THEN Financial = very_low (f.d. = 0.2)

Through the defuzzification, the final result for Financial is thus computed to 80%, as also shown in Table 7. In other words, *"the customer is assessed a sound financial background because of his pretty much excellent Security; The very_low Liquidity, combined with the fact, that the Security is only pretty much but not perfectly considered excellent, leads to a less than perfect financial background evaluation."*

Now, test rec_2 which describes a hypothetical customer with the same Security but a much better and more continuos Inc_Exp. This customer is evaluated by the first rule block to have a high Liquidity. In the evaluation of the second rule block, this is taken into account and leads to an even better financial background evaluation.

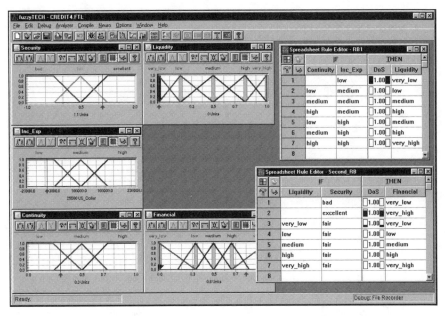

Figure 97: Inference flow for rec_1 of the file TEST5.IN.

rec_3 describes another hypothetical customer with the same Inc_Exp and Continuity as the customer before, however, having a much lower Security. His Security is considered to be pretty much fair, and in combination with a high Liquidity still results in an above average financial background assessment.

rec_4 describes the same customer again, but with a less continuous income. This leads to a less favorable Liquidity assessment and thus to a lower financial background rating. rec_5 is the same as rec_4 with an even lower Continuity and gets an even worse financial background rating. This shows that in cases where the Security is fair, the Liquidity assessment becomes the important differentiation factor.

rec_6 is the same as rec_5 with a much increased income. This leads to a much more favorable Liquidity assessment, however, this does not compensate the other factors much and only results in an average result.

This financial background evaluation is rather crude; these rules and membership functions have been designed to illustrate the design of a fuzzy logic system rather than to be part of a meaningful system. You can of course can change this. Use sample cases like the ones in TEST5.IN and evaluate the system in the debug mode. Decisions and evaluations that you consider to be wrong in the fuzzy logic system can be changed by manipulating the rules and membership functions. As all editors and analyzers of *fuzzy*TECH are dynamic, each change will be instantly reflected in all windows. This facilitates "What-If" analyses because you see the effects of every design step immediately.

2.3.3 Advanced Features of *fuzzy*TECH

This Section covers some of the advanced features of *fuzzy*TECH. In particular, you will learn how you can customize the *fuzzy*TECH user interface to your needs and preferences. Also, you will learn about the file formats that *fuzzy*TECH uses to exchange data in files and to store fuzzy logic systems.

Customization of the fuzzyTECH User Interface

The user interface of *fuzzy*TECH can be customized in several ways. For instance, you may turn off individual toolbars or the status bar to save screen space on low resolution monitors. Open the Preferences dialog box (Figure 98) by selecting "Options\Preferences..." from the menu bar. These options will be stored in the FTWIN.INI file contained in the directory where you installed *fuzzy*TECH.

The options are:

Toolbar group

For each window type, you can turn the toolbar on or off. All functions that you access through the toolbars can also be accessed through the menu bar or the properties menus invoked for some windows by clicking right in the respective window.

Miscellaneous group

■ Enable Confirm Dialogs:

When enabled, this option ensures that a confirmation dialog box is shown any time you delete or greatly alter a component of the fuzzy logic system. Experienced designers should disable this option because the UNDO function of *fuzzy*TECH reverses accidental deletions and modifications.

■ Show Termlistbox:

If enabled, all Linguistic Variable Editors show the Term list box when opened. Experienced designers should disable this option, because the Term dialog can also be opened by double clicking on the term name printed above the plot area of the Variable Editors. A single click on the term name selects the respective term membership function in the plot area.

■ Show Statusline:

Lets you turn the status bar on and off.

■ Debug Window Iconized:

The Debug window is active in any debug mode. It always displays the crisp values of all input and output variables of the system. Enabling this option iconizes the Debug window any time you start the Debug mode. If you have low video resolution, you can use this option to save screen space and computing time. Note that you can restore an iconized Debug window at any time.

■ Commented File Format:

If this option is enabled, *fuzzy*TECH starts writing and reading data records at Line 4. Line 1 and 3 are considered comments and Line 2 lists the linguistic variable names in the sequence they appear in each record. Also, the first word (not to be separated by space characters) in each row is considered the record name and displayed in some debug modes. However, when importing from or exporting to other software, you may need a "plain" ASCII format, that is, the records start with the first row in the file and there is no record name. For this file format, disable the option. For more details, see the on-line help system or [22].

■ Show ToolTip Comments:

When this option is enabled, the comments entered for linguistic variables, interfaces, and rule blocks are shown in a ToolTip type fashion when the Project Editor or Variables window is active and the mouse cursor rests over the respective object. You do not need to click on the object.

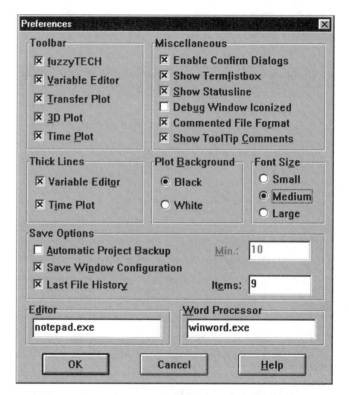

Figure 98: The Preferences dialog box lets you customize the user interface of *fuzzy*TECH.

Thick Lines group:

Use this option for high resolution monitors to increase the line thickness in Variable Editors and the Time Plot.

Plot Background group:

Use this option to select the background color to black or white. This is useful when obtaining screen shots of the Time Plot and the 3D Plot analyzer that shall later be printed on paper.

Font Size group:

Depending on the screen size, *fuzzy*TECH has pre-set the font size for many of its windows upon installation. You can change this using the Font Size option.

Save Options group:

■ Automatic Project Backup:

The full-featured version of *fuzzy*TECH can automatically save the current project in the \BACKUP\ subdirectory. Hence, the file you have opened will not be overwritten. To avoid confusing backup files with their originals, the file extension of backup projects is *.FT! rather than *.FTL for the originals. You may set a time interval for the automatic project backup.

■ Save Window Configuration:

If the "Save Window Configuration" option in the Preferences dialog box is enabled, *fuzzy*TECH saves the positions and sizes of all windows as well as the configuration of all open analyzers in a *.CFG file whenever you save the *.FTL file. If you open a FTL file, *fuzzy*TECH searches for a *.CFG file with the same project name (the project name consists of the first eight characters of the file name). If this *.CFG file exists, it will be opened, causing all windows to restore to their position and size and all analyzers (once you activate a debug mode) to their position size and configuration as was in use at the last save.

You may open the *.CFG file with an ASCII editor. If no *.CFG file with the same project name is found in the same directory, all windows open in default size and you must configure analyzers manually.

The functions "Save As..." and "Open..." also let you save and open *.CFG files under a different project name. This allows to have multiple configurations for the same FTL project. To reset the configuration to *fuzzy*TECH defaults, just erase the *.CFG with the same project name as the *.FTL file.

■ Last File History:

Specifies how many recently opened files the File menu of *fuzzy*TECH should list. The maximum number of files is nine (9).

Editor group:

Lets you specify your favorite text editor. This editor is used to display the contents of ASCII format files in *fuzzy*TECH. When you install *fuzzy*TECH, the Windows Notepad editor is selected as default text editor (NOTEPAD.EXE). If you like to use a different editor to display text, you can specify it in this field with the full MS-DOS path.

Word Processor group:

Lets you specify your favorite word processor. This word processor is used to display the contents of the RTF (rich text format) files produced by the documentation generator. When you install *fuzzy*-TECH, the setup routine tries to find an active installation of MS-Word. (WINWORD.EXE).

If you like to use a different word processor to display text, you can specify it in this field with the full MS-DOS path. Note that you can use any word processor supporting RTF format. If no other word processor is available, you can use the WORDPAD.EXE applet provided with MS-Windows 95 and MS-Windows /NT 4.0.

The FTL Format

*fuzzy*TECH uses the platform and vendor independent FTL format (Fuzzy Technology Language) to store a fuzzy logic system on disk. A detailed description of FTL is contained in [22] and [41]. Try making a modification of a fuzzy logic system in FTL format. Open the fuzzy logic system CREDIT4.FTL and open the Spreadsheet Rule Editor for the first rule base "RB1" (Figure 99). The first rule in the base states:

IF Inc_Exp = low THEN Liquidity = very_low

Now change this rule to:

IF Inc_Exp = high THEN Liquidity = very_low

using the FTL format directly.

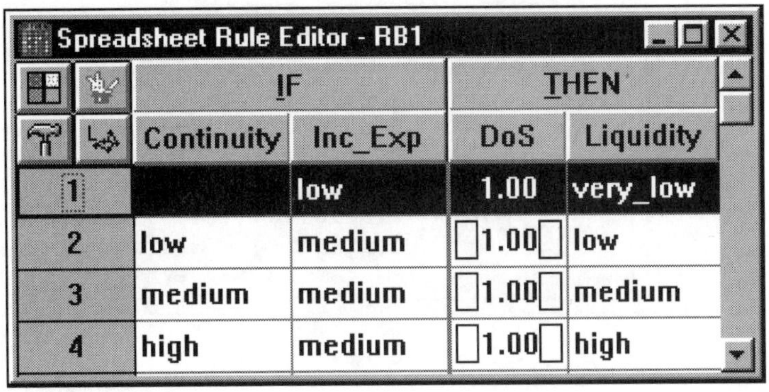
Spreadsheet Rule Editor - RB1
IF
THEN
Continuity
Inc_Exp
DoS
Liquidity
1 low 1.00 very_low
2 low medium 1.00 low
3 medium medium 1.00 medium
4 high medium 1.00 high

Figure 99: Spreadsheet Rule Editor for the first rule base "RB1".

Open an editor window (Figure 100) for the file CREDIT4.FTL by selecting File\View from the menu bar. Scroll the text to the line that displays "RULEBLOCK". FTL is a text format that uses two types of entities: objects and slots. Each object consists of an object name and an object body in "{}":

RULEBLOCK { .... }

Within an object body, other objects and slots can be defined. A slot consists of a slot name to the left of an "=" and a value for this slot to the right:

NAME = RB1;

There are defaults for most definitions, so even complex systems require only a few lines of code. When *fuzzy*TECH generates a FTL file to store the current fuzzy logic project, it will output all definitions even if the assignment is the default value because other software using FTL may make different default assumptions. Comments in FTL are put into "/* ... */" marks.

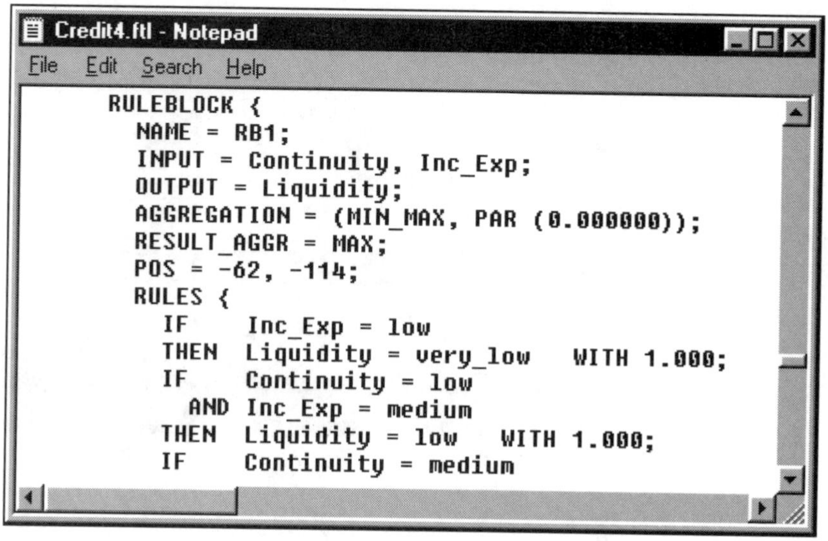

```
Credit4.ftl - Notepad
File   Edit   Search   Help
       RULEBLOCK {
         NAME = RB1;
         INPUT = Continuity, Inc_Exp;
         OUTPUT = Liquidity;
         AGGREGATION = (MIN_MAX, PAR (0.000000));
         RESULT_AGGR = MAX;
         POS = -62, -114;
         RULES {
           IF    Inc_Exp = low
           THEN  Liquidity = very_low    WITH 1.000;
           IF    Continuity = low
             AND Inc_Exp = medium
           THEN  Liquidity = low    WITH 1.000;
           IF    Continuity = medium
```

Figure 100: Text editor window for CREDIT.FTL.

Locate the first rule of the first rule block "RB1" in the FTL file

```
RULES {
  IF    Inc_Exp = high
  THEN  Liquidity = very_low    WITH 1.000;
```

and change the "If-Part" of the rule from "Inc_Exp = low" to "Inc_Exp = high". Now, save this FTL file in the \SAMPLES\BUSI-NESS\CREDIT\ subdirectory under the different name "CREDIT5.FTL". Open this file in *fuzzy*TECH and open the Spreadsheet Rule Editor for "RB1" (Figure 101).

The first rule in the Spreadsheet Rule Editor has now changed accordingly. Even though an entire fuzzy logic system can be programmed in FTL, this is not practical. The graphical editors of *fuzzy*TECH provide a much higher productivity, and fuzzy logic system components can be designed more transparently using this visual approach.

Note: if you manually edit an FTL file that was generated by *fuzzy*TECH, make sure to erase the line containing "SHELL = XXXX;". This forces *fuzzy*TECH to do a complete consistency check when opening the FTL file. If by analyzing the "SHELL" slot, *fuzzy*TECH for Business detects that it is the creator of this file, the file will not be completely checked. This expedites the opening of FTL files.

Spreadsheet Rule Editor - RB1				
		IF		**THEN**
		Continuity	**Inc_Exp**	**DoS**	**Liquidity**
1			high	■1.00■	very_low
2		low	medium	☐1.00☐	low
3		medium	medium	☐1.00☐	medium
4		high	medium	☐1.00☐	high

Figure 101: Spreadsheet Rule Editor for the
first rule base "RB1" with Modified Rule 1.

Data File Types

*fuzzy*TECH uses ASCII format files for input and output values for multiple purpose. The different suffixes classify the usage of the file:

- *.PTN   Files generated by the Patter Generator
- *.TRC   Files uploaded from a target hardware trace
- *.OUT   Files generated by the Batch Mode
- *.IN   Files recorded from a real process
- *.EXP   Files for NeuroFuzzy training
- *.DAT   Files containing data to be clustered
- *.SKP   Files containing data sets that were removed
         from a *.DAT file during clustering

The file type can be either plain ASCII tables or a file format containing comments as previously described.

2.3.4 *fuzzy*TECH's Revision Control System

Like most design software, *fuzzy*TECH stores the entire information on a system under development in a file. In the case of *fuzzy*TECH this is an ASCII format file in FTL syntax with the suffix *.FTL. Optionally, *fuzzy*TECH stores the information on editor and analyzer configuration in a *.CFG file that is an ASCII format file following the same syntax rules as most Windows *.INI files. While this is the standard way to handle project files in software development, often the modifications to a system under design must be documented. This is a must for developers that are required to document systems modifications in an ISO 9000-compliant fashion. In software engineering, such documentation is handled by a Revision Control System. The objectives of a Revision Control System are to:

- ensure that only the appropriate persons can conduct modifications,

- document the modifications and the associated comments of the developer, and

- allow the user to scroll back the project to an earlier stage.

Such revision control systems are available from a large number of vendors and you can integrate *fuzzy*TECH and its FTL files as source files with any commercial revision control system. However, revision control systems are powerful but complicated tools, and if you do not already use one, you may find it advisable to use the integrated Revision Control System of *fuzzy*TECH. Because of its tight integration with *fuzzy*TECH, revision control becomes an easy task, and the overhead required to work with a revision control system will more than pay for the time you have invested in setting it up the first time you decide to revert to an earlier stage of development.

fuzzyTECH's Revision Control System

*fuzzy*TECH's Revision Control System (RCS) uses *.REV files to store multiple *.FTL files plus additional information describing the modifications from previous development stages. Each development stage is represented by its *.FTL file. In brief, a *.REV file contains the sequence of *.FTL files of a development project. You can store each *.FTL file that represents a certain stage of development in the *.REV file and reclaim each *.FTL file from it later. The RCS uses a compressed and encrypted format for *.REV files. Hence, even a large number of *.FTL files can be stored in a *.REV file in a compact fashion. The RCS enforces password encryption to ensure that only authorized people can modify the fuzzy logic project.

Working with an Existing REV File

To become familiar with the RCS, open the existing file CREDIT.REV found in \SAMPLES\BUSINESS\CREDIT\. You can either select File\Open... from the menu bar and set the Filetype screen to show Revision Files (*.REV) only, or select File\Revision Control... from the menu bar and click on the [Open REV...] button. Both methods open the Revision Control dialog as shown in Figure 102.

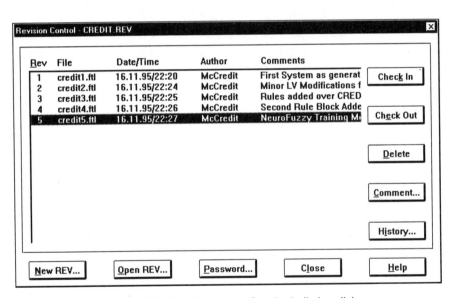

Figure 102: The Revision Control dialog lists
all stages of a fuzzy logic project's development.

Password Protection

The RCS enforces the use of passwords to protect the REV file from viewing and editing. For CREDIT.REV, the password is "fuzzy" (case sensitive!). You can change the password of an opened *.REV file by selecting the [Password...] button from the Revision Control dialog.

Working with Revisions

The list box in this dialog reports all revisions that are stored in the *.REV file. For CREDIT.REV, all five stages of CREDITx.FTL that this book used as examples are stored. The first column of the list box shows the revision number. This number is derived from the sequence in which revisions have been stored in the RCS and thus cannot be changed. The File column shows the original filename of the *.FTL file that was stored in the *.REV file. The Date/Time column shows when the *.FTL file was added to the *.REV file. The Author and Comments columns show who developed the revision and what was changed with respect to the previous revision. The column Comments only shows the first part of the first line of the comments. You may look at the comments in detail by selecting the revision in the list box and clicking on [Comment...]. To ensure consistency, you cannot modify the columns Rev, File, Date/Time, Author, and Comments of an existing revision.

Retrieving FTL Files from a REV file

If you want to view or modify a revision, you need to log this revision out of the RCS. First, select the revision in the list box. Then press [Check Out]. Because an *.FTL file with the same name exists, the RCS lets you now specify a new file name. Next, the revision is automatically opened with *fuzzy*TECH. You can store the file during development as any other *.FTL file.

Storing FTL Files in a REV File

When a new stage in development is reached that you would like to document and store in the RCS, you have to open the respective *.FTL file with *fuzzy*TECH. Then open the Revision Control dialog again by selecting File\Revision Control... from the menu bar. If you have restarted *fuzzy*TECH since the last time you opened the *.REV file, you have to open it again by clicking on the [Open REV...] button. Click on [Check In] to store the current *.FTL file as a new revision. This opens a dialog (Figure 103) that lets you specify the author's name and describe the modifications made.

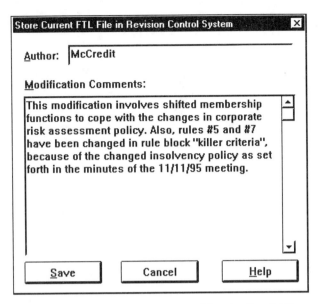

Figure 103: When you store a revision in the RCS, you specify the author's name and describe the modifications.

To create a new file, just click the [New REV...] button in the Revision Control dialog and specify a password for this *.REV file. Make sure that you note the password, as there is no way to access a *.REV file without this password. The password can only consist of standard alphanumeric characters and must be at least 5 characters long.

Printing a Complete Development History

To print a complete development history that covers all revisions, click on the [History...] button. This exports all the revision information plus all comments in a single text file that can be edited, printed, or integrated with other documents.

Note that the binary *.REV file format is much more compact than the textual *.FTL format. While the five CREDITx.FTL files together use more than 50 KB of disk space, the CREDIT.REV file that contains all of them in condensed format uses less than 10 KB of disk space. You can also use the *.REV file format to store only one *.FTL file if you either need a more compact version than *.FTL or if you want to protect the *.FTL file from being read by unauthorized persons.

2.3.5 Automated Documentation Generation

*fuzzy*TECH automatically creates complete documents describing all components of your current fuzzy logic system. The extend and level of detail of the description can widely be configured. Also, custom document format templates can be created with a standard word processor and automatically be used by *fuzzy*TECH.

To become familiar with the documentation generator, open the file CREDIT4.FTL that is contained in the subdirectory \SAMPLES\-BUSINESS\CREDIT\. Start the Documentation function by either selecting File\Documentation.. from the main menu bar or selecting the Documentation 🗎 button of the main toolbar of *fuzzy*TECH. This opens the Documentation Generator Configuration Dialog as shown in Figure 104.

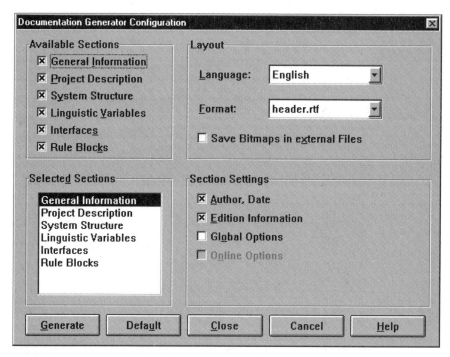

Figure 104: The Documentation Generator Configuration dialog lets you specify which parts of the fuzzy logic system shall be included and how detailed the documentation shall be.

Contents Selection and Level of Detail

The group Available Sections lets you specify which parts of your fuzzy logic system design shall be included with the generated document. By default, all sections are selected. To further specify how detailed each section shall be, select each included part in the Selected Section list box and define the level of detail in the Section Settings group. When you leave the dialog by selecting the [Close] button, all settings will be saved in the FTWIN.INI file for all your projects.

The group Layout lets you select language and format of the generated document. The Language drop list box specifies the language in which *fuzzy*TECH's explanations shall be generated. For each installed language, a subdirectory such as "\ENGLISH\" under the subdirectory \DOCIT\ exists. All text is stored in rich text format (*.RTF). To customize the text blocks refer to the *fuzzy*TECH Reference Manual for a format description.

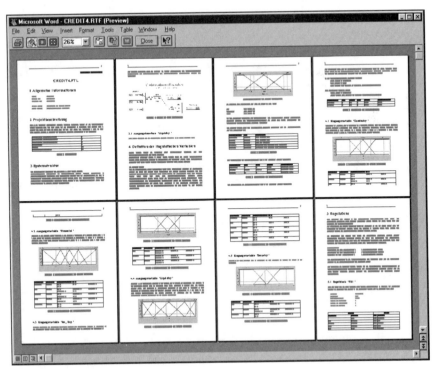

Figure 105: RTF file generated by *fuzzy*TECH in MS-Word.

The Format drop list box lets you select a document format template. The template defines the format styles of each part of the document (header, footer, title, text, subtitles, frames, ...). To generate a customized documentation template refer to the *fuzzy*TECH Reference Manual for a format description. Notice that you need a word processor that supports rich text format such as MS-Word or MS-Wordpad to change text blocks and documentation templates.

Generating RTF Files

To generate the documentation, select the [Generate] button from the Documentation Generator Configuration dialog, and choose a name and location for the generated RTF file. *fuzzy*TECH now automatically opens and closes its editors for each component of the fuzzy logic system that is to be included in the documentation. To view, edit, and print the generated documentation, open the file CREDIT4.RTF with a word processor (Figure 105).

Comments

To document your fuzzy logic system, *fuzzy*TECH analyzes your system and selects the appropriate text elements from its library. If you have enabled the General Information... options in the Section Settings group, *fuzzy*TECH even explains the principal function of these components in a fuzzy logic system. Notice that *fuzzy*TECH includes the Comments for each component of the fuzzy logic system and the project itself. To edit the comments, select the respective object and select Comments from the respective property menus.

3

Getting Started with NeuroFuzzy Design

To enhance fuzzy logic systems with learning capabilities, you can integrate neural net technologies. The combination of fuzzy logic and neural net technology is called "NeuroFuzzy," and it reaps the advantages from both technologies. The first section of this chapter introduces you to the basic principles of neural nets and shows how neural nets can be combined with fuzzy logic. In Section 3.2, you will learn how to apply the NeuroFuzzy Module in case studies. Section 3.3 discusses data clustering techniques and data pre-processing.

3.1   NeuroFuzzy Technology

Fuzzy logic is a technology that mimics the human decision-making process on the very high abstraction level of natural language. On the contrary, neural nets try to copy the way a human brain works on the lowest level, the "hardware" level. At first glance, this seems to put the two techniques in opposite corners. However, this is not the case. To introduce you to this technique, Section 3.1.1 covers the basics of neural net technology. In Section 3.1.2, the combination of fuzzy logic and neural nets is discussed, and Section 3.1.3 compares NeuroFuzzy with other adaptive technologies.

3.1.1 Adaptive Systems and Neural Networks

The imitation of the human mind with computer systems has inspired scientists for the last century. About 50 years ago, researchers created the first electronic hardware models of nerve cells. Since then, a large scientific community has been working on new mathematical models and training algorithms. Today, so-called "neural nets" receive most of the interest in this domain. Neural nets use a number of simple computational units called "neurons" that each try to imitate the behavior of a single human brain cell. In the following, the brain is referred to as a "biological neural net" and implementations on computers are "neural nets." Figure 106 shows the basic structure of such a neural net.

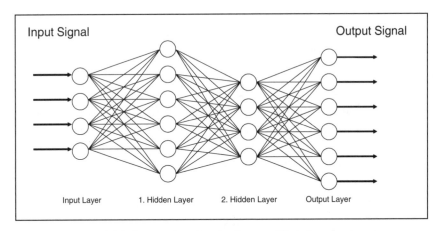

Figure 106: Basic structure of an artificial neural net.

Each neuron in a neural net processes the incoming inputs into an output. The output is then linked to other neurons. Some of the neurons form the interface of the neural net. The neural net shown in Figure 106 has both a layer for the input and the output signals. The information enters the neural net at the input layer. All layers of the neural net process these signals through the net until they reach the output layer.

The objective of a neural net is to process the information in the way in which it has been trained. Training involves either sample data sets of inputs and corresponding outputs or a teacher who rates the performance of the neural net. For this training, neural nets use "learning algorithms." Upon creation, a neural net is ignorant and does not reflect any behavior. The learning algorithm then modifies the individual neurons of the net and the weight of their connections in such a way that the behavior of the net reflects the desired behavior.

How to Mimic Human Nerve Cells

Researchers in the area of neural nets have analyzed various models of human brain cells. In the following, only the one most commonly used in industrial applications is described. For a detailed introduction to neural nets, refer to [2, 10, 15, 28].

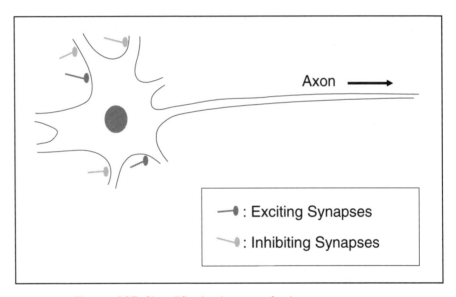

Figure 107: Simplified scheme of a human neuron.

The human brain contains about 10^{11} nerve cells with about 10^{14} connections to each other. Figure 107 shows the simplified scheme of such a human neuron. The cell itself contains a kernel and the outside is an electrical membrane. Each neuron has an activation level that ranges between a maximum and a minimum. Thus, in contrast to Boolean logic, more than two activation values exist.

Synapses exist to increase or decrease the activation of this neuron through other neurons. These synapses transmit the activation level from a sending neuron to a receiving neuron. If the synapse is an excitatory one, the activation level from the sending neuron increases the activation of the receiving neuron. If the synapse is an inhibiting one, the activation from the sending neuron decreases the activation of the receiving neuron. Synapses not only differ by whether they excite or inhibit the receiving neuron, but also by the amount of this effect (synaptic strength). The output of each neuron is transferred by the axon that ends in as many as 10,000 synapses influencing other neurons.

Can Neural Nets Copy Human Thinking?

This is the simple neuron model that underlies most of today's neural net applications. **Note:** this model is only a very coarse approximation of reality. You cannot exactly model even one single human neuron; it is simply beyond the current ability of humans. Hence, all work based on this simple neuron model is unable to exactly copy the human brain. It is instead an "inspiration" from nature rather than a "copy" of it. However, many successful applications using this technique have proven the benefit of neural nets based on this simple neuron model.

Simple Mathematical Model of a Neuron

Various mathematical models exist that are based on this simple neuron model. Figure 108 shows the most common one. First, the propagation function combines all inputs X_i that stem from the sending neurons. The means of combination is a weighted sum for which the weights w_i represent the synaptic strength. Exciting synapses have positive weights; inhibiting synapses have negative weights. To express a background activation level of the neuron, an offset (bias) Θ is added to the weighted sum.

The activation function computes the output signal Y of the neuron from the activation level f. The activation function is of sigmoid type as plotted in the box at the lower right of Figure 108.

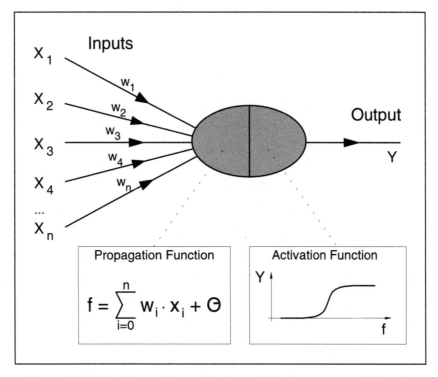

Figure 108: Simple mathematical model of a neuron. All inputs
are combined by a weighted sum (propagation function).
Then, the activation level of the neuron is computed with the
activation function. The activation level is also the output signal.

Training Neural Nets

A multitude of different methods and algorithms exist for building
a neural net. They differ by their architecture and the learning methods
they employ. This section describes learning methods for neural nets
based on the simple layer-type neural nets shown in Figure 106.

Learning Phase and Working Phase

The major step in designing a neural net solution is teaching the
net a desired behavior. This is called the learning phase. Here, you can
either use sample data sets or a "teacher." A teacher is either a mathematical function or a person that rates the quality of the neural net per-

formance. Since neural nets are mostly used for complex applications where no good mathematical model exists and rating the performance of a neural net is usually difficult for most applications, sample data training is common.

After completion of the learning phase, the neural net is ready to use. This is called the working phase. As a result of the training, the neural net will output values similar to those in the sample data sets when the input values match one of the training samples. For input values in between those of the sample data, it approximates output values. In the working phase, the behavior of the neural net is deterministic. That is, for every like combination of input values, the output value will always be the same. During the working phase, the neural net does not learn. This is important in most technical applications in order to ensure that the system never drifts to a hazardous behavior.

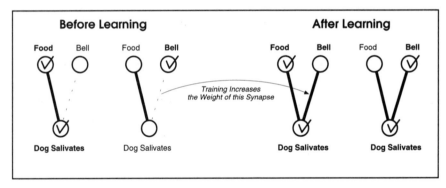

Figure 109: The principle of Pavlov's dog experiment. Before learning, the dogs salivated only when Pavlov showed them food. They ignored the bell. After they learned that the bell was linked to the food, the dogs also salivated if only the bell rang.

Pavlov's Dogs

So, how do you teach a neural net? Basically, it works like Pavlov's experiments with dogs. Over a hundred years ago, Pavlov experimented with canine behavior. When he showed the dogs food, the dogs salivated. He then installed a bell in the dogs' cages. When he rang the bell, the dogs did not salivate because they saw no link between the bell and the food. Then, Pavlov trained the dogs by always ringing the bell when he gave the dogs food. After a while, the dogs also salivated when the bell rang and no food was present.

Figure 109 shows how the simple neuron model can represent Pavlov's dogs. There are two input neurons: one representing the fact that the dog sees food, the other one the fact that the bell rings. Both input neurons have links to the output neuron. These links are the synapses. The thickness of the line represents synapse weight. Before learning, the dogs only react to the food and not the bell. Hence, the line from the left input neuron to the output neuron is thick, while the line from the right input neuron to the output neuron is very thin.

The Hebbian Learning Rule

Consistently ringing the bell when food is presented creates an association between the bell and the food. Hence, the right line also becomes thicker—the synapse weight increases. From this experiment, a researcher by the name of Hebb deducted the following learning rule[9]:

Hebb's Learning Rule:

Increase weight to active input neuron, if the output of this neuron should be active, decrease weight to active input neuron, if the output of this neuron should be inactive.

This rule, called the Hebbian rule, is the father of all learning algorithms. Today's most often used neural net learning algorithm, the "error back propagation algorithm" is based on the Hebbian learning rule. This algorithm first applies the input values of a sample data set to the inputs of the neural net to be trained. Next, it compares the outputs of the neural net with the given output value of the example and computes the error. This error is used to analyze which synaptic weight it shall modify in order to reduce the error for this example. The algorithm repeats these steps with every data set until the average error falls below a pre-defined threshold. **Note:** this iterative approach can never reduce the error for all data sets to zero because the data sets are not entirely clear in most applications.

3.1.2 Combining Neural and Fuzzy

The key benefit of fuzzy logic is that it lets you define the desired system behavior with simple "If-Then" relations. In many applications, this gets you a simpler solution in less design time. In addition, you can use all available engineering know-how to optimize the performance directly.

While this is certainly the beauty of fuzzy logic, it is also its major limitation. In many applications, knowledge that describes desired system behavior is contained in data sets. In this case, the designer has to derive the "If-Then" rules from the data sets manually, which requires a major effort with large data sets.

When data sets contain knowledge about the system to be designed, a neural net promises a solution because it can train itself from the data sets. However, the number of existing commercial applications of neural nets is limited. This is in contrast to fuzzy logic, which is a very common design technique in Asia and Europe.

	Neural Nets	Fuzzy Logic
Knowledge Representation	Implicit, the system cannot be easily interpreted or modified (-)	Explicit, verification and optimization are easy and efficient (+++)
Trainability	Trains itself by learning from data sets (+++)	None, you have to define everything explicitly (-)

Table 8: Both neural nets and fuzzy logic
have their strengths and weaknesses.

The sparse use of neural nets in applications is due to a number of reasons. First, neural net solutions remain a "black box." You can neither interpret what causes a certain behavior nor can you modify a neural net manually to influence a certain behavior. Second, neural nets require prohibitive computational effort for most mass-market products. Third, selection of the appropriate net model and setting the parameters of the learning algorithm is still a "black art" and requires much experience. Of the aforementioned reasons, the lack of an easy way to verify and optimize a neural net solution is probably the major limitation.

In simple words, both neural nets and fuzzy logic are powerful design techniques that have their strengths and weaknesses. Neural nets can learn from data sets while fuzzy logic solutions are easy to verify and optimize. If you look at these properties in a comparison table (Table 8), it becomes obvious that a clever combination of the two technologies delivers the best of both worlds. A combination of the explicit knowledge representation of fuzzy logic with the learning power of neural nets results in NeuroFuzzy.

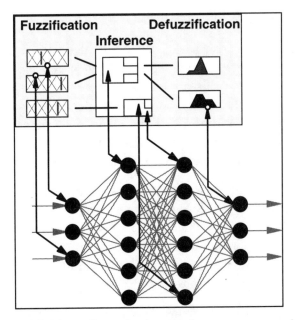

Figure 110: NeuroFuzzy technologies map a neural net to a fuzzy logic system. This enables the use of powerful neural net learning algorithms with fuzzy logic.

Training Fuzzy Logic Systems with NeuroFuzzy

Many alternative ways of integrating neural nets and fuzzy logic have been proposed in scientific literature [43]. Very few have been successfully applied in industrial applications. In this book, the focus is on methods that have been developed as an extension of the works of Zadeh, Zimmermann, and Kosko and have become the underlying technology used in recent successful system implementations.

The first artificial neural net implementation dates back over 50 years. Since then, most research has dealt with learning techniques and algorithms. One major milestone in the development of neural net technology was the invention of the error back propagation algorithm about ten years ago. The error back propagation algorithm soon became the standard for most neural net implementations due to its high performance [23].

Learning by Error Back Propagation

The error back propagation algorithm first selects one of the examples of the training data set. Second, it computes the neural net output values for the current training examples' inputs. Next, it compares these output values to the desired output value of the training example. The difference, called the error, determines which neuron in the net should be modified and how. The mathematical mapping of the error back into the neurons of the net is called error back propagation.

If the error back propagation algorithm is so powerful, why not use it to train fuzzy logic systems too? Alas, this is not so straight-forward. To determine which neuron has what influence, the error back propagation algorithm differentiates the transfer functions of the neurons. The main problem here is that the standard fuzzy logic inference step cannot be differentiated.

To solve this problem, some NeuroFuzzy development tools use extended fuzzy logic inference methods. The most common approach is to use so-called Fuzzy Associative Memories (FAMs). A FAM is a fuzzy logic rule with an associated weight. A mathematical framework exists that maps FAMs to neurons in a neural net. This enables the use of a modified error back propagation algorithm with fuzzy logic. For more details on the math behind this technology, refer to [14]. However, as a user of the NeuroFuzzy Module of *fuzzy*TECH, you do not need to worry about the details of the algorithm. The NeuroFuzzy Module works as an "intelligent" assistant with your design. It helps you to generate and optimize membership functions and rule bases from sample data. The next sections give you an overview of the design steps you take when you use NeuroFuzzy.

3.1.3 NeuroFuzzy vs. Other Adaptive Technologies

NeuroFuzzy advantages versus other adaptive techniques are:

- Because you start with a pre-structured system, the degree of freedom for learning is limited. In many applications, the experience is that the quantification of the input and output variables by membership functions and the structure of the information flow in the system already contain a lot of the information that an unstructured neural net needs to derive from the sample data sets.

- You can use any knowledge of the system right from the start. In most applications, a few things are usually perfectly clear. Using NeuroFuzzy, you can implement this knowledge in the initial fuzzy logic system.

- You can exclude parts of the system from training. For example, this is necessary in applications where some rules contain knowledge that is essential to the safe operation of a plant.

- You can always interpret the result or current stage of the system since it contains self-explained fuzzy logic rules and linguistic variables.

- You can manually optimize the result of NeuroFuzzy training.

- You can train the system interactively. After modification, you can start training all over again with the same or other sample data sets.

- The resulting fuzzy logic system is faster and more compact on most hardware platforms.

On the other hand, there are a few disadvantages of NeuroFuzzy compared with other adaptive techniques. First, there is much more experience with neural nets as extensive research has gone on for 50 years. NeuroFuzzy in contrast is still a "young" technology that was developed by practitioners rather than researchers. Second, NeuroFuzzy training features fewer degrees of freedom for the learning algorithm when compared to a neural net. In most real world applications, this proves to be an advantage rather than a drawback. However, in applications where you have massive amounts of data but no knowledge of the system's structure, NeuroFuzzy may not deliver a solution at all.

3.2   Training Examples

In the previous section, the discussion involved the basic technology required to set up a solution using NeuroFuzzy techniques. In this section, you will use three case studies to try this yourself. The first case study of an "exclusive or" is rather simple and given primarily to illustrate the use of *fuzzy*TECH for Business' NeuroFuzzy Module. The second case study will use the creditworthiness assessment that was used in Section 1.2 to illustrate the use of fuzzy logic. In the third case study, you will set up an entire fuzzy logic data analysis system from scratch.

3.2.1 Using *fuzzy*TECH's Build-In NeuroFuzzy Module

To show the development steps of a NeuroFuzzy solution and to illustrate the use of the NeuroFuzzy Module, you will now train a fuzzy logic system to represent the behavior of a digital exclusive or (XOR). Many researchers in the neural net area use the XOR case study to demonstrate certain capabilities of a neural training algorithm. As an additional exercise, you can also train other logical functions (OR, AND, NOR, NAND, NOT, $\Rightarrow$, etc.).

Training Data

First start *fuzzy*TECH for Business from the Windows Program Manager, select "File\View File..." in the menu bar, choose "Example

Data File (*.EXP)" as "File Type," and select the file "XOR.FTL" in the list box. This file is located in the subdirectory \SAMPLES\- NEUROFUZ\XOR\. The editor window shows the contents of the file (Figure 111). The first and third row of the file contain comments while the second row specifies the names of the linguistic variables: "Input_A", "Input_B" and "Output." The actual data records start with row 4. **Note:** the file may not contain any empty rows.

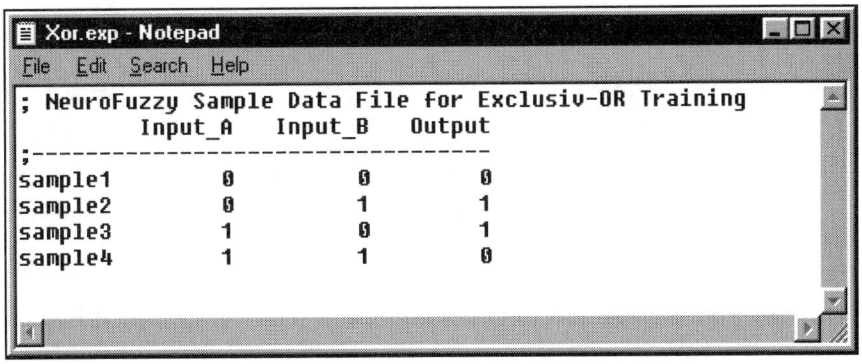

```
Xor.exp - Notepad                                    _ □ ×
File   Edit   Search   Help
; NeuroFuzzy Sample Data File for Exclusiv-OR Training
            Input_A      Input_B      Output
;----------------------------------------------
sample1         0            0            0
sample2         0            1            1
sample3         1            0            1
sample4         1            1            0
```

Figure 111: Contents of the file XOR.EXP.

The data record rows start with the record names "sample1" through "sample4." Then, the values of the two input and one output variables are shown. The values must follow the IEEE format for float values (see [22] or the on-line help system for details). You may use any ASCII editor to generate a training data file. Also, most spreadsheet, data base, or data acquisition software systems can generate the training data files.

Development Steps with the NeuroFuzzy Module

To develop a solution using the NeuroFuzzy Module of *fuzzy*TECH for Business, you have to follow these steps:

1. Acquire training data and cluster if necessary.

2. Create an "empty" fuzzy logic system.

3. Enter all existing knowledge of the solution.

4. Open the components of the fuzzy logic system to be trained by the NeuroFuzzy Module.

5. Configure the NeuroFuzzy Module.

6. Train the system with the sample data.

7. Evaluate the system performance.

8. Optimize manually if necessary.

9. Implement the result as a "pure" fuzzy logic system.

■ Step 1.

The training data for the XOR example is easy to obtain in the form of a decision table of the digital (Boolean) XOR. In practical applications, finding a representative set of sample data, however, can be the hardest part of the design.

When you use training data that was recorded from a real process, chances are that many data sets are redundant. Using training data sets with redundant records lengthens training significantly. Even worse, if most of the data records describe the same condition, they will have a much greater impact on the solution. For example, if you want to design a creditworthiness assessment application, and you only have records of good customers, the training will result in a solution that excels for good customers but performs poorly with other customers. To avoid this, training data should be clustered before it is used in NeuroFuzzy training. See Section 3.3 for details on clustering.

■ Step 2.

The NeuroFuzzy Module can only train an existing fuzzy logic system. Thus, the "empty" structure of the fuzzy logic system must be defined before training can start. This structure consists of linguistic variables, terms, membership functions, rule blocks, rules, and interfaces. *fuzzy*TECH supports this design step with the Fuzzy Design Wizard.

■ Step 3.

In this step, you enter all existing knowledge about the solution into the fuzzy logic system. The NeuroFuzzy Module uses this so-called *a priori* knowledge as the starting point of the training. The fact that existing knowledge can easily be used is a big advantage of the NeuroFuzzy approach over a neural net solution. If no knowledge on the solution exists, you must skip Step 3. In this case, the NeuroFuzzy Module must extract the necessary information solely from the sample data. Note that even if all information required to build the solution is already contained in the training data, entering existing knowledge will expedite the training. If the training data is of poor quality, using existing knowledge to help the NeuroFuzzy Module may be the only way to come up with a solution at all.

■ Step 4.

The NeuroFuzzy Module training paradigm is highly structured. You can exactly define which components of the system should be modified by the NeuroFuzzy Module. For linguistic variables you can open specific terms for training, and for rule blocks you can open the individual rules for training.

Use this to exclude specific rules from training. For example, you may not want the NeuroFuzzy Module to modify any of the rules that represent (non-fuzzy) legal issues. You can also exclude rules that you have identified as wrong.

When using multiple sample data sets for training, you can train different parts of the fuzzy logic system with different sample data. For example, if you want to design a creditworthiness assessment system, you may have data sets representing customers that are reliable in making payments as well as data sets representing customers that are not. If you use these data sets to train different parts of the rule base, you make sure that rules for the different customer types are separated.

■ Step 5.

To configure the NeuroFuzzy Module, you specify the learning method and its parameters. For details on different training methods, see [22]. For most applications, the default selections determined automatically by the NeuroFuzzy Module will be sufficient.

■ Step 6.

During the actual training, the NeuroFuzzy Module continuously selects training data records to test how well the current fuzzy logic system represents this record. It then uses a modified error back propagation algorithm to determine how the fuzzy logic system should be modified to better represent this one training data record. When reaching a pre-defined error threshold or a pre-defined number of steps, the training stops. You may start and stop the training at any time to run tests, alter parameters, modify rules or membership functions, or to select other training data sets.

■ Step 7.

After completion of the actual training, you can test the resulting fuzzy logic system using all debug modes and analyzers of *fuzzy*TECH. If the result is not satisfactory, you can repeat some development steps.

■ Step 8.

In contrast to neural nets, the result of NeuroFuzzy training is a fuzzy logic system that you can directly optimize by hand. How to manually optimize the system depends greatly on the type of application. If you have sample data, you can use the File Recorder to verify the evaluation process of the rules and membership functions; if not, you can use the Interactive Debug mode to create hypothetical situations.

■ Step 9.

The result of NeuroFuzzy training is a "pure" fuzzy logic system that can be implemented on PCs, workstations, or mainframes just like any "other" fuzzy logic system.

Now back to the XOR example. The training data already exists. Therefore, the next step is the creation of an "empty" fuzzy logic system using the Fuzzy Design Wizard.

Using the Fuzzy Design Wizard for the XOR Example

Start the Fuzzy Design Wizard by clicking on the "Fuzzy Design Wizard" button 🦅 of the toolbar. This opens the first dialog box of the Fuzzy Design Wizard. Select the option "Use a data file"

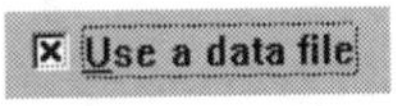

> ☒ <u>U</u>se a data file

and press the return key to open the "Read Project Information from…" dialog box. Select the file XOR.EXP in the subdirectory \SAMPLES\-NEUROFUZ\XOR\. Next, click [OK] to move to the second dialog box of the Fuzzy Design Wizard, shown in Figure 112.

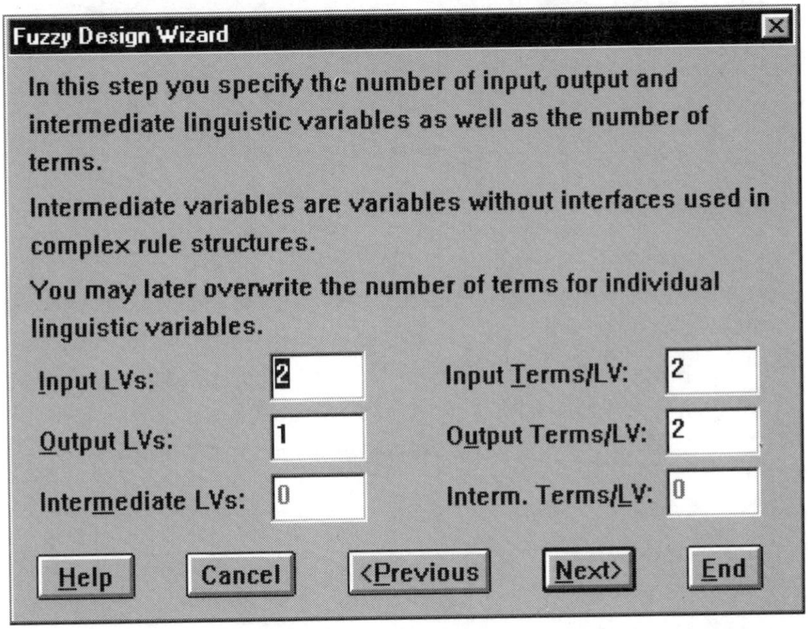

Figure 112: Fuzzy Design Wizard dialog box for the XOR Example.

By analyzing the file "XOR.EXP," the Fuzzy Design Wizard discovered that the system to be created has two input variables and one output variable. Also, the Fuzzy Design Wizard has found only zeros and ones in the file as values for the input and output variables, and it subsequently suggests two terms for input and output variables. Accept the values and press the return key to move to the next dialog box, shown in Figure 113.

Fuzzy Design Wizard   ☒

In this step you specify input variable 1.

Name: │Input_A   │

Range From: │0   │   To: │1   │

Number of Terms: │2   │

Term Names: │ false, true   ▼│

[Help]   [Cancel]   [<Previous]   [Next>]   [End]

Figure 113: Definition of input variable
Input_A in the Fuzzy Design Wizard.

Because just the values of "0" and "1" are in the file XOR.EXP for Input_A, the Fuzzy Design Wizard proposes a range of [0; 1] and the term names "false" and "true." Accept the values and press the return key to move to the next dialog box for the second input variable, Input_B. Accept the values and press the return key again. This opens the Fuzzy Design Wizard dialog box for the output variable Output. For the output variable, the Fuzzy Design Wizard proposes a range larger than from 0 to 1. This is due to the consideration that a later shift of the output membership functions out of the range 0 to 1 could be necessary. Overwrite the range value with -0.1 and 1.1, so the analyzers will zoom the interval and step to the next Fuzzy Design Wizard dialog box:

Next, press the return key to move to the next Fuzzy Design Wizard dialog box, which defines the defuzzification method for the output variable. Accept the default proposed by the Fuzzy Design Wizard by pressing the return key. The next dialog box, shown in Figure 114, defines the number of rule blocks and how the rules are to be created.

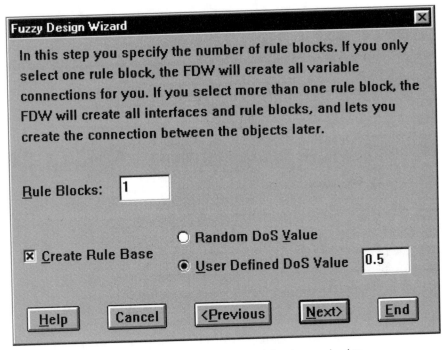

Figure 114: Definition of rule blocks and rules.

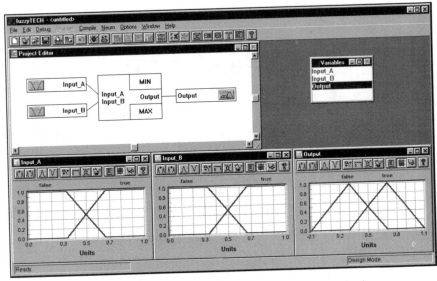

Figure 115: Structure of the system generated
by the FDW for the file XOR.EXP.

Accept the defaults of one rule block and the creation of a rule base with the DoS value of 0.5 by entering the value "0.5" and pressing the return key. The generated fuzzy logic system is shown in Figure 115.

Open Components of the Fuzzy Logic System for Learning

In this step, you open the components of the fuzzy logic system to be modified by the NeuroFuzzy training. For the XOR example, you open all rules and the output variables for training. First, open a Variable Editor window for the variable "Output" by double-clicking on the variable name in the Variables window. To open all membership functions for learning, click on the Learn MBFs button 🖼 in the toolbar of the Variable Editor. If you only want to partially open the membership functions, open the properties menu by clicking right somewhere in the Variable Editor and select the "Learn all MBFs..." option. This opens the dialog box, shown in Figure 116, where you can specify the range in which the NeuroFuzzy Module may modify the membership functions. To indicate membership functions opened for learning, a "L:" appears left of the respective term name in the Term list box of the Variable Editor.

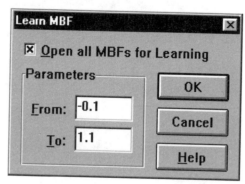

Figure 116: Open the membership functions for learning.

Now open the Spreadsheet Rule Editor for the Rule Block. The Fuzzy Design Wizard already opened all rules for learning, indicated by the gray background of the DoS values [0.50]. To open or close all rules for learning, click the Learn DoS button 🖼 in the Learn DoS dialog box. Here you can enter the interval in which the NeuroFuzzy Module may alter the DoS of the rules. To open and close individual rules, click on the DoS value in the Spreadsheet Rule Editor and select [Learn...]. Since the Fuzzy Design Wizard already opened all rules for learning, make no further setting changes here.

Configuring the NeuroFuzzy Module

In this step, you specify the learn method and set parameters for it. Open the NeuroFuzzy Configuration dialog box (Figure 117) by either clicking the respective button [■] in the main toolbar or by selecting "Neuro\Configuration..." in the menu bar. The upper right list box "Learn Methods:" shows all available training algorithms. You may also code your own training algorithm using the elements provided by the NeuroFuzzy Module and list them in the "Learn Methods:" list box.

Note: the *fuzzy*TECH for Business Demo software is limited to three input variables and one output variable for NeuroFuzzy training.

The group "Learn Parameters:" lets you set parameters for the algorithm. Leave these parameters at the proposed default values for the training of the XOR example. The group "Stop Conditions:" lets you specify when the training should automatically terminate. The three conditions are used alternatively. For instance, if you enable "Max. Steps:" with a value of 100 and "Max. Dev.: Factor" with a value of 0.1, the training stops after 100 training cycles or when the maximum error is lower than 10 percent, whichever occurs first. If you do not select any stop condition, you must stop training manually.

The "Save Best Project:" group lets the NeuroFuzzy Module save the result with the minimum error automatically during training. This is useful for unsupervised training sessions because with the NeuroFuzzy paradigm, the error can increase during training to avoid being trapped in local optima.

The group "Selection Mode:" lets you specify the sequence in which the samples are selected for training: "Sequential" always follows the sequence in the sample data file while "Random" selects an arbitrary sequence. Whenever the sample data is sorted in some way, you should select "Random." Because the XOR contains sorted samples, select

"Random." Make sure that all other options are specified as shown in Figure 117 and leave the dialog box by clicking [OK].

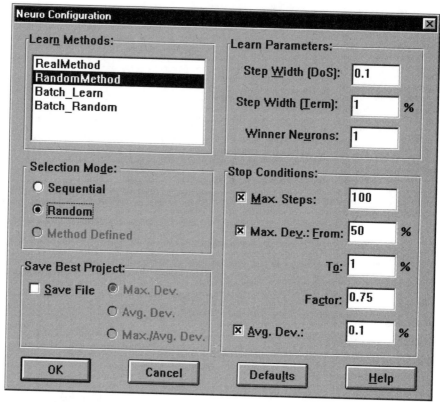

Figure 117: The Neuro Configuration dialog box lets you select a learning method and set the parameters for it.

Training and Analysis

All modifications that the NeuroFuzzy Module carries out become visible in the *fuzzy*TECH editors and analyzers. However, to make the training algorithm as computationally efficient as possible, you may not modify any of the *fuzzy*TECH windows during training. Consequently, you must configure and arrange all *fuzzy*TECH editors and analyzers before you start training. Figure 118 shows a window configuration that works well when training the XOR example. Activate the Interactive Debug mode, iconize the Debug window, open the 3D Plot analyzer, and activate the "Repaint" and "Background" options in the 3D Plot analyzer. Next, position the windows as shown in the figure 118.

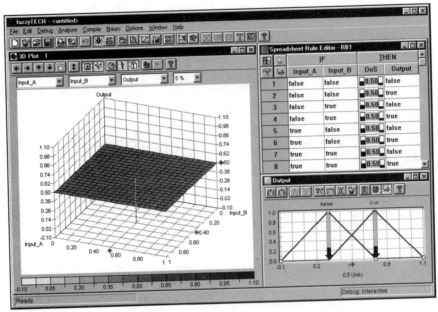

Figure 118: Possible window configuration for learning.

The 3D Plot analyzer shows a flat surface that is constant at 0.5. This is due to the fact that the rule base contains a rule for every possible combination of input and output variable terms. Each rule is valid with a degree of support of 0.5, which makes it as much true as false. Subsequently, all rules equalize each other and the result of the fuzzy logic inference is always 0.5. The following training steps will modify the degree of support for the rules and the membership functions of the output variable.

Initiate the training by either clicking the Learn button 🖾 on the main toolbar or selecting "Neuro\Learning…" from the menu bar. Because the NeuroFuzzy Module only generates fuzzy logic systems that are easy to comprehend, it operates with Standard MBFs. Therefore, all membership functions are converted to Standard MBFs at each initiation of training. Click [OK] on the confirmation dialog box for the conversion and select the file "XOR.EXP" for training. This opens the Learn Control dialog box.

Learn Control

The Learn Control dialog box lets you supervise and guide the training process. While the Learn Control dialog box is open, you cannot use any other function in any window of *fuzzy*TECH. However, you can close the Learn Control dialog box any time by clicking on the Close button ▣ of the Learn Control dialog box toolbar, use the other *fuzzy*-TECH functions, and open the Learn Control dialog box again later. All system modifications conducted by the NeuroFuzzy Module will be saved.

The three left buttons on the toolbar—Start, Stop, and Step ⏭⏹▶—let you initiate and halt the training. The next two buttons— Error Plot and Statistic ◹⏹—let you choose how the training progress is displayed in the "Errors:" group of the Learn Control dialog box. The Error Plot shows how the maximum and the average error are progressing over time, and Statistic displays a histogram of how many examples have trained the system to within a certain error. Both buttons are selected, thus, the "Error:" group appears as shown in Figure 118.

The next button, Error List ▣, displays a sorted list of all examples with an error above the threshold specified in the Neuro Configuration dialog box.

The button Perform ▣ updates the error computation in case the training is interrupted by the Stop button. For computational efficiency, the NeuroFuzzy Module automatically updates error computation only at the start of each iteration.

The next button, Update ▣, should be pressed for this XOR example. When pressed, every modification the NeuroFuzzy Module carries out is instantly reflected in all editors and analyzer windows that have been opened before the Learn Control dialog box was invoked. For details on these options and explanations of the other elements of the Learn Control dialog box, refer to [22] or the on-line help system.

Start Training

Now, initiate training by pressing the ⏭ button named Start. If you have followed all these steps you should now be able to monitor the training in the windows of *fuzzy*TECH. The NeuroFuzzy Module modifies the DoS of the rules and moves the membership functions of the output variable. The 3D Plot analyzer shows how this affects the transfer surface. Figure 119 shows the transfer surface after training. The input combinations (0,0), (0,1), (1,0), and (1,1) from the sample data file will be well represented with the trained fuzzy logic system. Between these points, the resulting fuzzy logic system performs a continuous approximation.

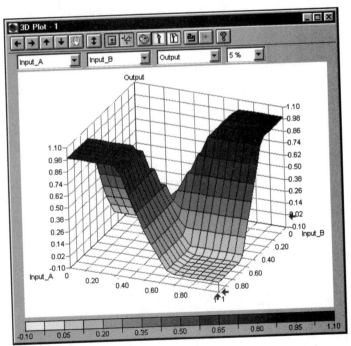

Figure 119: Learning result in the 3D Plot.

You may use the File Recorder debug mode to step through the samples in the "XOR.EXP" file. Try to train other logical functions ("AND", "OR",...) as an exercise. If you want to eliminate rules that only have a small influence on the system after training, you can use the "alpha cut" function from the Rule Block Utilities dialog box.

3.2.2. Training the Creditworthiness Evaluation

The XOR example is both an academic example and rather simple in its structure. In this section, the example of the credit assessment case study introduced in Section 2.2 is used as an example for rule induction from sample data.

Training Expert's Evaluation

To follow the example set forth in this section, you have to start *fuzzy*TECH and open the file CREDIT3.FTL, which is located in the \SAMPLES\BUSINESS\CREDIT\ subdirectory. This file contains the examples that you can use for NeuroFuzzy training. You can look at the contents of the file by selecting File\View File... from the menu bar and opening the CREDIT3.EXP file (Figure 120). It contains 51 examples of customers whose liquidity has been ranked by experts. In contrast to the TEST1.IN ... TEST3.IN files used in Section 2 to show the File Recorder debug mode, the CREDIT3.EXP file also contains a column for the output variable Liquidity, which contains the evaluation result of the experts.

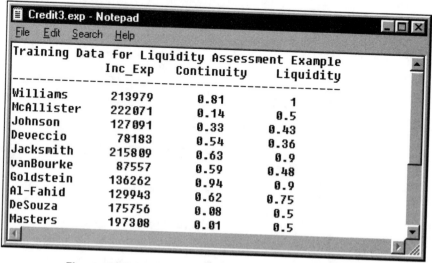

Figure 120: The file CREDIT3.EXP contains expert evaluations of customers for use during training.

For example, customers Jacksmith and Goldstein both get an excellent Liquidity rating of 0.9. Customer Jacksmith gets this because of his very high income, and customer Goldstein receives this because of the combination of his high income and the excellent continuity of his cash flow. Customer Masters gets a medium Liquidity assessment even though his income is very high because his income is highly non-continuous. Next, you can use this file with the experts' rating results for NeuroFuzzy training to extract the rules that the experts followed to come up with the decisions shown.

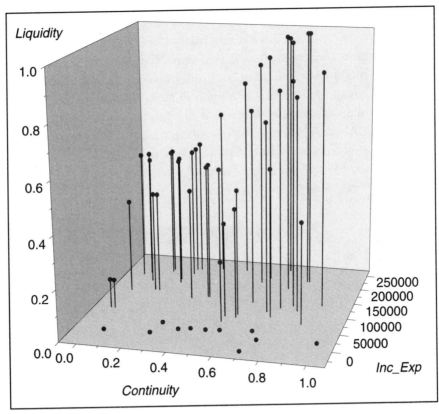

Figure 121: Three-dimensional plot of CREDIT3.EXP.

Figure 121 shows a three-dimensional plot of the contents of file CREDIT3.EXP.

Setting Up the Fuzzy Logic System

Because you already have a fuzzy logic system that is ready for training, you do not need to follow all the steps presented in Section 3.2.1. Rather, open the Spreadsheet Rule Editor for the CREDIT3.FTL system, click on the Utilities button 🖙, select the option "create full rule block"

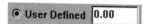

and set the "user defined value"

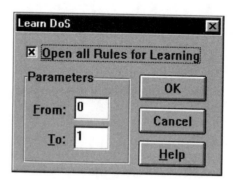

to zero. Then press the [OK] button. This will erase the existing rule base and create a new rule base that contains a rule for each possible combination of input and output terms, a total of 45 rules. All rules have a DoS of zero, and subsequently there is no information in the system. Enable the Interactive debug mode by clicking on the Interactive button 🐞 of the toolbar of the main window and open a 3D Plot analyzer by clicking the 3D Plot button 📊 of the toolbar of the main window. There is no surface plot because no rule has a non-zero weight. Next, close the 3D Plot analyzer.

Figure 122: Open the rules for learning.

To prepare the fuzzy logic system for training, you must open the system's components for learning. Since the membership functions have already been set up, only the rules need to be trained by the experts' assessment file. Select the Learn button 📝 from the Spreadsheet Rule Editor to open the Learn DoS dialog box shown in Figure 122. You can set the interval in which the NeuroFuzzy Module is to modify the DoS of the rules in the Parameters Group. Also, you may later change this interval individually for each rule by selecting the Learn option from the menu that pops up when you click on a DoS value in the Spreadsheet Rule Editor. Here, just accept the full training interval from 0 to 1 and press [OK].

Now, all DoS are displayed with a gray background color to indicate that they are open for NeuroFuzzy training.

Configuration of the NeuroFuzzy Training

Open the Neuro Configuration dialog box by pressing its button on the toolbar of the main window. Select "Learn Methods: Random-Method," select "Selection Mode: Random," disable all the Stop conditions, and close the dialog box by clicking on [OK]. Then start the learning by clicking the Learn button of the toolbar of the main window. Select the file CREDIT3.EXP as the training data file. Start training by clicking the Start button on the Learn Control dialog box toolbar. After the first learning step, the error histogram shows that while the system evaluates a few customer cases (examples) with little error, most are poorly evaluated and the error is rather high:

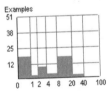

After more training steps, the error plots show that the system is converging to a solution that is representative of the training data samples:

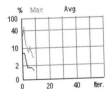 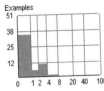

The error histogram above shows that the system represents the "knowledge" of most examples quite well and only a few indicate a need for further system refinement. The left plot shows the Maximum and Average error over time (iterations). Note that from the 5th to the 6th iteration, the maximum error slightly increased. Stop the training manually when the average error reaches a value smaller than 2 percent and close the Learn Control dialog box.

Analyzing Training Results

The best way to obtain a quick overview on the system's response is to use the 3D Plot analyzer. Enable Interactive debug mode and open a 3D Plot analyzer. Figure 123 shows a 3D Plot for a training result of CREDIT3.EXP.

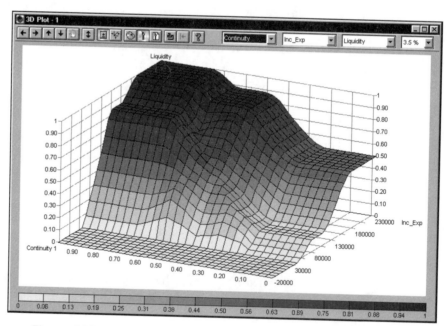

Figure 123: 3D Plot showing the training result of CREDIT3.EXP.

This training result very much resembles the behavior of the manually created rule base (Figure 58). As you can see in this example, incorporating the credit experts' knowledge directly as rules or by using their decision examples for training the rules delivered almost the same result.

However, the rules that the NeuroFuzzy Module trained are not the same as those defined manually. This is due to a number of reasons:

- The training data sets are not exact representations of the experts' knowledge as defined in the rules of Section 2.2.2. In the real world, a given expert's decisions are not reproduced with 100 percent accuracy.

- In real world sample databases (unlike the academic XOR example), there is always a certain degree of inconsistency in the sample data. Therefore, the NeuroFuzzy Module will not be able to deliver a final error of zero. As the NeuroFuzzy Module tries to find compromises between inconsistencies, the rules that result are often different from those directly entered.

- The NeuroFuzzy Module cannot combine rules. Rather, it can only modify existing rules. Thus, if you do not define "don't care" rules before training, these types of rules cannot result from training. The section on "Evaluating the Trained Rule Base" below contains more details on this.

- The NeuroFuzzy Module uses a fixed or variable training rate, depending on the learn method used. That is, it performs small modifications of the fuzzy logic system to make it better represent the sample data cases. However, modification steps are non-zero. Thus, a small discrediting error that is inherent to the NeuroFuzzy algorithm always remains and leaves a few rules with a small DoS that do not really represent anything useful in the fuzzy logic system. The section on "Deleting Rules" on page 173 covers this issue in more detail.

Note: you could have watched the entire training progress with the 3D Plot analyzer. Simply enable Interactive debug mode and open a 3D Plot analyzer with enabled Background Plot before learning. Then enable the button "Update Debug Windows" in the Learn Control dialog box and start learning.

Evaluating the Trained Rule Base

First erase all rules from the rule base that have no influence at all on the system. Click the Utilities button 🖳 on the Spreadsheet Rule

Editor, select "Utility: Alpha Cut," set "DoS value: User defined" to "0.0," and click the [OK] button. This causes all rules with a DoS of zero to be removed from the rule base. This leaves about 20 rules in the rule base. Note that the training results shown here and the ones you achieve may differ slightly due to the random selection function in the NeuroFuzzy training algorithm.

	IF		THEN	
	Continuity	Inc_Exp	DoS	Liquidity
1	low	low	0.98	very_low
2	medium	low	0.95	very_low
3	high	low	1.00	very_low
4	low	medium	0.98	very_low

Figure 124: Trained rules sorted by the terms of Inc_Exp.

Next, click on the [Inc_Exp] button to sort all remaining rules in the sequence of the terms of Inc_Exp. The first three rules in the rule block should now look similar to those shown in Figure 124. These three rules all cover the case "Inc_Exp = low." Whatever the Continuity assessment is, whether "low," "medium," or "high," the conclusion for Liquidity is always "very_low." This is because a low Inc_Exp assessment always results in a very_low Liquidity rating, regardless of the Continuity assessment. In Section 2.2.2, where you entered the rules manually, you therefore only entered the rule:

IF Inc_Exp IS low THEN Liquidity IS very_low

This is equivalent to the three rules the NeuroFuzzy Training produced for "Inc_Exp = low." You can manually change Rule 1 in Figure 124 by selecting [...] in the properties menu of the field "Continuity = low," and erasing Rules 2 and 3. This will give the same result as before, only using two less rules. The NeuroFuzzy Module does not automatically aggregate rules into "don't care" rules because automatically generated "don't care" rules often make the entire rule base harder to understand for a developer. For more details, see [22].

Deleting Rules

As pointed out before, a number of the trained rules have very little influence on the system behavior (DoS is small). Often, it is helpful to delete such rules because a smaller rule base is easier to analyze and to modify manually. However, you need to be careful when deleting rules because a small DoS is only an indicator that a rule has little influence on system behavior.

To delete low-DoS rules, you can either use the Alpha Cut utility of the Spreadsheet Rule Editor or you can erase rules manually. In any case, it is helpful to open a 3D Plot analyzer in Background Paint mode to visualize the effects of any rule deletion. First, use an Alpha cut to erase all rules with a DoS of less than or equal to 0.05. This should have very little effect on the system behavior as visualized by the shape of the surface shown in the 3D Plot window. Second, click on the [DoS] button in the Spreadsheet Rule Editor to sort rules by their DoS value. Then start to manually erase rules starting with the last rule in the sequence. As you proceed, the effects on the surface become more significant and eventually you will start to create areas that are not covered by rules at all.

If you use rule deletion after a training step, follow these guidelines:

- You can always delete all rules with a DoS of zero because these rules have no effect on the behavior of the system. However, do not erase rules with a DoS of zero if you want to proceed with NeuroFuzzy training later. Remember, the NeuroFuzzy Module can only train existing rules. All rules you delete now cannot be accessed in subsequent training steps.

- Deletion of rules with a small DoS value can result in a smaller rule base that is easier to comprehend and easier to maintain. However, care must be taken to not erase rules that represent important parts of the system behavior.

- A small DoS value is an indicator but not a proof that a rule has a very minor effect on a system's behavior.

For more details, see [22].

3.2.3 NeuroFuzzy Training in Data Analysis

This section presents the case study of a glass sorter in a recycling plant. The glass sorter is provided as an interactive simulation SIMULATE.EXE in the subdirectory \SAMPLES\NEUROFUZ\-NFSENSOR\. You will obtain the training data directly from this simulation, set up an entire fuzzy logic system for the classification, and train the classification rules using the recorded data. The case study presented in this section and the software simulation stem from a real-world application that runs in a recycling plant. The case study presented in this section has been simplified for teaching purposes.

Glass Sorter Software Simulation

When recycling glass, the problem is that the color of the glass produced is a mixture of the glass types used. Thus, if many types go into the recycling process the result will be dark brown glass. In Germany, where the amount of glass that is recycled is rather high, the amount of dark brown glass produced by recycling can easily exceed the demand. Thus white, blue, and green glass need to be produced from raw materials because glass mix recycling cannot produce these colors. One solution to this is to manually separate the different glass colors before recycling and then process them in separate batches. However, manual separation is too expensive.

Glass Sorter Application

Thus, the sorting procedure must be automated. The objective of this automated sorter is to feed the bottles to be recycled into a number of containers. For recognition, a RGB color sensor is used, and for the sorting, a pneumatic-mechanical system is used. When full, a container becomes a batch for the glass ovens, where the different colors of glass are produced. The simplified simulation model is shown in Figure 125. It considers only four different containers.

The interesting part is that for this selection, no exact criteria can be formulated for the tolerance of the colors for the different batches.

Also, these tolerances can change over time as the same color output of a batch can be achieved with different glass mixes. The strategy on what type of glass shall be blended in one batch changes over time depending on the volumes of the incoming glass. Hence, the solution has to be easy to re-tune and must be based on the experience of the operators.

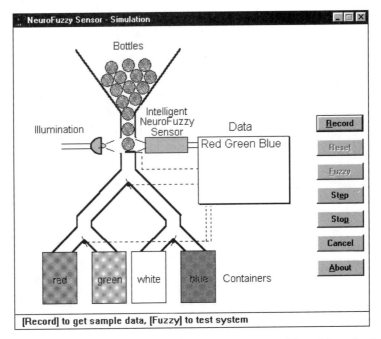

Figure 125: The NeuroFuzzy Sensor Simulation of the Glass Sorter Application. Note that the Simulation lets you both record training data as well as test a NeuroFuzzy solution.

The following procedure follows the NeuroFuzzy development steps introduced in Section 3.2.1.

Step 1: Obtain Training Data

The NeuroFuzzy Module can automatically convert the experience of the operators into a solution, if training data is present. This training data can be obtained by letting the operator look at a number of bottles and decide in which container he would put the bottle. At the same time, the RGB color sensor records the color pattern of the bottle. This data together forms the training data for the NeuroFuzzy Module.

Start the glass sorter simulation by double-clicking on the NeuroFuzzy Sensor icon ⚏ in the *fuzzy*TECH for Business group of the Program Manager. Figure 125 shows the simulation window.

To start recording training data, press the [Record] button on the sensor simulation. Next, press the [Step] button. This places a bottle in front of the sensor and the operator. The operator then sorts the bottle into the appropriate container. At the same time, this is recorded in the file NFSENSOR.EXP, a file the sensor simulation automatically generates while recording in the \SAMPLES\NEUROFUZ\NFSENSOR\ subdirectory. Record eight bottles to start with by pressing the [Step] button seven more times. A text display in the lower part of the simulation shows the progress of the training data recording.

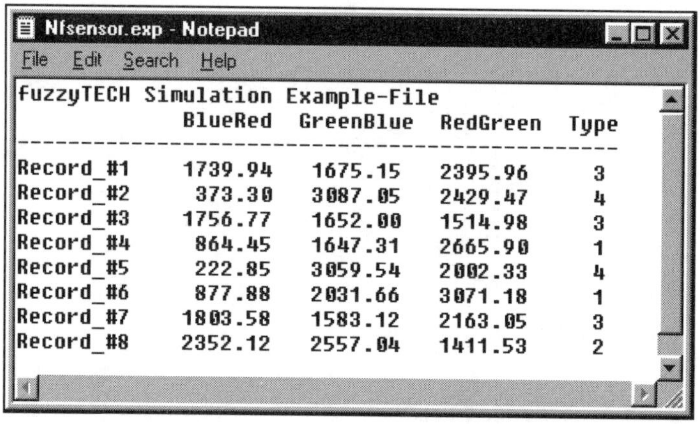

```
▤ Nfsensor.exp - Notepad                              _ □ ✕
 File  Edit  Search  Help

fuzzyTECH Simulation Example-File
                 BlueRed   GreenBlue   RedGreen   Type
-----------------------------------------------------------
Record_#1       1739.94    1675.15    2395.96     3
Record_#2        373.30    3087.05    2429.47     4
Record_#3       1756.77    1652.00    1514.98     3
Record_#4        864.45    1647.31    2665.90     1
Record_#5        222.85    3059.54    2002.33     4
Record_#6        877.88    2031.66    3071.18     1
Record_#7       1803.58    1583.12    2163.05     3
Record_#8       2352.12    2557.04    1411.53     2
```

Figure 126: The Sensor simulation has generated eight records containing training data.

When eight records are stored, press the [End] button to close the file NFSENSOR.EXP. Now, start *fuzzy*TECH, select File\View File..., and open the file NFSENSOR.EXP. Figure 126 shows what the file contents could look like. Note that the bottles are "generated" by the simulation following a statistical distribution. Now any time you generate a training data file, you will be presented with "new" bottles. The column "Type" contains the operator's container choice.

Step 2: Generate an Initial System with the Fuzzy Design Wizard

Close the Editor window and activate the Fuzzy Design Wizard by clicking on the 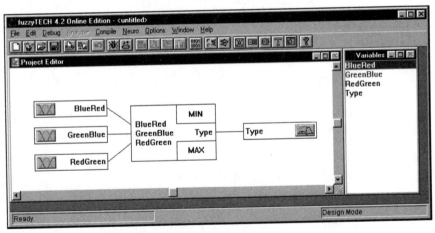 button of the main window toolbar. Enable the check box "Use Data File" in the first Fuzzy Design Wizard window and press the return key. Specify the NFSENSOR.EXP file in the "Read Project Information From..." dialog box.

This opens the second Fuzzy Design Wizard dialog box. The Fuzzy Design Wizard found three input and one output variable in the file. Because of the simple data structure, the Fuzzy Design Wizard suggests the use of three terms per input and five terms per output variable. Because you have four containers to sort the bottles into, select four terms for the output variable and a range from zero (0) to five (5). Then press the [End] button to accept all other suggestions of the Fuzzy Design Wizard. This automatically generates a complete fuzzy logic system as displayed in Figure 127.

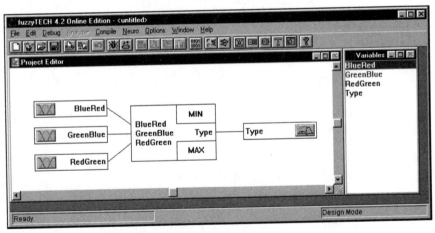

Figure 127: The Fuzzy Design Wizard has created a complete fuzzy logic system from the recorded sample data.

Step 3: Enter Existing Knowledge

Because there is no knowledge on the system's performance available at this time, you must skip this step.

Step 4: Open the Components to Be Trained

The Fuzzy Design Wizard always opens all generated rules for training but no linguistic variables. Since this is the starting point for the training, you do not need to open any further components of the system.

Step 5: Configuration of the NeuroFuzzy Module

Open the NeuroFuzzy Configuration Dialog box by clicking on the respective icon ▨ in the toolbar of the main window. Select "Learn Method: RandomMethod," select "Selection Mode: Random," and leave the other options at their defaults. Close the dialog box by clicking on [OK].

Step 6: Training

Start the actual training by clicking the Learn button ▨ in the toolbar of the main window. Specify the NFSENSOR.EXP file in the "Read Example File..." dialog box and click [OK] to open the Learn Control dialog box. Initiate training by clicking the Start button ▶ of the toolbar of the Learn Control dialog box. The learning progress is now shown in the "Errors:" group of the Learn Control dialog box. When training stops, close the File Control dialog box by clicking the Close button ▣ on the toolbar in the Learn Control dialog box.

Step 7: Evaluate Performance

To evaluate the performance of the fuzzy logic system you just trained from the recorded sample data, start the NeuroFuzzy Sensor Simulation again and put *fuzzy*TECH in fT-Link debug mode by selecting Debug\fT-Link from the menu bar. In the NeuroFuzzy Sensor Simulation window, the button [Fuzzy] is now enabled. Click on the button to start the classification. This visualizes the classification process and you can observe whether the bottles are placed in the appropriate containers. The lower part of the simulation window counts hits (TRUE) and misses (FALSE).

Most likely, many bottles are classified correctly while some are not. Your results may vary, because the eight bottles you recorded for training were selected randomly by the NeuroFuzzy Sensor Simulation. For the training data example shown in Figure 126, at least one bottle of each color is present in the data set. Due to the random generation of bottles in the recording step and the fact that you "only" recorded eight samples, you could even have selected bottles so that those of a specific color (Type) were excluded. In this case, the NeuroFuzzy Module was unable to use them for training. However, in the training data example shown in Figure 126, only one bottle of Type = 2 exists. Thus, it is no surprise that the performance is not completely satisfactory.

If the performance analysis results in unsatisfactory performance, you should analyze why. In this case, the answer was easy: the number of data records was too low. Hence, start over at Step 1 but record 30 sample bottles this time. The results of the sorting should be much better this time.

Step 8: Optimize Manually

If you still find unsatisfactory behavior, you can use the File Recorder debug mode to browse the NFSENSOR.EXP file and manually modify the rules.

Step 9: Implement as a Fuzzy Logic System

Now you can implement the resulting fuzzy logic system in a manner as discussed in Chapter 4.

Conclusion

The objectives for the system solution were:

■ To adapt the operator sorting strategy.

■ To allow easy re-tuning.

The designed system achieves these quite well. The operator only needs to sort a few dozen bottles manually to allow the NeuroFuzzy

Module to create a solution that copies the operator's strategy quite well. Because of the low effort of this task, re-tuning also becomes an easy task.

3.3   Data Clustering

The NeuroFuzzy techniques that you experimented with in the previous section are a powerful method for converting information contained in sample data into fuzzy logic rules. The benefit of this is enormous. Fuzzy logic rules can be interpreted and optimized by humans in a straightforward manner, in contrast to sample data files. However, in many cases the training data for the NeuroFuzzy learning must be pre-processed. Such pre-processing is necessary for two reasons:

- It removes redundant data.
- It resolves conflicts in the data.

For instance, consider a situation in which you would like to derive a credit granting policy from past data. In this past data, typically 98 percent of the cases cover standard situations, while only two percent of the cases cover more unusual customer profiles. As any training algorithm treats each case with the same importance, it will spend most of its attention on the standard cases and very little on the unusual cases. If you use such sample data directly for training, it will take a long time for the system to converge on a solution and the performance on the more unusual cases is likely to be low. Hence, removal of redundant data will greatly improve the training result in this situation.

Also, you may have a certain degree of inconsistency in the cases because multiple credit experts have processed them. These inconsistencies may be very hard to spot because credit experts may certainly agree in certain situations but may strongly disagree in others. If you use inconsistent training data, the NeuroFuzzy module will average between the inconsistencies to minimize total training error. For small inconsistencies, this may be the desired result, but if you have a few strong inconsistencies in the training data set, the training result may be poor. It follows the well known adage, "garbage in, garbage out." Thus, you're better off removing these strong inconsistencies before training.

To help you with pre-processing of sample data, *fuzzy*TECH contains a built-in clustering function. This clustering function helps you both in removing redundant data and in resolving strong inconsistencies in the data. Before you experiment with the software in Section 3.3.2, Section 3.3.1 introduces you to the clustering techniques employed by *fuzzy*TECH's clustering function. Section 3.3.3 introduces you to Fuzzy Clustering, a method that employs fuzzy logic in making the decisions regarding which data points should be clustered together.

3.3.1 Clustering Techniques

To illustrate the function of a clustering algorithm, consider a simple data set as shown in Figure 128. A single output input variable is related to a single input variable.

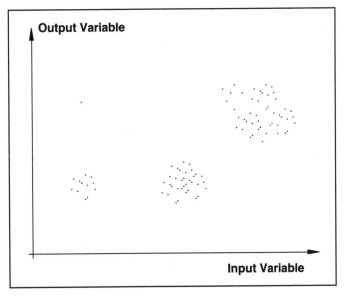

Figure 128: Sample data set containing
one input and one output variable.

Removing Redundant Data

As Figure 128 shows, most data points in the set are grouped with others in one of three clouds. These clouds are called "clusters." To reduce the number of data points, a single data point can replace all of the members in each cluster. Such data points are referred to as "typicals."

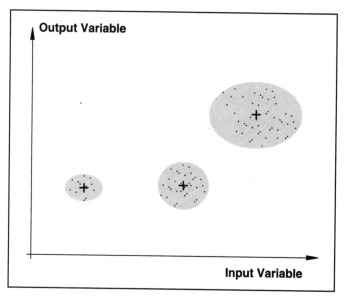

Figure 129: The data points of Figure 128 can be grouped into three clusters. Each cluster is represented by a "typical" data point (cross).

Figure 129 shows the location of the three typicals for the data set of Figure 128. If only the three typicals are used for subsequent NeuroFuzzy training, the resulting rules might be:

IF Input IS low THEN Output = low
IF Input IS medium THEN Output = low
IF Input IS high THEN Output = high

With only three typicals for training, the training time for the NeuroFuzzy Module would be much shorter than with the original sample data. **Note:** the leftmost cluster contains significantly fewer data points than the middle cluster. If this sample data was used without pre-processing, this area would attract more attention from the NeuroFuzzy algorithm because the NeuroFuzzy training algorithm treats each data sample with the same importance.

Resolving Conflicts

The second objective of the data pre-processing step is to identify and resolve conflicts between data points. In the example of Figure 128, there exists a single data point that cannot be grouped in a cluster. Figure 130 indicates this data point with an arrow. It does not belong to the leftmost cluster because the distance to the other data points of this cluster is too great. Consequently, this data point conflicts with the other points and should be removed since otherwise the later NeuroFuzzy training cannot deduce a clear rule from the sample data.

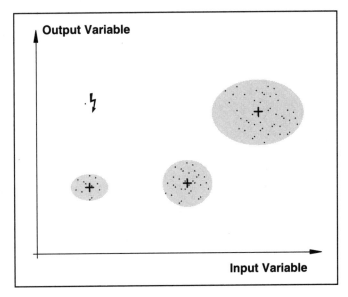

Figure 130: If a data point is too far away from a cluster, it is considered a conflict.

The Clustering Algorithm

*fuzzy*TECH's clustering function employs the standard Isodata clustering method, as well as the innovative FuzzyCluster clustering method. Both methods are similar but use different distance measures for the determination of the distances between data points. Also, *fuzzy-*TECH's clustering function integrates a data consistency check within the clustering procedure.

Configuration of the Cluster Algorithm

Clustering means to combine "similar" data points into a single cluster. The result of the clustering is the set of typicals, where each typical denotes one cluster. Now the question becomes: what is "similar"? The similarity of data points is specified by an "accuracy" for each variable. Thus, "accuracy" is actually a vector. Its dimension is the total number of inputs plus outputs. Data points that are within the boundary established by the corresponding accuracy measure are considered "similar" and thus belong to the same cluster.

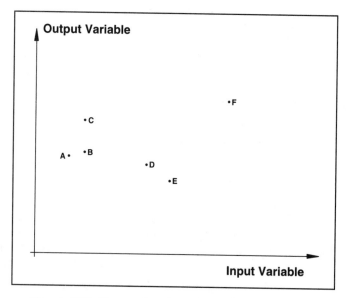

Figure 131: Example of a set of six data points.

Computing Distances and Data Sample Reduction

The first step of the clustering algorithm is to compute the geometric distances between all the data points. Next, all data points that are closer to each other than the geometric length of the accuracy vector are marked and sorted. Starting with the closest pair of data points, all "similar" pairs are combined. This results in a new data point and the two original data points are erased from the data set. Each time a new data point is inserted, the distances from this new data point to all others must be re-computed.

Figure 131 shows an example of a set of six data points. After all distances are computed, the distance AB proves to be the shortest one. Hence, A and B are combined into a new data point X, and A and B are removed.

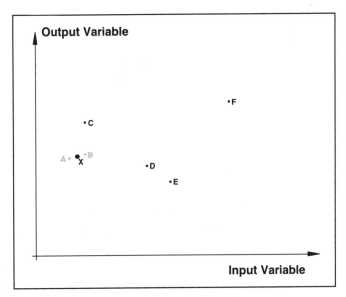

Figure 132: Data points A and B have been combined into data point X.

The result of this step is shown in Figure 132. Now the distances from the new point X to all other points are computed. Points D and E are closest to each other and are thus combined to form a new point, Y. Points D and E are removed. Figure 133 shows the situation now.

After computing the distances to the new point, Y, the closest two points now are X and C. Figure 134 shows how X and C are combined to form the new point, Z. Since point X stemmed from a combination of two points and point C is only one point, the new point Z will be located closer to X because Z has to represent the original points A, B, and C. The position of Z is computed as the linear combination of X and C weighted by the number of original data points.

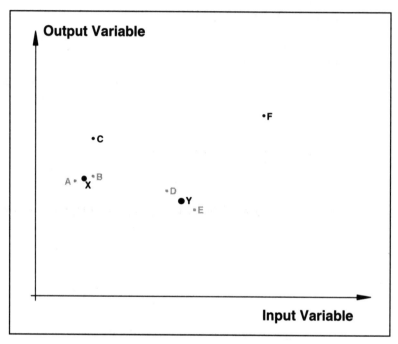

Figure 133: Data points D and E have been combined to data point Y.

No further combination of points can be made because the distances between Z, F, and Y are too great to be considered "similar." Clustering halts and outputs data points Z, Y, and F as typicals.

Consistency Analysis

If the "Check Data Consistency" option of *fuzzy*TECH's clustering function is enabled, data points that are considered similar according to the input variable values but not similar with respect to the output variable values are marked and presented to the user to resolve the conflict. Figure 135 shows an example.

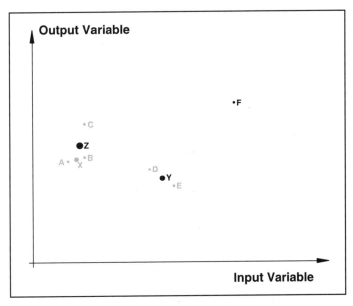

Figure 134: Data points C and X have been combined into data point Z.

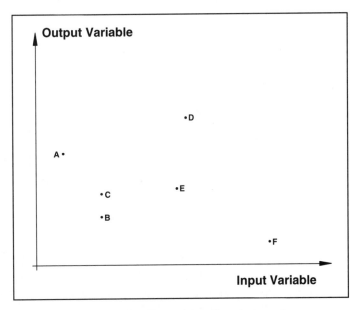

Figure 135: Example of a data set containing conflicting data points.

Data points D and E are considered to have a similar input variable value. However, the corresponding output variable value is not similar. This puts these two points in conflict with each other. Data points B and C are not considered conflicting because the respective output variable values are close enough to be considered similar. Data points A and B are not considered conflicting since the input variable values are not close enough to be considered similar. *fuzzy*TECH's clustering function brings these conflicts to the user's attention. The user must decide if only one, both, or neither point should be used.

Fuzzy Clustering

The clustering method as discussed in the previous section has proven itself useful in many application areas. However, the fuzzy logic extension, dubbed "fuzzy clustering," has been an equally useful extension. Fuzzy clustering uses a more sophisticated means of determining the "similarity" of data points. First, it does not use a "threshold" type definition as presented with the Isodata method. Second, it considers different similarity definitions for each variable.

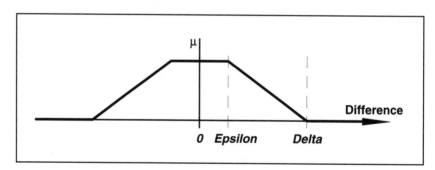

Figure 136: In fuzzy clustering, the similarity of two data points is expressed using a membership function.

In fuzzy clustering, each variable is associated with a membership function that assesses how similar two data points are depending on the difference in value for the given variable. In contrast to the Isodata method, first the similarity of two data points for each variable v is assessed as degree of truth (μ_v). The distance d_{xy} between two points is then computed as the negative minimum of the similarities

($d_{XY} = -\min_v \{\mu_v\}$). The two points that have the lowest d_{XY} are considered closest.

The interpretation of Epsilon and Delta is as follows:

- Epsilon defines the largest allowed difference in value of two data points that will result in the points being considered completely similar.

- Delta is the smallest allowed difference in value of two data points that will result in the points being considered as completely dissimilar.

3.3.2 Clustering with *fuzzy*TECH

This section guides you through a simple clustering example with the built-in clustering module of *fuzzy*TECH. You will learn the basic steps it takes to use clustering techniques as a means of data reduction.

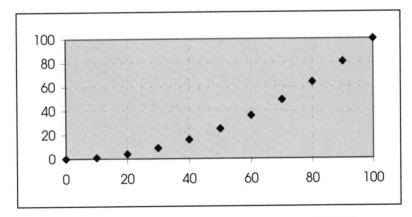

Figure 137: The file CLUSTER1.EXP contains 11 data samples describing a simple mathematical function.

To illustrate the use of the clustering module, a simple mathematical function with one input and one output is used as an example:

$$Output = \left(\frac{Input}{10} \right)^2$$

For input values ranging from 0 to 100 with a stepwidth of 10, the input and output values are given in the file CLUSTER1.EXP located in the subdirectory \SAMPLES\NEUROFUZ\CLUSTER\. Figure 137 shows the contents of this file.

Training the CLUSTER1.EXP Data

You can use the file CLUSTER1.EXP for NeuroFuzzy training. Start *fuzzy*TECH, start the Fuzzy Design Wizard, enable "Use a data file," and specify the file CLUSTER1.EXP. Because of the simple structure of the sample data file, the Fuzzy Design Wizard proposes five terms per input and three terms per output variable. Overwrite both values with "7" to create seven terms each for input and output variables. Overwrite the input variable range from the proposed [0;100] to [-15;115] and accept all other proposed values to generate the project.

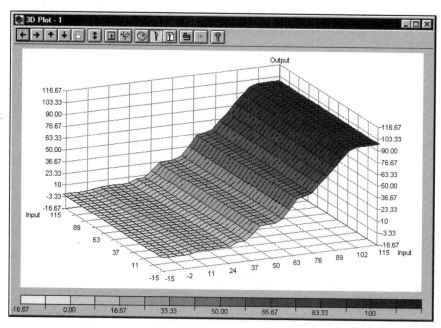

Figure 138: NeuroFuzzy training result from file CLUSTER1.EXP.

Enable the Interactive debug mode and open a 3D Plot analyzer. Open the Neuro Configuration dialog box, set "Learn Method:" to

"RandomMethod" and "Selection Mode:" to "Random." Initiate NeuroFuzzy training with the file CLUSTER1.EXP. After a few iterations, the training should stop with an average error of less than one percent and show a result similar to Figure 138. Note the "flat" portions of the curve are outside the training interval of [0;100].

Data Reduction

The small training test has shown that the 11 data points contained in CLUSTER1.EXP can be converted into fuzzy logic rules rather quickly by the NeuroFuzzy module. Now, what would happen if many more data points were available? The file CLUSTER2.DAT contains 100 data points following the same mathematical function as the data points contained in CLUSTER1.EXP. Figure 139 shows the locations of the data points.

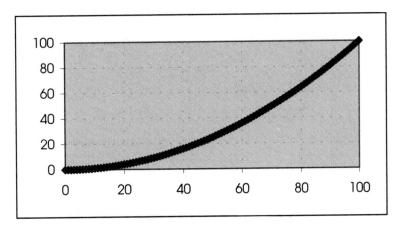

Figure 139: The file CLUSTER2.DAT contains 100 data samples describing the same mathematical function as shown in Figure 137.

What would be the result if this file were to be used for NeuroFuzzy training? The fuzzy logic system to be trained contains seven terms each for input and output. Obtaining a significantly better representation of the mathematical function than with the training data contained in CLUSTER1.EXP would thus be impossible. Hence, using file CLUSTER2.DAT instead of CLUSTER1.EXP would only slow down the training process and would most likely not deliver a better result. **Note:** with a small problem such as the one used here for illustration, the NeuroFuzzy module will deliver reasonable results in either case, but if problems get more complex, using large data files can result in prohibitive computational effort.

Clustering Data

For these reasons, the data contained in CLUSTER2.DAT should be clustered into typicals before being used for NeuroFuzzy training. Start *fuzzy*TECH's clustering function by selecting Neuro\Isodata-Cluster... from the menu bar of *fuzzy*TECH. Specify the file CLUSTER2.DAT in the Cluster Data from... dialog box. This opens the IsoData Configuration dialog box as shown in Figure 140.

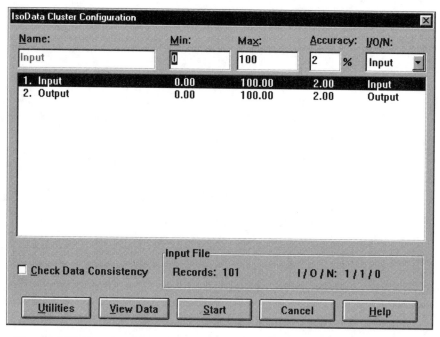

Figure 140: The configuration dialog box for the IsoData clustering lets you specify Range, Accuracy, and Usage of each variable.

The IsoData Cluster Configuration dialog box contains a large list box that lists each variable contained in the file. In each row of the list box, the variable's position, its name, minimum and maximum, its accuracy, and its usage are shown. To change these values, select the variable in the list box and enter the new values in the edit fields above the list box. Modify Accuracy of both variables to 10%. To start clustering, press the [Start] button.

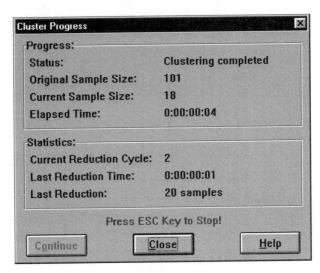

Figure 141: The Cluster Progress dialog box
updates you on the status of the clustering.

This opens the Cluster Progress dialog box shown in Figure 141, which updates you on the status of the clustering. **Note:** if you use *fuzzy*TECH's clustering function with an operating system such as Windows 3.1 that does not support preemptive multitasking, you may not use or start other programs while clustering is in progress. If you want to use other programs, you need to interrupt clustering by pressing the [Esc] key of the keyboard. This opens another control dialog box that lets you continue, end, or reset clustering. While this dialog box is open, you can work with other programs.

After clustering is completed, the Write Typicals to... dialog box opens. Store the typicals under the name CLUSTER2.EXP in the subdirectory \SAMPLES\NEUROFUZ\CLUSTER\ and press [Cancel] in the Cluster Progress dialog box to end *fuzzy*TECH's clustering function. Figure 142 shows the 16 data points that the clustering function computed as typicals from the CLUSTER2.DAT file. The 18 typicals can now be used for NeuroFuzzy training where they can be converted into fuzzy logic rules.

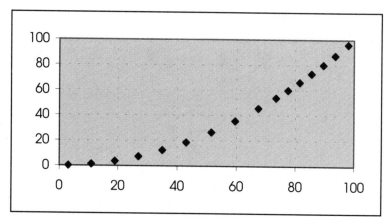

Figure 142: The output file of the clustering step, CLUSTER2.EXP, contains only the typical points of file CLUSTER2.DAT.

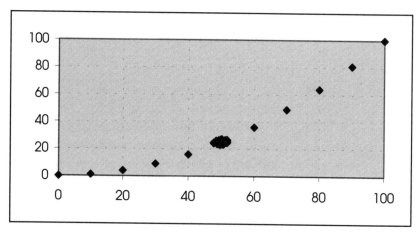

Figure 143: The file CLUSTER3.DAT contains 100 data points where most points are redundant.

Removing Redundant Data

A different case is contained in the file CLUSTER3.DAT. This file contains 100 data points as well. However, as shown in Figure 143, most data points are located very closely to the data point (50, 25). All of these data points can be replaced by a single typical by using a clustering method, because a single data point is sufficient for the Neuro-Fuzzy training.

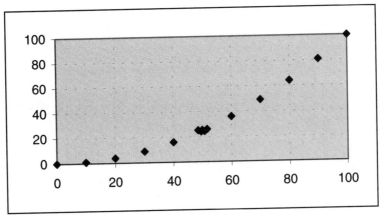

Figure 144: The IsoData clustering method has removed most of the redundant data points.

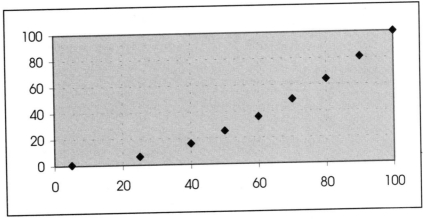

Figure 145: With a accuracy setting of seven percent, clustering removes all redundant data points.

If you cluster the file CLUSTER3.DAT with an accuracy of three percent for all variables, the IsoData clustering will remove most redundant data points as shown in Figure 144. However, the accuracy of

3% was not large enough to remove all redundancies. If you cluster the file CLUSTER3.DAT with an accuracy of 7% for all variables, the IsoData clustering will remove all redundant data points, as shown in Figure 145. Determining the best accuracy setting for the IsoData clustering may require a few test cycles.

Resolving Conflicts

*fuzzy*TECH's clustering function can resolve conflicts during clustering if the "Check Data Consistency" option is enabled in the IsoData Cluster Configuration dialog box. Use the file CLUSTER6.DAT, which contains the same samples as file CLUSTER2.DAT plus two conflicting data points. Figure 146 plots the contents of file CLUSTER6.DAT.

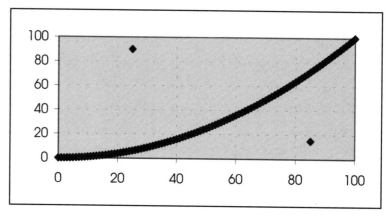

Figure 146: CLUSTER2.DAT, plus two conflicting data points.

Initiate the IsoData clustering for the file CLUSTER6.DAT, enable the "Check Data Consistency" option in the IsoData Cluster Configuration dialog box, and set Accuracy of all for the input variable to 2% and for the output variable to 10%. When you start the clustering, the Resolve Data Discrepancy dialog box opens, as shown in Figure 147.

The Resolve Data Discrepancy dialog box opens for each conflicting pair of data points. The dialog box in Figure 147 shows the detected conflict between data points #24 and #103. While the input variable values are close enough (≤ 2%) to be clustered in the same typical, the outputs differ greatly (> 10%) from each other. The buttons of the right side of the dialog box show the options for resolving the conflict. The upper two buttons let you decide on just using one of the data points, causing the clustering function to remove the other one from the data point set. If you select one of these options, the other data point will automatically be written to a Skip file.

The button [Use Both] leaves the conflicting pair of data points in the set and the button [Use Neither] removes both data points. The button [Skip All] removes all conflicting data points while the button [Cancel] causes the clustering function to use all the data points. [Cancel] is similar to having not enabled the "Check Data Consistency" option in the IsoData Cluster Configuration dialog box in the first place.

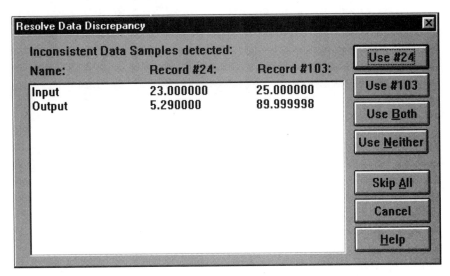

Figure 147: The Resolve Data Discrepancy dialog box opens for every detected pair of conflicting data points.

Now select [Use #24] because data point #103 is wrong. The Fuzzy-Cluster module now prompts you for a file and location where it is to write the data points removed from the data sample while solving conflicts. Accept the proposed filename and location. The Resolve Data Discrepancy dialog will open again and display the discrepancy between data points #85 and #102. Select [Use #85] because data point #102 is wrong. Then clustering proceeds as with the examples before.

3.3.3 Fuzzy Clustering of NeuroFuzzy Training Data

In the previous section, you worked with the "academic" example of clustering and training a simple square function. In this section, you will use real "raw" data for the design of a fuzzy logic system. This raw data first needs to be clustered to create a training data set of typicals. This data set is then used for NeuroFuzzy training to create a fuzzy logic system.

Raw Data Sample File

The raw data sample file is contained in the file CREDIT4.DAT located in the subdirectory \SAMPLES\BUSINESS\CREDIT\. It contains 500 data points. Because of the large number of data points, they can hardly be plotted in a transparent fashion.

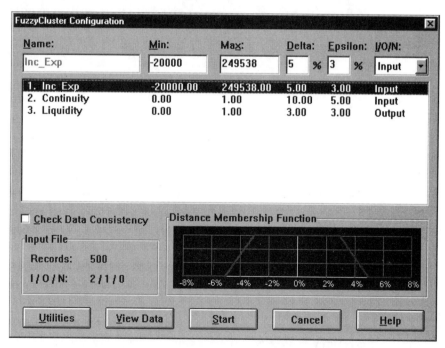

Figure 148: The Fuzzy Cluster Configuration dialog
box lets you define membership functions
to express the similarity between two data points.

Fuzzy Clustering Configuration

Because the variables Continuity, Inc_Exp, and Liquidity have different interpretations for how similar data point differences are interpreted, select the "FuzzyCluster..." option of the "Neuro" menu of the menu bar. The Fuzzy Cluster Configuration dialog box shown in Figure 148 looks similar to the IsoData Cluster Configuration dialog box. However, the distance measure between two data points is defined by membership functions rather than by an accuracy measure.

All membership functions are defined by the two parameters Delta and Epsilon. Epsilon describes the distance under which two values for the variable are considered to be completely similar and Delta describes the distance above which two values for the variable are considered to be completely dissimilar. For the variable Inc_Exp, enter a Delta of 5 and an Epsilon of 3. The resulting membership function is shown in the Membership Function Fuzzy Clustering group as shown in Figure 148. For the variable Continuity, enter a Delta of 10 and an Epsilon of 5. The resulting membership function is:

For the variable Liquidity, enter both a Delta and an Epsilon of 3. The resulting membership function is:

This type of membership function does not allow for any "fuzziness"; the interval in which two values of Liquidity are considered similar is crisp as with the IsoData method.

Fuzzy Clustering

Start FuzzyCluster by clicking the [Start] button in the "Fuzzy Cluster Configuration" dialog box. On a Pentium™100 class PC running Windows 95™, FuzzyCluster reduces the 500 samples in the data file to 72 typicals in about 2 minutes. Store the typicals as CREDIT4.EXP, open the file CREDIT1.FTL in *fuzzy*TECH, and train the fuzzy logic system using the RandomMethod with the Selection Mode set to Random. If you have the 3D Plot analyzer open with Background Paint and Trace enabled, you can follow the NeuroFuzzy Module as it approximates the typicals by modifying the rules. **Note:** the Neuro-Fuzzy Module will only reach an average error on the order of ten percent. This is due to the fact that because real world data was used, it still contains inconsistencies or typicals that cannot be represented with just three terms per input variable.

If you would like to try an even smaller set of typicals, you can repeat FuzzyCluster with the following settings for Delta and Epsilon:

Variable	Delta	Epsilon
Inc_Exp	10	5
Continuity	20	10
Liquidity	5	5

These settings assume that the variable Continuity is derived from a calculation of the balance fluctuation of the applicant. Thus the information this variable delivers to the assessment is rather "fuzzy." Hence, the similarity membership function has been widened. Also, the membership functions for Inc_Exp and Liquidity are expanded as well, giving the cluster function a looser interpretation of what points should be considered similar. When you use FuzzyCluster with these settings, the generated set of typicals contains 26 data points.

Clustering of Large Data Files

You can use *fuzzy*TECH's integrated clustering function from within *fuzzy*TECH or as a stand-alone application. The clustering function is a separate EXE file located in the directory in which you installed *fuzzy*TECH. Simply call up CLUSTER.EXE from the File Manager or install it in a program group. When installed in a program group, the clustering function provides its own icon 📇. Because Fuzzy-Cluster is a separate program, multi-tasking operating systems can run it in the background. If not called up from *fuzzy*TECH, the clustering function starts with its own main window. However, this window does not contain new functions; primarily, it lets you select the clustering method.

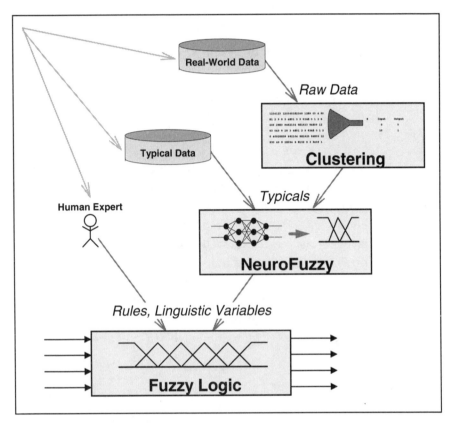

Figure 149: The combination of fuzzy logic, NeuroFuzzy, and clustering techniques provides a complete workbench for the design of intelligent systems.

What is Clustering Bringing to the Party?

To summarize the previous chapters, consider the following conclusions:

■ A fuzzy logic system can approximate any nonlinear, multi-variable system.

- The representation of a fuzzy logic system is linguistic rather than mathematic.

- Thus, human experience and experimental results can be used directly for system design.

- Typical data samples can be converted into a fuzzy logic system with the NeuroFuzzy module.

- Real-world sample data can be converted into typicals using clustering techniques.

Thus, the combination of multiple techniques, such as fuzzy logic, NeuroFuzzy, and clustering, constitutes a powerful workbench for the design of intelligent systems. Figure 149 illustrates the different methods of system design that the combination of techniques allows you. Explicit knowledge of desired system behavior, such as decision-making policies, are put into a system directly by human experts in the form of fuzzy logic rules and linguistic variables. If typical data is available, the NeuroFuzzy module automatically converts it into the rules and linguistic variables for the fuzzy logic system. If only raw real-world data is available, *fuzzy*TECH's clustering function will resolve conflicts in the data and remove redundancies to generate the typicals.

4

Integration of Fuzzy Logic with Standard Software

Two ways exist to integrate a fuzzy logic system developed in *fuzzy*TECH with other software:

- Integrate the complete *fuzzy*TECH software system with the other software.

- Use a runtime module (stand-alone operation).

Integrating the Complete fuzzyTECH Software

Figure 150 provides an overview of the different alternatives to integrate the complete *fuzzy*TECH software with other software products. *fuzzy*TECH itself (FTWIN.EXE) provides access to ASCII formatted data by its File Recorder and Batch debug modes. The DDE-Link is also provided by *fuzzy*TECH itself and discussed in Section 4.4. However, DDE is inter-program communication technique implemented for early MS-Windows operating systems and should not be used if more advanced communication techniques provided by *fuzzy*TECH can be used.

All other integration techniques use the so-called Remote Control Unit (RCU) of *fuzzy*TECH. The RCU is provided as a Dynamic Link Library (DLL) both as a 16-bit (FTRCU.DLL) and a 32-bit version (FTRCU32.DLL) in the *fuzzy*TECH directory. The RCU serves the functionality of *fuzzy*TECH to other programs. If you want to integrate *fuzzy*TECH in your own programs and you are not using MS-

VisualBasic, this is the method of choice. Section 4.4 covers the direct access to the RCU by programming languages.

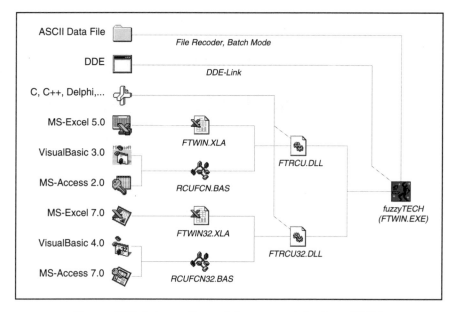

Figure 150: Integration of the complete *fuzzy*TECH system with other software products.

For MS-Excel, a "*fuzzy*TECH Assistant" (FTWINxx.XLA) provides plug-and-play type integration. It integrates fuzzy logic functions in a spreadsheet by just point-and-click. Section 4.1 contains a complete description of the *fuzzy*TECH Assistant for MS-Excel.

A special Basic source code module (RCUFCNxx.BAS) features the call of a fuzzy logic computation in VisualBasic and MS-Access as a single line of code. Sections 4.2 and 4.3 treat this interface in detail.

Using a Runtime Module

The advantage of integrating the complete *fuzzy*TECH software system is that all editors and analyzers can be used while *fuzzy*TECH processes the input data. If you use a runtime module, you will not be able to analyze or modify the system at runtime. On the other side, the computing performance of the complete *fuzzy*TECH software system is much lower than with just a runtime module because computation involves all editors and analyzers. Also, using the complete *fuzzy*TECH software system limits you to a integration in the MS-Windows environment. A runtime module in contrast can be ported to workstation and mainframe computers. Section 4.5 discusses *fuzzy*TECH's runtime modules.

4.1   Integration of *fuzzy*TECH with Excel

To integrate with MS-Excel, a special *fuzzy*TECH Assistant is provided that functions like any other standard Excel Function Assistant. To work with the examples in this section, you need to have Excel installed on your PC. The discussion assumes you have installed Excel release 5.0 or 7.0. If you use a later version than this, refer to your Excel user's manual on how to integrate the *fuzzy*TECH Assistant. All screen shots show MS-Excel 5.0.

4.1.1 Installing the *fuzzy*TECH Assistant

The installation procedure is simple and straightforward. *fuzzy*TECH provides the following files in the \EXCEL\XLA\ sub-directory of your *fuzzy*TECH installation :

- FTWIN.XLA   (the *fuzzy*TECH Assistant for MS-Excel 5.0)

- FTWIN32.XLA   (the *fuzzy*TECH Assistant for MS-Excel 7.0)

- FA_CONT.HLP (the help system of the *fuzzy*TECH Assistant)

To install the *fuzzy*TECH Excel Assistant, first launch Excel and open the Add-In-Manager by selecting Tools\Add-Ins... from Excel's menu bar. Then install the respective add-in FTWIN.XLA for MS-Excel 5.0 or FTWIN32.XLA for MS-Excel 7.0 which is located in the subdirectory \EXCEL\XLA\ of your *fuzzy*TECH installation. Figure 151 shows the successful installation. Click [OK] to close the Add-In-Manager.

This installation generates a new "fuzzyTECH" menu bar entry in Excel as well as a tool bar with only one button:

You can dock this tool button to another tool bar or hide the *fuzzy-*TECH toolbar by clicking the systems icon on the toolbar. At the same time that the Add-In-Manager installed the *fuzzy*TECH Assistant, it also started *fuzzy*TECH to make sure that fuzzy logic server operation is provided by *fuzzy*TECH. The *fuzzy*TECH Assistant finds *fuzzy*TECH by the path entry in the [FTWIN] section of the WIN.INI file. This path was established upon installation of *fuzzy*TECH.

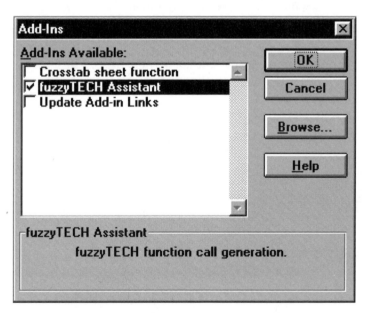

Figure 151: MS-Excel 5.0 Add-In-Manager
with the *fuzzy*TECH Assistant installed.

For additional information and troubleshooting support, refer to the help file of the *fuzzy*TECH Excel Assistant. To open this file, either select fuzzyTECH\Assistant Help from Excel's main menu or open the file FA_CONT.HLP located in the subdirectory \EXCEL\XLA\ of your *fuzzy*TECH installation directly with Windows Help.

4.1.2 Creating a Fuzzy Logic Spreadsheet

Now that the *fuzzy*TECH Assistant is installed within Excel, you can begin to set up your first fuzzy logic spreadsheet. From within Excel, open the file TEST1.XLS, which is located in the subdirectory \SAMPLES\BUSINESS\CREDIT\. Figure 152 shows the opened spreadsheet in Excel. The table contains the same data used in Section 1.2 to introduce the basic concepts of fuzzy logic.

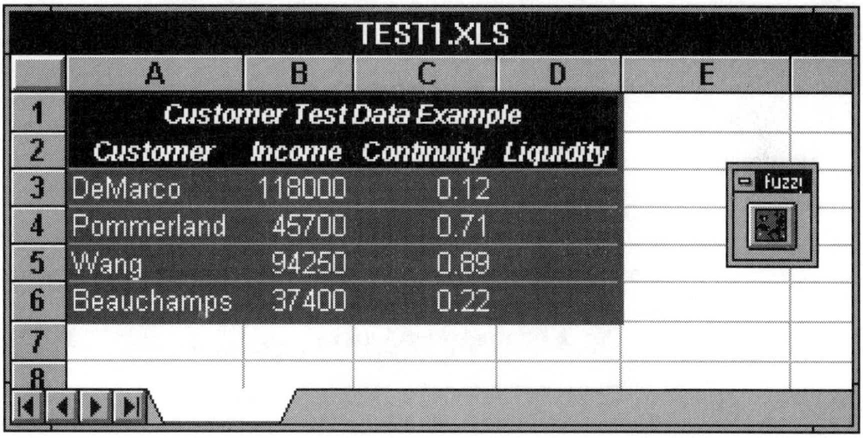

Figure 152: Spreadsheet TEST1.XLS in Excel.

Now click on the *fuzzy*TECH icon in the Excel toolbar [icon] or select "fuzzyTECH\Start Assistant" from Excel's menu bar. This opens the *fuzzy*TECH Assistant dialog box shown in Figure 153.

Note: the [Help] button opens specific help pages on the use of the *fuzzy*TECH Assistant.

With the *fuzzy*TECH Assistant, you can select the fuzzy logic systems you want to use in your spreadsheet with the [Select New...] button. Every fuzzy logic system selected is listed in the list box. If you want to use a fuzzy logic function in the current spreadsheet, select the function in the list box and then click [Connect] to list the inputs and outputs in the "Input Interfaces" and "Output Interfaces" groups.

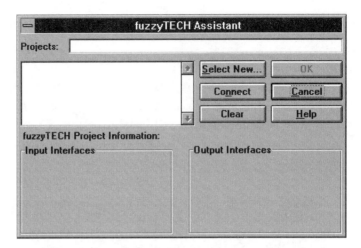

Figure 153: The *fuzzy*TECH Assistant in MS-Excel.

Next, click on [Select New...] and select the file CREDIT3.FTL to add it to the list box. Then highlight this project in the list box and click on [Connect]. Now, the *fuzzy*TECH Assistant opens the project remotely in *fuzzy*TECH and fetches the interface information. The input and output interfaces are now listed in their respective groups as shown in Figure 154.

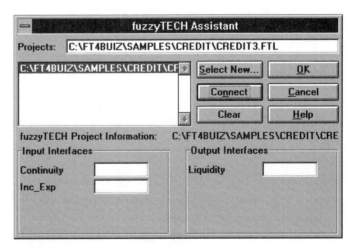

Figure 154: When a fuzzy logic project is selected and connected, the lower groups of the *fuzzy*TECH Assistant list all input and output interfaces.

Next, enter the cell references to the respective spreadsheet cells. Click in the edit field to the right of the input variable Continuity, which is in the "Input Interfaces" group, until the "|" cursor begins to blink in this edit field. Move the mouse pointer to the customer data table in the spreadsheet and select the four values under the column Continuity:

By doing this, the edit field displays the addresses of the fields as "$C$3:$C$6." Next, click in the edit field to the right of the input variable Inc_Exp, move the mouse pointer to the customer data table, and select the four values under the column Income. Continue this process with the output variable Liquidity until the *fuzzy*TECH Assistant shows the appropriate addresses:

Continuity	$C$3:$C$6		Liquidity	$D$3:$D$6
Inc_Exp	$B$3:$B$6			

Press [OK] to close the *fuzzy*TECH Assistant dialog box and create the cell links for the output cells. The spreadsheet now looks as shown in Figure 155. The column Liquidity contains the computation results of the fuzzy logic system. The link is dynamic. You can change the values in the columns Income and Continuity, and the respective fields in the column Liquidity are automatically updated (provided you enabled Excel's Automatic Calculation Option).

You can also link single cells rather than columns with the *fuzzy*TECH Assistant. Likewise, you can also link matrices by simply selecting the appropriate edit fields in the *fuzzy*TECH Assistant and highlighting the respective area in the spreadsheet. When you click [OK] in the *fuzzy*TECH Assistant, it automatically checks whether the dimensions of the input and output cells are consistent. As an alternative to this method, you can type in the cell coordinates for the input and output variables of the fuzzy logic system in the edit fields. You may include different fuzzy logic functions in the same spreadsheet. All of these functions get automatically loaded when you open your spreadsheet. For example, save the spreadsheet TEST1.XLS now and leave

Excel. Next, launch Excel again and open the file TEST1.XLS. The fuzzy logic function embedded in the spreadsheet comes up as it was the stored within Excel.

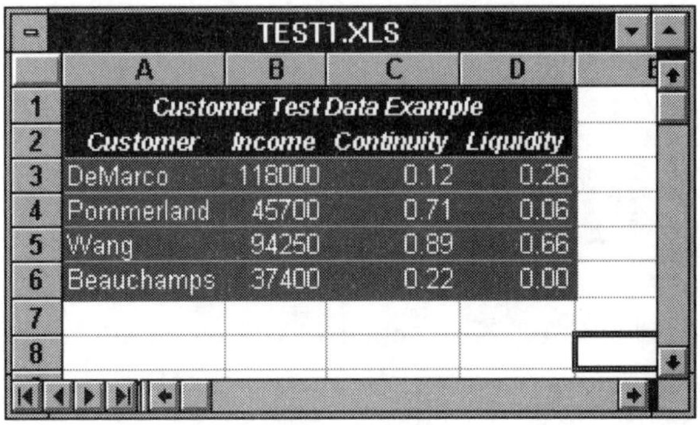

Figure 155: The spreadsheet TEST1.XLS with the fuzzy logic function.

The fuzzyTECH Interface from MS-Excel

The *fuzzy*TECH Assistant provides a quick and easy way to integrate fuzzy logic functions into Excel spreadsheets. However, you can also enter the fuzzy logic calls directly in the cell. For example, the cell D3, containing the liquidity assessment of customer DeMarco, has the following contents:

```
=FTWIN.XLA!FuzComp("C:\FT4BUIZ\SAMPLES\CREDIT\CREDIT3.FTL";2;1;1;Tabelle1!$C$3;Tabelle1!$B$3)
```

This function call contains all the information the FTWIN.XLA add-in (the *fuzzy*TECH Assistant) needs to carry out the computation. For a reference regarding function call syntax, refer to [22]. When you use the *fuzzy*TECH Assistant, you never need to worry about the call syntax because it sets up the call automatically for you.

Note: when Excel is active and the *fuzzy*TECH Remote add-in is loaded, the *fuzzy*TECH Assistant places *fuzzy*TECH in RCU debug mode. In RCU debug mode, certain operations, such as opening other files, are disabled to ensure consistency. However, you may change the fuzzy logic system in *fuzzy*TECH and store the modifications. This is useful if you use data in a spreadsheet for debugging a fuzzy logic system.

Further Operations within Excel

You can use the fuzzy logic function the same way you use other cell operations from within Excel. For example, you can use the results of a fuzzy logic system for further analysis in Excel. From within Excel, open the file TEST4.XLS, which contains the time series data from Section 2.2.4. This spreadsheet is shown in Figure 156.

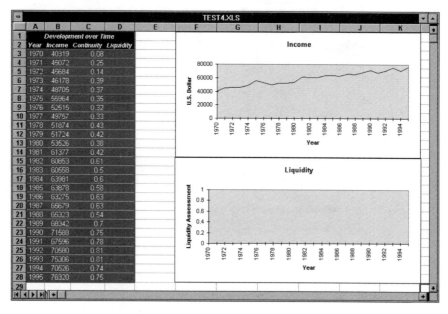

Figure 156: Spreadsheet TEST4.XLS in Excel.

Next link the fuzzy logic functions for the columns Income, Continuity, and Liquidity as was done for the spreadsheet TEST1.XLS. The resulting spreadsheet is shown in Figure 157, where the results are further displayed as curves of Income and Liquidity over time. You can create another curve for Continuity.

4.1.3 Stock Analysis Case Study

In Section 1.1.1, we looked at an overview of a stock analysis system using fuzzy logic that is implemented in Excel. This section guides you through that case study on your PC. To follow this example on your PC, you must have the *fuzzy*TECH Assistant installed as described in Section 4.1.1.

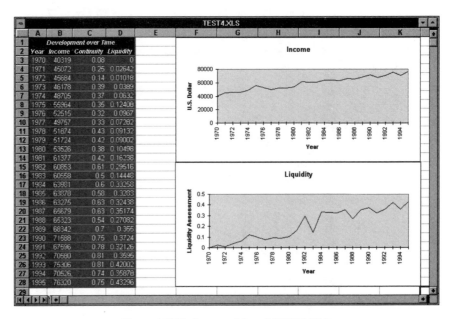

Figure 157: Spreadsheet TEST4.XLS with fuzzy logic functions in Excel.

The Stock Analysis Spreadsheet

From within Excel, open the file STOCK.XLS located in the subdirectory \SAMPLES\BUSINESS\STOCK\. Figure 158 shows an overview of the spreadsheet. It contains multiple columns in which the stock prices, trade volume, and trend indicators, computed from the first two fields, are contained. Each row represents a work day. For visualization purposes, three charts show the values over time. The upper left chart shows the stock prices, the lower left chart shows the investment strategy as computed by the fuzzy logic system, and the right chart shows the computed trend indicators.

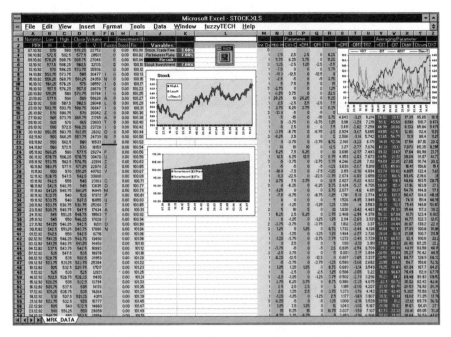

Figure 158: Fuzzy-logic-assisted technical chart
analysis to optimize an investment strategy.

Spreadsheet Contents

Column A shows the date (international format) of each row, and Columns B, C, D, and E show the stock prices and their respective sales volume. Column G contains the output of the fuzzy logic trend identification system, which is "1" for buy, "0" for hold, and "-1" for sell. Columns H and I show where the money is currently invested and the current amount of the investment.

Note: the trend indicators computed need a 20-day initialization period for the averaging. Thus, the first time the fuzzy logic system can perform a decision is in Row 23. The investment starts with $100 on the first day (Cell I3) in a market rate account. The respective market rate is stored in Cell K3 and set to 7%. You may modify this rate and analyze the differences in the investment strategy. **Note:** because of the high amount of calculations required to update the spreadsheet's computations, automatic re-computation is set to off in Excel. To refresh the computation, you need to press the [F9] key after each change. Figure 159 shows an enlarged view of the left side of the spreadsheet of STOCK.XLS.

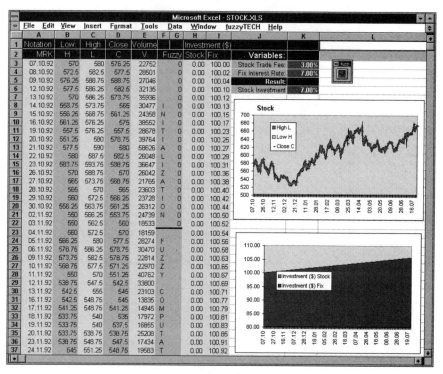

Figure 159: Left part of the spreadsheet listing stock information, the stock price chart, and the investment strategy chart.

The spreadsheet also considers a stock trading fee that is automatically subtracted from the total investment each time the investment is transferred from the market rate account to the stock investment. You may also change this fee and re-compute the spreadsheet. The total profit rate of the investment strategy is computed in Cell K6.

Note: in the spreadsheet you just opened, the fuzzy logic trend identification is not yet integrated. Thus, the buy/hold/sell decision of the fuzzy logic trend identification is always "0" (Column G), which is equivalent to "hold." Because the investment started on the first day in the market rate account, this decision is never revised throughout the

200-day period considered. Consequently, the lower chart of Figure 159 shows the sole investment placed in the market rate account.

Technical Chart Analysis

Columns M to AA contain indicators and indexes based on the stock price and volume. They are:

■ Column M: Number of past days for which interest has to be computed.

■ Column N: Difference between today's highest stock price and the last trade day.

■ Column O: Difference between today's closing stock price and the last trade day.

■ Column P: Today's highest stock price minus the closing price of the last trade day. The value is zero if the closing price of the last trade day is lower than today's highest price (+DM = "positive directional movement").

■ Column Q: Today's lowest stock price minus the closing price of the last trade day. The value is zero if the closing price of the last trade day is lower than today's lowest price (–DM = "negative directional movement").

■ Column R: True Range (TR), defined as the largest of: (a) the distance between today's high and today's low, (b) the distance between today's high and yesterday's close, or (c) the distance between today's low and yesterday's close.

■ Columns S to U: The 7-day average of Columns P to R.

■ Columns V and W: Positive and negative Directional Indicator (±DI). Computed as DI = DM / TR. Both variables are inputs to the fuzzy logic trend identification system as B_DI_PL and C_DI_MIN.

■ Column X: Intermediate value to compute ADX, DIdiff7 = (+DI7) – (–DI7).

■ Column Y: Intermediate value to compute ADX, DIsum = (+DI7) + (−DI7).

■ Column Z: Intermediate value to compute ADX, DX7 = DIsum / DIdiff7.

■ Column AA: Average Directional Index (ADX), computed as the seven-day average of DX7. This variable is an input to the fuzzy logic system as D_ADX.

This technical chart analysis strategy is discussed in detail in [6]. **Note:** the input columns of the fuzzy logic trend identification system are cyan colored in the spreadsheet. The chart located in Column S to Z plots the value of some of the computed indicators.

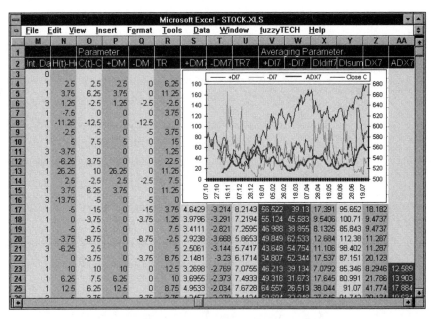

Figure 160: Right part of the spreadsheet listing the computed indicators.

The Fuzzy Logic Trend Identification System

Next, open the file STOCK.FTL located in the subdirectory \SAMPLES\BUSINESS\STOCK\ with *fuzzy*TECH. Figure 161 shows the structure of this fuzzy logic system. In addition to the three trend indicators B_DI_PL, C_DI_MIN, and D_ADX, the fuzzy logic system uses the interest rate of the market rate account, Int_Rate, and the trade fee rate, Trade_Fee, as input variables.

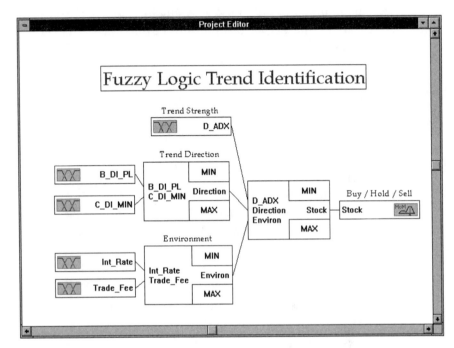

Figure 161: Structure of the fuzzy logic trend identification system.

When using MoM defuzzification, the output variable, Stock, has only the three terms "buy," "hold," and "sell." Thus, the output value of Stock can only be "1," "0," or "–1." This value is used in the Excel spreadsheet to execute buy and sell decisions.

The rightmost rule block computes the value of Stock by analyzing trend strength, trend direction, and environment. The trend strength is indicated by the input variable D_ADX computed in the Excel spreadsheet. Trend direction is computed by another rule block from the input variables B_DI_PL and C_DI_MIN. Environment is computed by a third rule block from the input variables Int_Rate and Trade_Fee. The environment assessment analyzes how attractive putting money in the market rate account is.

Integrating Trend Identification in Excel

In the previous case studies of integrating fuzzy logic functions with Excel spreadsheets, you used the *fuzzy*TECH Assistant to automatically create the links. In this case study, you will create the link manually. You only need to manually enter one call to the fuzzy logic system. Thereafter, use the AutoFill function of Excel to fill the entire column.

To enter the fuzzy logic system call manually, select the Cell G23 and enter the following string:

```
=FTWIN.XLA!FuzComp("C:\FT4BUIZ\SAMPLES\BUSINESS\STOCK\STOCK.FTL",
    5, 1, 1, MRK_DATA!$V23,MRK_DATA!$W23,MRK_DATA!$AA23,
    MRK_DATA!$K$4,MRK_DATA!$K$3)
```

The FTWIN.XLA specifies to Excel where the function called is located. The function name is FuzComp and it contains the path name of the fuzzy logic system, the interface information, and the cells that point to the input variable values as function parameters. **Note:** you need to enter a different path name if you have installed *fuzzy*TECH for Business in a different directory than "C:\FT4BUIZ." The parameter after the path and file name is the number of input interfaces of the fuzzy logic system—in this case, the number is "5." The next parameters are the number of output interfaces of the fuzzy logic system and the number of the output interface, the value of which shall be stored in Cell G23 where this function call is contained. Both parameter values are "1" as only one output interface exists in the fuzzy logic system. The next parameters are the locations of the input variables. **Note:** the second two input variables—interest rate and trade fee—are constant for all rows. Thus, the cells are referenced by "$" characters before the address, such as "$K$4" for interest rate and "$K$3" for trade fee.

To insert the same fuzzy logic function call in the entire Column G under Row 23, and use the AutoFill function of Excel. Select Cell G23 and drag the AutoFill handle with the mouse down to Cell G203. If you do not know how to use the AutoFill function, refer to the Excel manual or its online help system. After you have copied the fuzzy logic function call to all cells from G24 to G203, press the [F9] key to recalculate the spreadsheet. This can take some time if you use a slow PC because the entire spreadsheet will be re-computed.

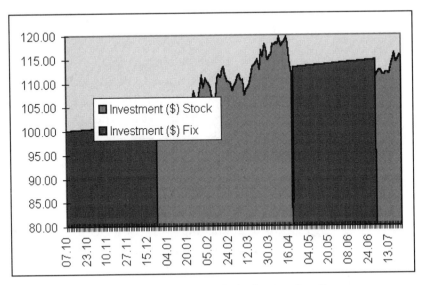

Figure 162: Investment strategy using the fuzzy logic trend identification system.

Figure 162 shows the lower left chart of the spreadsheet, which displays the investment strategy. The red areas show the periods in which the money was invested in the market rate account, the blue area shows the periods the money was invested in stock. The height of the curve shows the total value of the investment. In the red areas, the total of the investment increases steadily because of the fixed interest rate. In the blue areas, the total of the investment follows the stock price.

Buy/Sell/Hold Decisions

Now look at Column G. In Row 57, the cell value (an output of the fuzzy logic system) changes to "+1," which denotes a "buy" decision. The current amount of the investment, $101.49, is thus transferred from Column I (market rate account) to Column H (stock investment). The value that is now listed in Column H, $98.44, is lower because the trade fee is deducted from the investment upon stock purchase.

In Row 138, the decision is reversed. The value of "–1" in Cell G138 denotes a "sell" decision. Hence, the total investment is put in the market rate account again. The total profit rate on the investment is shown in Cell K6. The profit rate of 18.92% is significantly higher than the fixed interest rate of 7% on the market rate account.

The case study presented in this section can only show a simplified example for one stock and can only decide either to put all money into the market rate account or into stock. Also, even a fuzzy logic system cannot guarantee successful investment decisions by itself. A fuzzy logic system can only help you to put your investment strategy into a consistent systems solution.

Real-World Application of Fuzzy Logic in Investment Banking

A real-world application of fuzzy logic in investment banking uses a similar approach for the technical analysis of stocks. However, the buy/sell/hold strategy does not rely on only the technical analysis. Rather, the fuzzy logic system also analyzes the fundamental position of the stock-issuing company as well as the situation of similar companies. An evaluation of how suitable for an investment a stock may be is then made by fuzzy logic on the basis of all three of these factors. Because the cited application makes investment decisions for different funds the bank issues, the suitability rating of each stock is combined with an assessment of how well the considered stock fits with the scope of the fund. Thus, a decision to buy a certain stock will always take multiple factors into account. For example, a very promising stock could be bought for a fund even if it only basically fits the scope of the fund. The cited fuzzy logic system runs on a workstation as a C code implementation where it is linked to an online brokering system. It evaluates about 1500 stocks in less than a minute. The bank that has implemented this system neither wants to publish the fuzzy logic system details nor the figures of its performance. It does not want its name to be published for reasons of confidentiality.

While the use of fuzzy logic in investment banking is still relatively new in the U.S., many European and Asian banks already have long-term experience with fuzzy logic. For example, Yamaichi Securities of

Tokyo uses fuzzy logic to make decisions for an investment fund, and Nikko Securities of Yokohama uses a NeuroFuzzy system for a bond-rating program [12].

4.2   Integration of *fuzzy*TECH with Visual Basic

In order to integrate *fuzzy*TECH with Visual Basic, *fuzzy*TECH provides a DLL interface. This DLL integrates easily with all Visual Basic applications. The interface is completely integrated in a Visual Basic module called RCUFCN.BAS for MS-VisualBasic 3.0 and RCUFCN32.BAS for MS-VisualBasic 4.0. This module can be added to your application by selecting File\Add-File from the menu bar of MS-VisualBasic 3.0 or 4.0. The Visual Basic modules RCUFCNxx.BAS are located in the \RCU\VB\SAMPLES\ subdirectory of your *fuzzy*TECH installation. In the same directory, you will find the file RCUTEST.BAS, which contains an example of how to use the interface procedures.

There are two different ways to call *fuzzy*TECH from VisualBasic: the single call interface (SCI) and the standard call interface (STCI). The SCI calls the entire fuzzy logic system in a single line of code, but is computationally slower than the STCI. The standard call interface is more efficient, but requires more lines of code to implement in VisualBasic. Section 4.2.1 shows the integration of the single call remote interface, Section 4.2.2 the integration of the standard call remote interface. To illustrate this, you can follow an easy example on your PC in Section 4.2.3.

4.2.1 Single Call Remote Interface Using Visual Basic

The remainder of this section assumes that you have Visual Basic version 3.0 or 4.0 installed on your PC. If you use a newer version of Visual Basic, refer to the MS-VisualBasic manual for how to handle MS-VisualBasic 4.0 projects. Most file name reference include the letters "xx" that stand for "32" for the 32-bit version to be used with MS-

VisualBasic 4.0. Both 16-bit and 32-bit versions are located in the same directory. All following screenshots and code samples shown in screenshots use MS-VisualBasic 3.0 and may look slightly different with MS-VisualBasic 4.0.

Interface Procedure

The remote control unit (RCU) allows you to call *fuzzy*TECH from your Visual Basic application, load a fuzzy project, and switch *fuzzy*TECH into debug mode. You can pass values for the inputs of the fuzzy project to *fuzzy*TECH, let the fuzzy project calculate the outputs, and receive the calculated values in your application.

Visual Basic Example

The following example code in Visual Basic shows the principal elements of the single call interface (SCI). The lines printed in boldface denote the calls to functions in RCUFCNxx.BAS:

```
Sub Main ()
    RCUHandle = 0                  ' reset Handle of RCU-DLL
    LoginRCU                       ' connect VB to FTRCU.DLL

    Dim Out As Double              ' define output variable
    Dim In1 As Double              ' define input variables
    Dim In2 As Double

    In1 = 2.3                      ' assign input values
    In2 = 1.9
    Out = FTWINRTE_SCI04 ("...\CREDIT.FTL",2,1,1,In1,In2, 0, 0)

    LogoutRCU                      ' terminate connection
EndSub
```

After a reset of the handle of the FTRCUxx.DLL, you connect Visual Basic to FTRCUxx.DLL by the LoginRCU function call.

The SCI in Visual Basic does not support variable numbers of input variables. For this reason, the RCUFCNxx.BAS module provides you with the following functions to call up *fuzzy*TECH:

FTWINRTE_SCI04()	for projects with up to 4 input variables
FTWINRTE_SCI08()	for projects with up to 8 input variables
FTWINRTE_SCI12()	for projects with up to 12 input variables
FTWINRTE_SCI16()	for projects with up to 16 input variables
FTWINRTE_SCI20()	for projects with up to 20 input variables

If your project has n input variables, select the function that supports $\geq n$ inputs and leave the unused variables assigned values of 0. Each function call delivers you the value of exactly one output variable. Thus, if you want to access more than one output variable, you need to call the function more than once. All functions uses the same parameter list where you define:

- Filename   the name of the fuzzy project with complete path
- NumInputs   number of input interfaces in project
- NumOutputs   number of output interfaces in project
- Output_i_Idx   index of the referenced output
- InputValues   variables or values passed to the inputs

Output interfaces are referenced by an index counting from one on and sequenced alphabetically by the variable names in the interfaces.

To illustrate the use of the SCI, you can follow an easy example on your PC in Section 4.2.3.

4.2.2 Standard Call Remote Interface Using Visual Basic

The standard call remote interface (STCI) not only provides a more efficient but also a more sophisticated way to access information provided by *fuzzy*TECH. In addition to the SCI functionality, it allows you to access information about a specified project in *fuzzy*TECH and to pass on or retrieve arrays of data. Usage of the STCI involves the steps listed in this section.

Connect the FTRCUxx.DLL

As with the SCI, you must first reset the handle of the FTRCU DLL and connect Visual Basic to the FTRCUxx.DLL:

```
RCUHandle = 0                    ' reset Handle of RCU-DLL
LoginRCU                         ' connect VB to FTRCU.DLL
```

Start fuzzyTECH, Load a Project, and Enable Debug Mode

To use a fuzzy logic system in your Visual Basic application, start *fuzzy*TECH from your application, load a project, and switch *fuzzy*TECH into debug mode. FTRCU commands initiate these tasks:

```
Dim n As Integer
Dim ret As Integer
ret = FTWINRTE_State(RTESTD_STE_STARTNORMAL)
    ' start fuzzyTECH
n = FTWINRTE_LoadProject("C:\FT4BUIZ\SAMPLE\CREDIT\CREDIT.FTL")
    ' load the project
n = FTWINRTE_State(RTESTD_STE_DEBUG)
    ' enable debug mode
```

Acquire Project Structure

Before using a fuzzy logic system, you should check to be certain that the appropriate project is loaded in *fuzzy*TECH. Also, the number of input and output interfaces must be known. This information about the project structure can be fetched via FTRCU functions:

```
Dim PData As FUZZYSTRUCT
    ' structure defined in RCUFCNxx.BAS
n = FTWINRTE_CMGetProjectInfo
        (RTESTD_PRJ_COMPACTMODE,PData,0)
```

```
' get project information in PData, e.g.:
' PData.NumIn contains # input interfaces
' PData.NumOut contains # output interfaces
PData.PrjName = NullString(PData.PrjName)
  ' PData.PrjName contains the project name
  ' to use it in VB convert the null terminated
  ' string into a Visual Basic string
```

Read Interface Items

To determine the specifics of the interfaces in your fuzzy logic project, you can retrieve information about the interface type, the variables used, and the computation methods:

```
Dim ITFCData As ITFCSTRUCT
  ' structure defined in RCUFCNxx.BAS
n = FTWINRTE_CMGetInterfaceInfo
  (RTESTD_ITFC_COMPACT, RTESTD_ITFC_RESET * 65536, ITFCData)
  ' get information of the first interface
ITFCData.LVName = NullString(ITFCData.LVName)
  ' ITFCData.LVName contains the LV name
  ' to use it in VB convert the null terminated
  ' string into a Visual Basic string
n = FTWINRTE_CMGetInterfaceInfo(RTESTD_ITFC_COMPACT,
  RTESTD_ITFC_NEXT * 65536, ITFCData)
  ' gets information of next interfaces
  ' If the return value is non-zero than:
  ' no more interfaces are available or an error
  ' occurred, the data structure is not filled
```

Transfer and Compute Values

Before you can use the functions for sending input and retrieving output values to and from *fuzzy*TECH, it is necessary to declare the type of data transfer to be used. FTRCU supports the transfer of single data elements as well as the transfer of arrays. You can reference variables though an index or by their variable names:

```
Dim CMode As Integer
n = FTWINRTE_SetConversation(RTESTD_CONV_SINGLE,
       RTESTD_CONV_DOUBLE, RTESTD_CONV_NAME, CMode)
   ' sets single data transfer and text reference
   ' the function sets CMode, that is used in
   ' SetCrisp- and GetCrisp- functions.
Dim VData As DOUBLESTRUCT
VData.LV1 = 4.09
n = FTWINRTE_NAMSetCrispInput(CMode, "Inc_Exp", VData)
   ' sets the input variable Inc_Exp
n = FTWINRTE_Compute()                ' initiate a computing step
Dim OData As DOUBLESTRUCT
n = FTWINRTE_NAMSVGetCrispOutput(CMode, "Liquidity", OData)
   ' get output Liquidity in OData.LV1
```

Disconnect FTRCU.DLL

As with the single call interface, the FTRCU interface can be disconnected when your application is terminated or fuzzy logic computation is no longer required:

```
   LogoutRCU          ' disconnect VB from FTRCU.DLL
```

FTRCU Interface

This section only gave a brief introduction to the functionality of the *fuzzy*TECH remote control unit with Visual Basic. Not all features of the FTRCU interface are supported under Visual Basic due to limitations of the programming language. A complete reference of the Visual Basic functionality is given in [22].

4.2.3 A Case Study Using Visual Basic

To follow the case study of the quality control system already introduced in Section 1.1.1, you need to have MS-VisualBasic 3.0 or 4.0 installed on your PC. The source files for this example and the fuzzy logic system are located in the subdirectory \SAMPLES\BUSINESS\-WHEELS\.

The fuzzy logic system for the comfort evaluation is contained in the file WHEELS.FTL. Figure 163 shows the structure of the system in the Project Editor window. The details of the entire system containing a total of 31 linguistic variables and 14 rule blocks are described in [25].

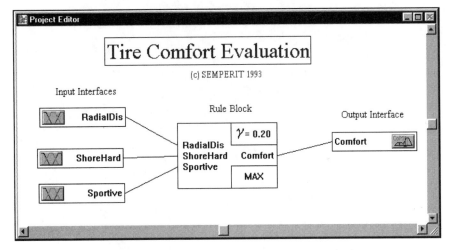

Figure 163: The subset of the tire comfort evaluation system contained in WHEELS.FTL.

Open the Project in Visual Basic

The following programming example in MS-VisualBasic comprises only a set of forms that let you enter the input values and visualize the output values to illustrate the Visual Basic interface.

To open the project, launch MS-VisualBasic and create a new project by selecting File\New Project... from the menu bar. Then add the three *.FRM files WHEELSxx.FRM, ABOUTxx.FRM, and HELPxx.FRM to the project using File\Add File... from the menu bar.

The *.FRM files are located in the \SAMPLES\BUSINESS\- WHEELS\ subdirectory of the *fuzzy*TECH installation. Next add the file RCUFCNxx.BAS located in the subdirectory \RCU\VB\- SAMPLES\ of the *fuzzy*TECH installation that contains the interface functions.

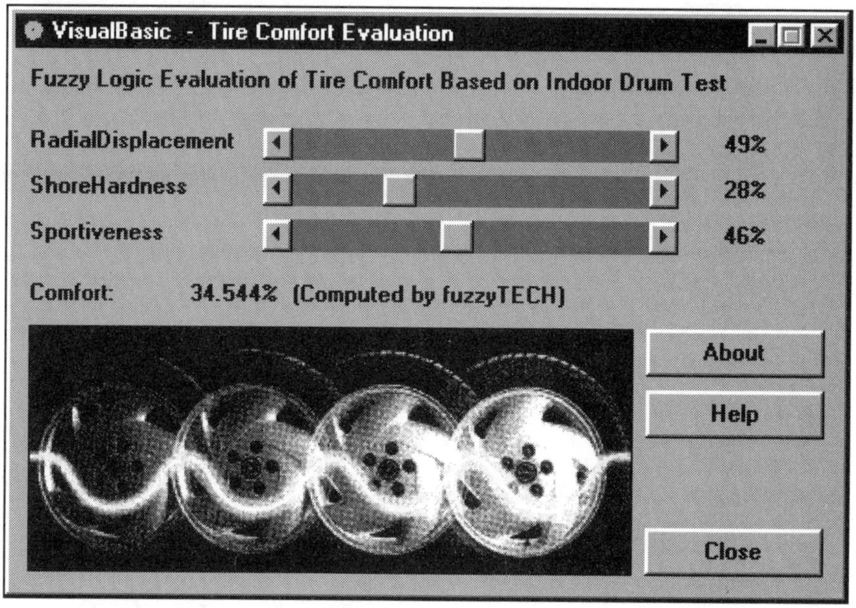

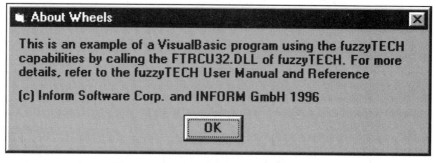

Figure 164: Main form of the Visual Basic user interface.

Figure 165: About Wheels form.

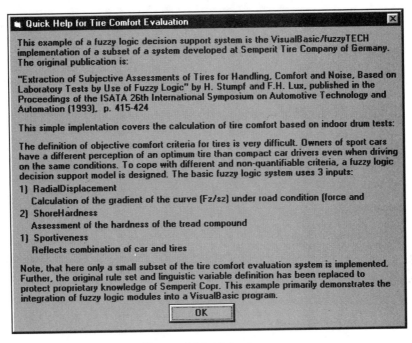

Figure 166: Help form.

Define the frmWheels form as the Start Up Form in the Project Options dialog box of Visual Basic, which is opened by selecting Options\Project... from the menu bar.

```
WHEELS.FRM

Object: Form        Proc: Load

Sub Form_Load ()
  ' initialize the FTRCU functionality
  RCUHandle = 0                    ' reset handle of FTRCU.DLL
  LoginRCU                         ' connect UB to FTRCU.DLL
  If RCUHandle <= 32 Then          ' error handling
    DgDef = MB_OK + MB_ICONSTOP
    Msg = "Could not locate FTRCU.DLL"
    Title = "Error"
    Response = MsgBox(Msg, DgDef, Title)
    End
  End If
  ' execute the call to the SCI of FTRCU once, so fuzzyTECH gets started
  DoFuzzy
End Sub
```

Figure 167: The initialization of the FTRCU functions is contained in the load procedure of the Wheels form.

Figure 164 shows the main form frmWheels from the tire comfort evaluation system. It contains three scroll bars that let you enter the three input variables of the fuzzy logic system. The output variable Comfort to be computed by *fuzzy*TECH is displayed under the scroll bars. The two upper push buttons open the About Wheels form (Figure 165) and the Help form (Figure 166), respectively.

Note: the function LoginRCU is defined in the RCUFCNxx.BAS module that you added to the project. The Visual Basic functions contained in RCUFCNxx.BAS comprise all the necessary code to connect to the FTRCU.DLL, so you only need to call the simple subroutines described in this section.

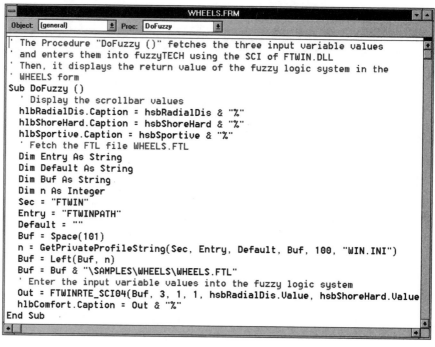

```
' The Procedure "DoFuzzy ()" fetches the three input variable values
' and enters them into fuzzyTECH using the SCI of FTWIN.DLL
' Then, it displays the return value of the fuzzy logic system in the
' WHEELS form
Sub DoFuzzy ()
  ' Display the scrollbar values
  hlbRadialDis.Caption = hsbRadialDis & "%"
  hlbShoreHard.Caption = hsbShoreHard & "%"
  hlbSportive.Caption = hsbSportive & "%"
  ' Fetch the FTL file WHEELS.FTL
  Dim Entry As String
  Dim Default As String
  Dim Buf As String
  Dim n As Integer
  Sec = "FTWIN"
  Entry = "FTWINPATH"
  Default = ""
  Buf = Space(101)
  n = GetPrivateProfileString(Sec, Entry, Default, Buf, 100, "WIN.INI")
  Buf = Left(Buf, n)
  Buf = Buf & "\SAMPLES\WHEELS\WHEELS.FTL"
  ' Enter the input variable values into the fuzzy logic system
  Out = FTWINRTE_SCI04(Buf, 3, 1, 1, hsbRadialDis.Value, hsbShoreHard.Value
  hlbComfort.Caption = Out & "%"
End Sub
```

Figure 168: The subroutine DoFuzzy contains the Single Call Remote Interface function call.

The actual call of the fuzzy logic system is contained in the subroutine DoFuzzy, listed in Figure 168. The subroutine is called every time the user touches a scroll bar. First, DoFuzzy updates the values displayed on the scrollbar. Next, it locates the WHEELS.FTL file by reading the directory in which you installed *fuzzy*TECH for Business from the WIN.INI entry which was set up by the installation routine of *fuzzy*TECH. The actual call to the fuzzy logic system is just a single function that returns one output value to the variable Out. The parameters of the FTWINRTE_SCI04() function call are:

- Buf: path and file name of the fuzzy logic system (*.FTL)

- 3: the number of input variables of the fuzzy logic system

- 1: the number of output variables of the fuzzy logic system

- 1: the number of the output variable that shall be returned

- the input variables of the fuzzy logic system

The total number of input variables entered in the parameter list of the FTWINRTE_SCI04() function call is four. Hence, the RCUFCNxx.BAS module provides different function calls depending on the number of input variables (refer to Section 4.2.1 for details). No function is provided for three inputs. Therefore, the function with four input variables was selected and the fourth input variable was set to zero in the parameter list.

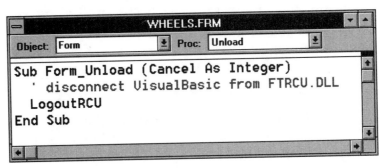

Figure 169: The termination of the FTRCU functions is contained in the unload procedure of the Wheels form.

When you leave the Wheels program, the FTRCUxx.DLL must be unloaded and all Windows resources used for communication must be freed. In Visual Basic, all you need to do is to call the LogoutRCU procedure defined in RCUFCNxx.BAS. In Wheels, this procedure is called in the Form_Unload function of the Wheels form (Figure 169).

4.3   Integration of *fuzzy*TECH with MS-Access

In this section, the case study of a customer profiling system presented in Section 1.1.1 is used again to illustrate the integration of fuzzy logic functions with MS-Access. To follow the case study, you need to have MS-Access 2.0 or 7.0 installed on your PC. The source files for this example and the fuzzy logic system are located in the subdirectory \SAMPLES\BUSINESS\FTINVEST\. Section 4.3.1 describes the steps required to integrate fuzzy logic functions in MS-Access in general. Section 4.3.2 presents the fuzzy logic customer profiling system. Section 4.3.3 shows the integration of this fuzzy logic system in the MS-Access database. Programming details of the presented FT Investment Bank database are contained in Section 4.3.4.

4.3.1 Integration of Fuzzy Logic Functions

If you already have a database written in MS-Access or you want to create your own, follow these steps:

- Open MS-Access.

- Either open your database or create a new database.

- Create a new Module in the Database window of MS-Access. Select the window titled Module: Module1 that was created by this action.

- Select File\Load Text from the main menu of MS-Access 2.0, or select Insert\File from the main menu of MS-Access 7.0.

- Select the file RCUFCN.BAS for MS-Access 2.0 and press the [Merge] button, or select the file RCUFCN32.BAS for MS-Access 7.0. Both files are located in the \RCU\VB\SAMPLES\ subdirectory of the *fuzzy*TECH installation.

The new module now has a declaration section and three functions: LoginRCU, LogoutRCU, GetFTWINDir, and NullString. These functions are listed in the drop list box

of the Module tool bar. You can close the Module: Module1 window and rename it to RCUFCNxx ("xx" := "32" for MS-Access 7.0; "xx" := "" for MS-Access 2.0). Now you can use the same functions in your MS-Access database as described in the prior Section for MS-VisualBasic. To lock *fuzzy*TECH for your application, you call LoginRCU. Next, you can use the fuzzy logic system by accessing the FTWINRTE_SCI calls. After you have completed the computation, call LogoutRCU to free *fuzzy*TECH for other tasks. All these steps are described in detail with regards to a larger database project in the Sections that follow.

4.3.2 The FT Investment Bank Case Study

The FT Investment Bank case study that you will work with here stems from a customer profiling application that is currently implemented and in everyday use at a financial services provider. The case study provided here is a very small fraction of the original system, because it only serves the purpose of illustrating the integration of MS-Access and databases with *fuzzy*TECH in general. Also, the linguistic variables, structure, and rules were changed to protect the intellectual property of the financial services provider. Any data contained in the database is fictional.

Note: the original application was conducted in England, where the financial behavior pattern of customers depends largely on the neighborhood in which the customer lives. Thus, the demographic analysis plays a strong role in the fuzzy logic assessment of the target group. Also, the original application does not run on a PC using MS-Access, but rather on a mainframe computer with the fuzzy logic system implemented in COBOL (cf. Section 2.3.5).

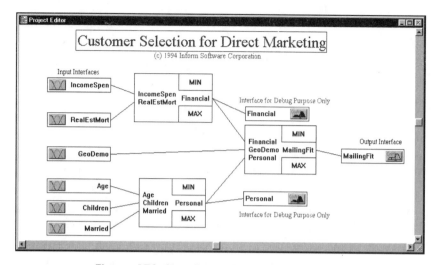

Figure 170: Structure of the FT Investment
Bank fuzzy logic customer profiling system.

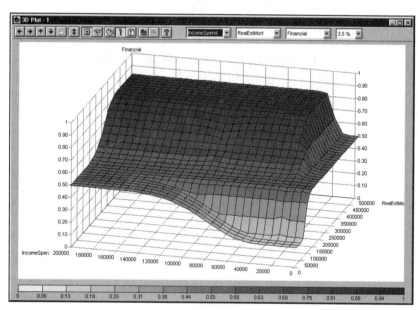

Figure 171: The Financial output interface
is for debugging purpose only.

Open the file FTINVEST.FTL located in the subdirectory
\SAMPLES\BUSINESS\FTINVEST\ with *fuzzy*TECH. Figure 170

shows the structure of this fuzzy logic project. It has been limited to only six input variables and 42 rules. There is only one output, which is used in the database, MailingFit, that rates the degree to which a customer is considered to be a member of the target group. The other two output interfaces for Financial and Personal are for debugging purposes only. These output interfaces allow you to open a 3D Plot analyzer with either Financial or Personal as the output variable and study how these parameters are assessed from the input data. For example, you can select Financial as the output and IncomeSpend plus RealEstMort as input variables in a 3D Plot analyzer, resulting in a transfer curve similar to Figure 171. As can be seen from the curve, both real estate and income can result in a favorable assessment of the financial background. However, if both are present, the rating is even higher.

4.3.3 FT Investment Bank's MS-Access Database

Close *fuzzy*TECH, and then start MS-Access. Open the file FTINVEST.MDB in MS-Access 2.0 or FTINVE32.MDB in MS-Access 7.0 located in the subdirectory \SAMPLES\BUSINESS\FTINVEST\ which contains the complete database of the FT Investment Bank case study. The database automatically opens the Main Menu form shown in Figure 172. It accesses the primary functions of the database.

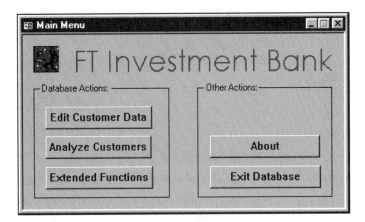

Figure 172: The Main Menu window comes up automatically when opening FTINVEST.MDB.

Also, a window titled Database: FTINVEST opens, which lets you browse through the components of the FTINVEST database. This window contains several lists of the different component groups. FTINVEST contains four tables listed in the Tables list

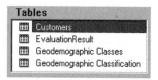

which contain the data records of the database. To edit the data records and manage the database, FTINVEST contains a number of forms listed in the Forms list:

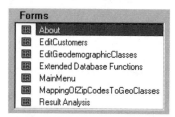

Also listed here is the Main Menu form that automatically starts when FTINVEST is opened. FTINVEST also contains a report

that provides a visualization of the statistical analysis of the results of the fuzzy logic customer profiling. The macro AutoExec

of FTINVEST opens the Main Menu form automatically each time you open the database. The entire AccessBasic code that links the fuzzy logic functions to the database tables is stored in two modules

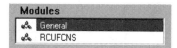

of the database. The RCUFCNxx module, supplied with *fuzzy*TECH for Business, contains all functions necessary to remotely control *fuzzy*-

TECH from MS-Access. The General module contains the code that performs the computations specific to FTINVEST.

Table Relations

In a relational database, tables are linked to form a model of the data to be stored in the database. The table Customers contains all the information specific to one customer, for example, their name and address as well as personal and financial background data. FTINVEST stores the ten pre-defined demographic classes in the Geodemographic Classes table, where each class is distinguished by a class number, a linguistic description, and a rating associated with the class. These tables are linked by relations to a third table, Geodemographic Classification, which maps each zip code to a demographic class.

You can display the relations graphically by activating the Database: FTINVEST window and selecting Edit\Relationships... from the menu bar of MS-Access. This opens the Relationships window as shown in Figure 173.

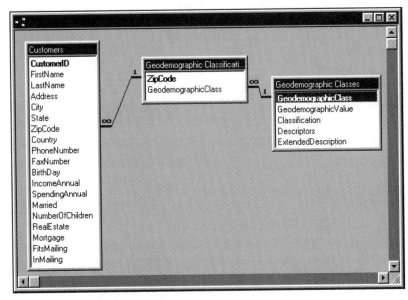

Figure 173: The Relationships window of MS-Access displays visually how the tables are related.

Using the FTINVEST Database

Press the [Edit Customer Data] button in the Main Menu window to open the Edit Customer window shown in Figure 174. The different fields in this form let you edit and enter a name and an address, as well as personal and financial background data. The arrow buttons at the bottom part of the window let you browse through the customers. FTINVEST contains 30 pre-defined fictional customers.

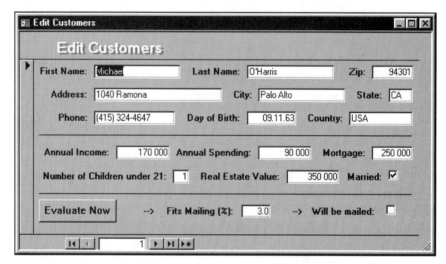

Figure 174: The Edit Customers window contains the customer data.

The lower part of the window contains one button, a field, and a check box. When you press the button [Evaluate Now], the mailing fitness degree is computed by the fuzzy logic system in *fuzzy*TECH for all customers in the database. The resulting degree is displayed in the "Fits Mailing (%):" field and cannot be edited.

To select a target group from this result, a threshold has to be defined in the Extended Database Functions menu (Figure 175). You open this menu by pressing the [Extended Functions] button in the Main Menu window. In the Extended Database Functions menu, click on [Define Mailing Threshold]. Every customer that belongs to the target group to a degree higher than or equal to the threshold will now be selected as a member of the target group. In the Edit Customer window shown in Figure 174, you must execute [Evaluate Now] again if you change the Mailing Threshold. The check box "Will be Mailed:" indicates whether the customer is selected as a member of the target group. This field can be used in later database functions that execute the direct marketing action.

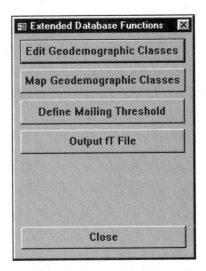

Figure 175: The Extended Database Functions menu accesses more functions.

Demographic Classification

As mentioned before, customer profiling makes extensive use of customer neighborhood assessment. Based on the assumption that the financial behavior patterns of customers strongly relate to their environment, ten primary demographic classes have been defined. You can browse through these classes by clicking [Edit Geodemographic Classes] in the Extended Database Functions window. Figure 176 shows the Edit Geodemographic Classes window, which displays each class.

By relating the neighborhood classification to the personal and financial background pattern (Figure 170), certain conclusions can be made. For example, if the customer lives in a posh, new neighborhood, but their income is still relatively low and they just started a family, then they will be more receptive to certain financial services ("keeping up with the Joneses"). Another customer with a better financial background who lives in a modest neighborhood might lead more of an "understated" lifestyle, thus they might be receptive to different financial products.

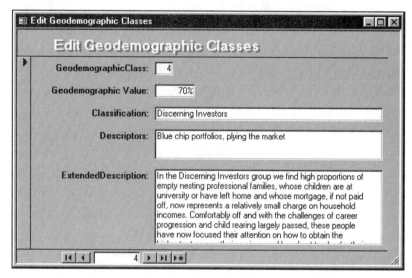

Figure 176: The FT Investment Bank uses ten pre-defined demographic classes to describe the customer's neighborhood.

Fuzzy Classification

Each demographic class has a class number, which is the reference number in the Geodemographic Classification table (Figure 173), a class name (Classification), a number of short descriptors (Descriptors), and a more descriptive text (Extended Description). Each class is assigned a value that becomes the input for the fuzzy logic system. **Note:** evaluating the demographic classes just by a single number is an over-simplification only done in this case study to keep system complexity down. The original application used all ten classes as inputs of one fuzzy input variable. Thus, each class becomes a term in the linguistic variable. Also, this enables a fuzzy classification. In a fuzzy classification, a neighborhood should not be assigned to one and only one class. For example, a neighborhood could be classified as "mostly equity-holding elders (class), just a few capital accumulators (class)." This could be translated to a value in linguistic variables as follows:

Gclass := {Class1, Class2, Class3, Class4, Class5, Class6,

Class7, Class8, Class9, Class10} = {0, 0, 0.2, 0, 0.8, 0, 0, 0, 0, 0}

The original application contains 170 rules and 9 input variables.

Matching Zip Codes to Demographic Classes

In this simplified database, the demographic classification only depends on the zip code rather than zip code plus street address. The table Geodemographic Classification links the tables Customer and Geodemographic classes in the relational database architecture (Figure 173). You can edit the relation by clicking [Map Demographic Classes] in the Extended Database Function menu window. Figure 177 shows the Geodemographic Classification window.

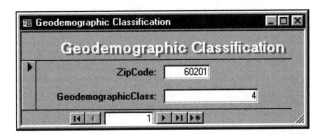

Figure 177: The Geodemographic Classification window maps each zip code to a demographic class.

Statistical Analysis

The FT Investment Bank database can be used in many different ways. You can linguistically define a target group in *fuzzy*TECH and then select the customers that belong to the target group to at least a certain degree (mailing threshold). This works fine if you already have an idea of how well the selection should satisfy the target group definition, that is, you already know the mailing threshold value. In other cases, you may not know in advance where to set the mailing threshold. Or you may have a limited size for a direct mail campaign. For instance, you can call ten of your customers directly and you want to call the ten that best satisfy the target group definition.

To help you set the mailing threshold, the FTINVEST database provides an analysis function. This function is activated by pressing the [Analyze Customers] button in the Main Menu. Figure 178 shows the report page with the graphical analysis of how many customers satisfy the target group definition to a certain degree. The degree (mailing fitness threshold) is plotted on the horizontal axis, while the number of customers is plotted on the vertical axis.

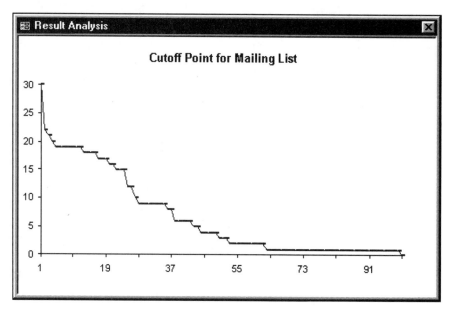

Figure 178: Customers satisfy the target group definition to a certain degree.

In this example, if you require a 100% satisfaction of the target group definition, then not a single customer would be in the selection. If you require an 80% fit, only one customer would be in the selection. A 50% mailing threshold will select three customers, and a 30% fit selects nine customers. The result analysis for the currently defined target group and the current customer selection in the database subsequently indicates that the customers in general do not satisfy the target group very well.

Also, the analysis results can help you to define the mailing threshold value. If you can only call ten customers directly, set the mailing threshold to 27%, and the ten customers that best satisfy the criteria of the target group will be selected.

You can also use the FTINVEST database to design new products and optimize them so that they best fit the customers you already have in your database. When you have designed a product and have defined the target group, you can use the Result Analysis function to find out how well such a product could be marketed to the customer database.

Using fuzzyTECH and MS-Access in Parallel

The FTINVEST database is linked directly to the fuzzy logic system in *fuzzy*TECH by a DLL link. This allows you to interactively follow the fuzzy logic inference in all *fuzzy*TECH editors and analyzers. Just open the respective windows in *fuzzy*TECH. You can now change the customer data in FTINVEST, push [Evaluate Now], and watch the computation in *fuzzy*TECH's windows. Likewise, you can modify the fuzzy logic system in *fuzzy*TECH, press [Evaluate Now] or [Analyze Customers] in FTINVEST, and see the effects of the modification in MS-Access.

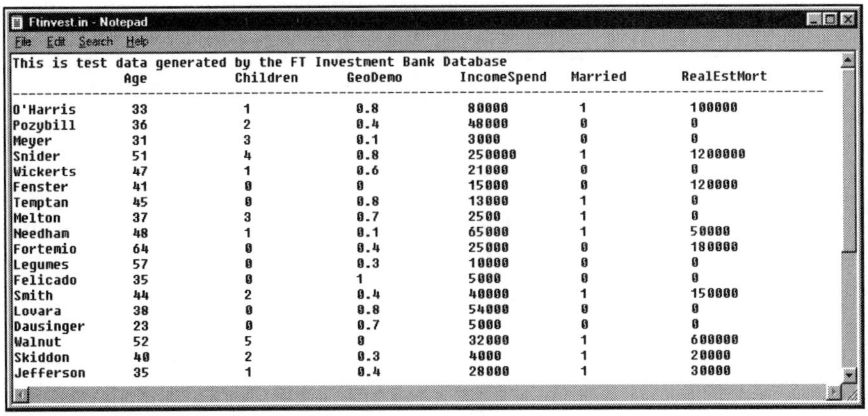

```
 Ftinvest.in - Notepad                                                    _ □ ×
 File  Edit  Search  Help
 This is test data generated by the FT Investment Bank Database
                Age        Children      GeoDemo      IncomeSpend   Married      RealEstMort
 ---------------------------------------------------------------------------------
 O'Harris        33         1             0.8          80000         1            100000
 Pozybill        36         2             0.4          48000         0            0
 Meyer           31         3             0.1          3000          0            0
 Snider          51         4             0.8          250000        1            1200000
 Wickerts        47         1             0.6          21000         0            0
 Fenster         41         0             0            15000         0            120000
 Temptan         45         0             0.8          13000         1            0
 Melton          37         3             0.7          2500          1            0
 Needham         48         1             0.1          65000         1            50000
 Fortemio        64         0             0.4          25000         0            180000
 Legumes         57         0             0.3          10000         0            0
 Felicado        35         0             1            5000          0            0
 Smith           44         2             0.4          40000         1            150000
 Lovara          38         0             0.8          54000         0            0
 Dausinger       23         0             0.7          5000          0            0
 Walnut          52         5             0            32000         1            600000
 Skiddon         40         2             0.3          4000          1            20000
 Jefferson       35         1             0.4          28000         1            30000
```

Figure 179: File FTINVEST.IN generated by
the FT Investment Bank database.

Linking to fuzzyTECH's File Interface

Rather than using the interactive link to *fuzzy*TECH, you can also generate an input file for *fuzzy*TECH using the [Output fT File] button of the Extended Database Function menu window. If you press this button, the file FTINVEST.IN file is generated in the \SAMPLES\-BUSINESS\FTINVEST\ subdirectory. Figure 179 shows the contents of this file. You can use this file in *fuzzy*TECH's File Recorder and Batch debug modes.

4.3.4 AccessBasic Integration

In this section, the focus is on the programming issues around the integration of fuzzy logic within MS-Access databases. MS-Access 2.0 and 7.0 both provide a built-in programming language, called Access-Basic, which is similar but not identical to Visual Basic. Despite some differences, you will find that integration of fuzzy logic functions is almost identical to integration with Visual Basic. All screenshots in this section show MS-Access 2.0. Both screenshots and screenshot contents may vary with MS-Access 7.0.

Note: in this book, lines that are longer than the page width are split into two or more lines. Both Visual Basic and Access Basic do not allow for this. Hence, if you copy source code parts from this book, make sure that you write each statement on only one line.

The fuzzyTECH RCU Interface in AccessBasic

As described in Section 4.3.1, you need to include the Visual Basic source code file RCUFCNxx.BAS, located in the \RCU\VB\SAMPLES\ subdirectory, within your project. Open a new module and select File\Load Text... to include the source code in your database. This source code module then becomes a part of the database listed in the Modules

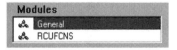

list of the Database: FTINVEST window. All other AccessBasic functions of FTINVEST are located either in the General module or tied in with the forms as Event Procedures.

The RCUFCNxx.BAS module provides three Basic functions to integrate the fuzzy logic system: one for login, one for computing the fuzzy logic system, and one for logout. Because AccessBasic and Visual Basic do not provide variable parameter lists in function calls, multiple functions are provided for computation that let you compute a fuzzy logic system with 4, 8, 12, etc.... input interfaces. Because the computing function can only return one output variable, you also have to provide the number of the output variables you want to have returned in the parameter list of the function.

Initialization

Before you can use the FTINVEST database, a number of initializations need to be made. The AccessBasic code for this is located in the form load event procedure of the Main Menu form. To open the code module, select the Main Menu window, enable View\Form Design, enable View\Code..., and then select the Form Load procedure of the module "Module: Form.MainMenu." The following code executes the initializations:

```
Sub Form_Load ()
 MailThreshold = 50
 ' first fetch the location of the ftinvest.ftl file
 Dim Sec As String
 Dim Entry As String
 Dim Buf As String
 Dim Default As String
 Dim n As Integer
 Sec = "FTWIN"
 Entry = "FTWINPATH"
 Default = ""
 FTWINpath = Space(101)
 n = GetPrivateProfileString(
```

```
Sec, Entry, Default, FTWINpath, 100, "WIN.INI")
FTWINpath = Left(FTWINpath, n)
Buf = FTWINpath & "\SAMPLES\BUSINESS\FTINVEST\FTINVEST.FTL"
' load and initiate the FTRCU (fuzzyTECH Remote Control Unit)
RCUHandle = 0
LoginRCU          ' this sub is defined in RCUFCNxx.BAS
End If
End Sub
```

There are two main tasks in this procedure. The first is to locate the FTINVEST.FTL file on your hard disk or network drive. Because the installation routine of *fuzzy*TECH writes the current path of the *fuzzy*TECH executable files in the WIN.INI file, it can be read from there. The GetPrivateProfileString function is a Windows function that returns the path of *fuzzy*TECH as the variable FTWINpath. In the declarations section of the General module, the variable FTWINpath is defined as a global string variable, so all procedures may use the variable once it is initialized.

The second task of this procedure loads and initializes the FTRCU module. The entire interfacing between MS-Access and *fuzzy*TECH is controlled by the FTRCUxx.DLL dynamic link library. You do not need to call this DLL from your code because the RCUFCNxx.BAS module does this for you. RCUFCNxx provides the procedure LoginRCU, which locates the FTRCUxx.DLL and loads this under Windows. If the RCU-Handle variable that is set by the LoginRCU procedure returns with a value of lower than 32, the FTRCUxx.DLL was not locatable. A possible reason for this could be a false entry of FTWINPATH in the WIN.INI file.

Computing the Fuzzy Logic System

To make the call to the fuzzy logic system computation more transparent, the FTINVEST database has a function ComputeFuzzy defined in the General module that uses the FTWINRTE_SCI08 function provided by the RCUFCNxx module:

```
Function ComputeFuzzy (in1, in2, in3, in4, in5, in6)
 ComputeFuzzy = FTWINRTE_SCI08(
  FTWINpath + "\SAMPLES\BUSINESS\FTINVEST\FTINVEST.FTL",
  6, 3, 2, in1, in2, in3, in4, in5, in6, 0, 0)
End Function
```

The FTWINRTE_SCI08 function requires the following parameters:

- Path of the *.FTL file.

- Number of input variables of the fuzzy logic system.

- Number of output variables of the fuzzy logic system.

- Number of output variables that shall be returned by the FTWINRTE_SCI function.

- Eight input variables. Because the FTINVEST system only uses six input variables, the last two inputs are set to 0.

Evaluating All Customers

When the [Evaluate Now] button in the Edit Customer window or the [Analyze Customers] button of the Main Menu window is pressed, the FitsMailing value of the Customers Table is computed by the fuzzy logic system. The code for this is contained in the EvaluateAllCustomers subroutine located in the General module:

```
Sub EvaluateAllCustomers ()
 Dim DB As Database
 Dim Tab1 As Recordset
 Dim Tab2 As Recordset
 Static E(100) As Integer
 Static Inputs(5) As Single
 Dim ZipCode As String
 Dim Class As String
 Dim i As Integer
```

```
Dim Result As Single

Set DB = DBEngine.Workspaces(0).Databases(0)
Set Tab1 = DB.OpenRecordset("Customers", DB_OPEN_TABLE)
Set Tab2 = DB.OpenRecordset("EvaluationResult",DB_OPEN_TABLE)

' compute FitsMailing for all records by fuzzy logic system
Tab1.MoveFirst
Do While Not Tab1.EOF

  ' compute inputs of the fuzzy system and store in Inputs()
  Inputs(0) = DatePart(
    "yyyy", Date) - DatePart("yyyy", Tab1![BirthDay])
  Inputs(1) = Tab1![NumberOfChildren]
  ZipCode = Tab1![ZipCode]
  Class = Dlookup(
    "[GeodemographicClass]", "Geodemographic Classification",
    "[ZipCode] = " & ZipCode)
  Inputs(2) = Dlookup(
    "[GeodemographicValue]", "Geodemographic Classes",
    "[GeodemographicClass] = " & Class)
  Inputs(3) = Tab1![IncomeAnnual] - Tab1![SpendingAnnual]
  If Tab1![Married] = -1
    Then Inputs(4) = 1
    Else Inputs(4) = 0
  Inputs(5) = Tab1![RealEstate] - Tab1![Mortgage]

  ' call the fuzzy logic computation
  Result = Fix(
    ComputeFuzzy(Inputs(0), Inputs(1), Inputs(2), Inputs(3),
    Inputs(4), Inputs(5)))
  If Result < 1 Then Result = 1

  ' update the record
  Tab1.Edit
  Tab1![FitsMailing] = Result
  If Result >= MailThreshold
```

```
   Then Tab1![InMailing] = True
   Else Tab1![InMailing] = False
  Tab1.Update
  Tab1.MoveNext
 Loop
End Sub
```

This subroutine starts with a loop through all records of the database. Within the loop, all the inputs of the fuzzy logic system as required by *fuzzy*TECH are computed for the columns of the Customers table and stored in the array Inputs(). Then the fuzzy logic computation is called using the function ComputeFuzzy, as described before. A result lower than one is clipped. The last part of the loop code is to update the FitsMailing and InMailing columns of the Customers table.

Computing the Histogram

Because the report generator of MS-Access uses a database table to store the data to be displayed, the EvaluationResult table is always filled with the histogram before the report generator is invoked. When [Analyze Customers] is pressed, first the EvaluateAllCustomers procedure is called, then the CreateHistogram procedure is called, and finally the report generator in the EvaluationResult table is invoked to display the histogram graphically.

```
Sub CreateHistogram ()
 Dim DB As Database
 Dim Tab1 As Recordset
 Dim Tab2 As Recordset
 Static E(100) As Integer
 Set DB = DBEngine.Workspaces(0).Databases(0)
 Set Tab1 = DB.OpenRecordset("Customers", DB_OPEN_TABLE)
 Set Tab2 = DB.OpenRecordset(
  "EvaluationResult", DB_OPEN_TABLE)
 Dim i As Integer
```

```
' reset histogram
For i = 0 To 100
 E(i) = 0 .
Next i


' compute histogram of fuzzy evaluation results, store in E()
Tab1.MoveFirst
Do While Not Tab1.EOF
 For i = 0 To Tab1![FitsMailing]
  E(i) = E(i) + 1
 Next i
 Tab1.MoveNext
Loop


' store histogram in the EvaluationResult data table
Tab2.MoveFirst
i = 1
Do While Not Tab2.EOF And i <= 100
 Tab2.Edit
 Tab2![MailingVolume] = E(i)
 Tab2.Update
 i = i + 1
 Tab2.MoveNext
Loop


End Sub
```

The CreateHistogram procedure performs three tasks. First, it resets the E() array, which stores the histogram before it is written into the EvaluationResult table. Next, the histogram is computed. The Do...While loop runs through every customer row in the Customers data table and numerically integrates the E() histogram array. The third task is to store the result of E() permanently in the Evaluation-Result table, so it may be graphically displayed by the report generator.

Generating a File for the File Interface of fuzzyTECH

By selecting the [Output fT File] button of the Extended Database Functions menu window, an input file for the *fuzzy*TECH file interface is generated. Processing the input data for the fuzzy logic system is thus similar to the processing in the subroutine EvaluateAllCustomers.

```
Sub OutputFTfile ()
 ' Generates a file in the fuzzyTECH file format for off-line
 ' analyses and tests


 Dim DB As Database
 Dim Tab1 As Recordset
 Set DB = DBEngine.Workspaces(0).Databases(0)
 Set Tab1 = DB.OpenRecordset("Customers", DB_OPEN_TABLE)


 ' path and file name for the output file
 FileName=FTWINpath + "\SAMPLES\BUSINESS\FTINVEST\FTINVEST.IN"


 ' write header for fuzzyTECH file format with comments
 Open FileName For Output As #1
 Print #1, "This is test data
  generated by the FT Investment Bank Database"
 Print #1, " ", "Age", "Children", "GeoDemo",
  "IncomeSpend", "Married", "RealEstMort"
 Print #1, "-------------------------------------------
 ----------------------------------------------------"


 ' fetch each customer row, process inputs for fuzzy system,
 ' and write input variable values in a row of the output file
 Tab1.MoveFirst
 Do While Not Tab1.EOF
  Age = DatePart("yyyy", Date)
     - DatePart("yyyy", Tab1![BirthDay])
  Children = Tab1![NumberOfChildren]
  ZipCode = Tab1![ZipCode]
  Class = DLookup("[GeodemographicClass]",
```

```
        "Geodemographic Classification","[ZipCode] = " & ZipCode)
    Geodemo = DLookup("[GeodemographicValue]",
        "Geodemographic Classes","[GeodemographicClass]="& Class)
    IncomeSpend = Tab1![IncomeAnnual] - Tab1![SpendingAnnual]
    If Tab1![Married] = -1 Then Married = 1 Else Married = 0
    RealEstMort = Tab1![RealEstate] - Tab1![Mortgage]
    Print #1, Tab1![LastName], Age, Children,
      Geodemo, IncomeSpend, Married, RealEstMort
    Tab1.MoveNext
  Loop
  Close #1
  MsgBox "The file FTINVEST.IN has been generated in
    the \SAMPLES\BUSINESS\FTINVEST\ subdirectory"
End Sub
```

The OutputFTfile procedure performs two tasks. First, it opens a file named FTINVEST.IN located in the subdirectory of the FTINVEST sample and writes the variable names header in the *fuzzy*TECH file format with comments. Second, it runs through the entire Customers table and outputs all of the fuzzy logic systems' input variables and writes them in a text file.

Releasing the fuzzyTECH RCU Interface

To free Windows resources that were required for communication between FTINVEST and *fuzzy*TECH and to unload the FTRCUxx.DLL, you must call the LogoutRCU function. In the FTINVEST database, this is performed in the Form Unload procedure of the module "Module: Form.MainMenu" as follows:

```
Sub Form_Unload (Cancel As Integer)
  ' unload the FTRCU (fuzzyTECH Remote Control Unit)
  LogoutRCU
End Sub
```

Event Procedures

The functions described in detail in this section contain the basic computation routines and all the interface points with the fuzzy logic computation. The calls of these functions and the invocation of windows and forms through buttons in the windows are contained in the event procedures for these buttons.

4.4   Using DDE and DLL links with *fuzzy*TECH

This section describes how you can integrate *fuzzy*TECH with other software packages and how you can use *fuzzy*TECH in your own programs. Section 4.4.1 explains the DDE link in detail, and Section 4.4.2 discusses the programming of *fuzzy*TECH using FTRCUxx.DLL.

4.4.1 Interfacing to *fuzzy*TECH Using DDE

DDE is a universal communication standard that Windows programs can use to exchange data. This section shows you how to access *fuzzy*TECH computation capabilities from another program.

Communication Procedure

When you use DDE, *fuzzy*TECH acts as data server. To initiate a DDE connection between a Windows client and *fuzzy*TECH, the client must use the following procedure:

- Start *fuzzy*TECH.

- Initiate the connection to *fuzzy*TECH by sending a DDE_INITIATE command using the keywords FTWIN and FUZZY.

- Send a DDE_EXECUTE command with a string specifying the required project file in *fuzzy*TECH. This will immediately load the project and switch to RCU debug mode.

- Send a DDE_POKE command using the keyword FUZDATA and the data file as text string.

- Send a DDE_REQUEST using the keyword FUZDATA. You will receive a text string containing the output data.

- A DDE_TERMINATE command closes the connection between client and server if required.

Data Format

The data text string contains the values for input variables (DDE_POKE) or the output values (DDE_REQUEST) in the alphabetical order of their names. The values use ASCII float data format. The values are separated by a carriage return and a line feed.

Data Format Example:

123 (ASCII(13)) (ASCII(10))
0.07 (ASCII(13)) (ASCII(10))
2.3E+3'(ASCII(13)) (ASCII(10))

4.4.2 Programming *fuzzy*TECH Using the DLL Link

By using the *fuzzy*TECH Remote Control Unit Dynamic Link Library (FTRCUxx.DLL), you can integrate *fuzzy*TECH seamlessly with your application. You can use any programming language that lety you call a DLL function to interface with *fuzzy*TECH. There are two ways you can use this interface:

- Single Call Interface (SCI)

The SCI provides quick, easy interfacing to *fuzzy*TECH but limits you to exchange of input/output variable values. Thus, it is ideal for using *fuzzy*TECH just to compute the outputs for a given set of inputs. Because SCI performs all checks on every call, it is slower than STCI. Further documentation is located in \RCU\C\SAMPLES\ SINGLE\.

■ Standard Call Interface (STCI)

The STCI gives you separate functions to initiate, load, and execute a fuzzy logic system within *fuzzy*TECH. Thus, it provides a better computation performance and more flexibility than the SCI. You will find the programming documentation for the STCI in \RCU\C\-SAMPLES\STANDARD\.

To locate FTRCU for your application, you can access the path via the WIN.INI file. The section [FTWIN] in the WIN.INI file contains the path information that is established during the installation routine of *fuzzy*TECH. For a more detailed reference on programming the interfaces from any programming language, refer to [22].

4.5 Creating Stand-Alone Solutions

Because of the wide difference in application's needs, *fuzzy*TECH provides different ways to implement stand-alone solutions:

■ Generation of C or COBOL source code that can be ported to any target computer system (Section 4.5.1).

■ Using FTOLE.EXE runtime module OLE server (Section 4.5.2).

■ Using FTRUN.DLL runtime module as DLL (Section 4.5.2).

Notice that the creation of stand-alone solutions is only supported by the full-featured *fuzzy*TECH for Business software product. Also, FTRUN.DLL and FTOLE.EXE are only contained with the full-featured *fuzzy*TECH for Business software product.

4.5.1 Generation of Portable Source Code

*fuzzy*TECH provides code generators that deliver royalty-free, stand-alone solutions from the fuzzy logic system. These code generators are add-on modules to *fuzzy*TECH for Business. During installation, *fuzzy*TECH for Business will provide a new main menu entry, named Compile:

This menu invokes built-in compilers that generate either C, COBOL, or M source code. You can use this source code to implement the fuzzy logic system independent of *fuzzy*TECH on nearly any computer:

- For a PC running MS-Windows, OS/2, or MS-Windows-NT: generation of DLL C code.

- For workstations running UNIX or a similar operating system: generation of ANSI-C or Kernighan&Ritchi-C code.

- For mainframe computers running COBOL compilers: generation of COBOL85 code.

- For other simulation software: generation of M Code.

Integration of a Stand-Alone Solution

The Global Options dialog box contains selections that let you define how your application shall interface with the generated code. The various options are found in the group "Code Generator":

If the option "Comments" is enabled, the generated code is annotated with comments describing the various parts of the computational routines. These comments provide useful information when you want to understand how *fuzzy*TECH has converted the fuzzy logic system into source code. If you do not want to analyze the generated C code, leave this option disabled. If you enable the "File Code" option, the generated source code can be directly compiled to a standalone executable program. Inputs and outputs are transferred via files in this case. Refer to [22] or the on-line help system of *fuzzy*TECH for details.

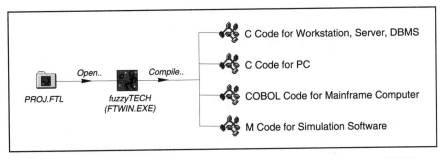

Figure 180: To generate portable source code from *fuzzy*TECH, open the FTL file and use the Compile.. menu options.

For some applications, you may need to cross debug the running fuzzy logic system from a separate PC running *fuzzy*TECH. This is facilitated by the "Online Code" option that lets you generate source code that can be remotely debugged from another computer. Refer to [22] or the on-line help system of *fuzzy*TECH for details.

If the option "Public Input and Output" is enabled, the code generator produces source code which uses public variables for the interface between the fuzzy logic code and the user written code. system. If this option is disabled, the fuzzy logic computation receives the inputs and passes outputs of the fuzzy logic system as function parameters.

Computational Resolution

*fuzzy*TECH lets you select the resolution for the input and output variables of the fuzzy logic system. The internal computational resolution is selected automatically to ensure most efficient computation. Select the variable data type in the group "Base Variable Data Type" of the "General Options" dialog:

Base Variable Data Type
- ○ 8 Bit Integer
- ○ 16 Bit Integer
- ● Double

If your fuzzy logic system shall run on a PC, workstation, or mainframe computer, select "Double" as data type as these computers compute Double type variables in a Floating Point Processing Unit.

Code Interface Example

The following example illustrates how you integrate the code generated by *fuzzy*TECH with your application using non-public input and output. For COBOL code generation, the principle is similar. Refer to [22] or the on-line help system of *fuzzy*TECH for details.

Example 5

```
#include "credit1.h"          /* include the header for the */
...                           /* fuzzy logic system code    */
double Continuity, Inc_Exp, Liquidity;
                              /* define the input/output    */
...                           /* variables                  */
void main(void) {
                              /* start main program         */
  initcredit1();              /* initialize fuzzy logic sys*/
  while(!stop) {
  ...                         /* assign input variables     */
    credit1(Continuity, Inc_Exp, &Liquidity);
                              /* call fuzzy logic system    */
  ...                         /* the variable Liquidity now */
                              /* contains the output value  */
  }
}
```

In the definition section of the main program that you write, you must include the file CREDIT1.H which is generated by the *fuzzy*TECH code generator. Then you must define the input and output variables of the fuzzy logic system with the other variables you use in your code. In the main routine, you must first call the function initcredit1() that is located in the file CREDIT1.C which is generated by the *fuzzy*TECH code generator. Then you can call the function credit1() which contains the fuzzy logic computation, possibly in a loop as illustrated in Example 5.

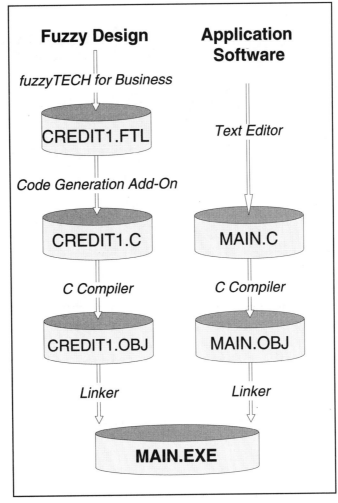

Figure 181: Implementation of a fuzzy logic system on a PC or workstation.

Compilation Sequence

Figure 181 shows how the different source code modules are combined to the final executable program. Refer to [22] or the on-line help system of *fuzzy*TECH for details.

Code Compatibility

For C code, the code generator supports the ANSI conventions as supported by most PC compilers and workstations and also the older Kernighan&Ritchie (K&R) convention some workstations may require. The group "Compatibility" lets you select the appropriate standard:

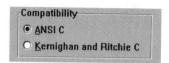

For COBOL, *fuzzy*TECH generates the COBOL85 standard that is most common on mainframe computers.

Performance of a Stand-Alone Solution

The generated source code of *fuzzy*TECH is highly efficient and allows the implementation of fuzzy logic systems that can compute many thousands of inputs in a second. For example, Table 9 shows benchmarks of typical fuzzy logic systems of various sizes. Each benchmark system is described by the number of rules, input variables, output variables, and terms. All benchmarks were run on a low-end i486SX-PC at 33 MHz using the MS-C Compiler 8.0. The "Time" column gives the computation time required for one full fuzzy logic computation, or more simply, the time required to compute all output variable values from the input variable values. The column Speed gives the number of complete fuzzy logic computations that can be computed in one second. Experience has shown that the implementation of a fuzzy logic system as a stand-alone module in C code is by far more efficient than using *fuzzy*TECH for Business directly, due primarily to the overhead of the *fuzzy*TECH shell. The code size required for these systems ranges from 1 KB RAM to 3.5 KB RAM.

	Benchmark	Time	Speed
System 1	20 Rules, 2 Inputs, 1 Output, 15 Terms	0.05 ms	20,000 Computations per Second
System 2	80 Rules, 3 Inputs, 1 Output, 20 Terms	0.09 ms	11,000 Computations per Second
System 3	500 Rules, 8 Inputs, 4 Outputs, 84 Terms	0.35 ms	2,800 Computations per Second

Table 9: Benchmarks of typical fuzzy logic systems on a 486SX-33 PC.

4.5.2 Using the *fuzzy*TECH OLE and DLL Stand-Alone Servers

The advantage of using *fuzzy*TECH's source code generators is, that you can port the system to about any computer. The disadvantage is, that you always need to deal with source code and a compiler. If your target for the fuzzy logic system is a PC running under MS-Windows 3.1x, MS-Windows 95, or MS-Windows/NT, then you find it easier to use one of the ready-to-use runtime modules of *fuzzy*TECH. They require no compilation and are available as OLE server or as DLL module.

Figure 182 sketches the principle: N software client can each call fuzzy logic systems by calling functions in FTRUN.DLL, and M software clients can each call fuzzy logic systems using the FTRUN.EXE OLE server:

- Use the DLL server (FTRUN.DLL or FTRUN32.DLL) whenever the client software can call DLL routines. Because DLL calls require much less Operating System overhead, they are faster and more robust.

- Use the OLE server (FTOLE.EXE) when the client cannot call DLL routines or when you want to use network object distribution provided by MS-Windows/NT.

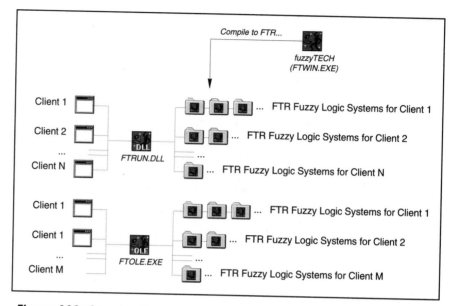

Figure 182: Client software can either call a stand-alone fuzzy logic computation as a DLL function or as a OLE service.

The DLL and OLE servers are functionally similar: Each client software first tells the server which fuzzy logic systems it intends to use. The fuzzy logic systems must first be compiled into the FTR format using *fuzzy*TECH's Compile menu:

The FTR format contains the binary description of the fuzzy logic system, and can directly be used by the DLL and OLE servers.

5

Case Studies of
Fuzzy Logic Applications

In this book, case studies and examples that stem from real-world fuzzy logic system solutions have been used to illustrate the technology and show its utility. However, most of these case studies and examples were greatly simplified. In this chapter, presentations are made of more complete fuzzy logic system solutions that have been implemented in industry. Some of these solutions stem from consulting work done by the fuzzy logic application group at Inform Software Corporation over the past decade. Other examples were taken from application work completed by independent *fuzzy*TECH users and others still were taken from publications and conference proceedings. Whenever the applications discussed here were published, the reference is provided for your further information.

5.1   Fuzzy Logic in Finance Applications

In the area of financial decision making, decisions involving some kind of assessment often have to be made in large quantities. For example, these evaluations can be about risk, creditworthiness, or likelihood of fraud. This section covers areas where work has been completed and was subsequently published.

Note: if an application area is not covered in this section, this by no means indicates that there is no ongoing work in this area.

Particularly in the financial area, the enthusiasm for publishing successful applications or allowing others to publish them is unfortunately very low. Section 5.1.5 lists brief abstracts of applications that are not treated in detail in this book.

5.1.1 Fuzzy Scoring for Mortgage Applicants

For the first case study, an application that INFORM GmbH did for a Home & Savings bank in the area of mortgage application assessment is presented. This application is very instructive for several reasons. First, criteria of greatly varying types are aggregated into the same fuzzy logic system. Some describe the building project, some the mortgage applicant, and some the repayment plan. Second, the entire project is described, that is, how the fuzzy logic solution was conceptualized, designed, debugged, tested, and implemented during the daily operations of a bank.

Note: some simplification of the system structure, linguistic variables, and the rule base is necessary to protect the intellectual property of the bank. The bank itself does not publish the fact that it is using fuzzy logic scoring models nor does it want its name to be referenced in a publication. Hence, the reference is simply "Home&Savings Bank" in the remainder of this section.

The Mortgage Advisory Support Software Project

During a large past project, the Home&Savings bank provided each of their mortgage advisors with a notebook PC for their visits to prospective customers. This PC runs a dedicated mortgage advisory support software (MASS), programmed using MS-Access, which contains forms to fill in regarding the mortgage application, as well as additional information on the different financial services of the bank. One of these pieces of information is the policy on acceptance of mortgage applicants. This is a document written by members of the corporate staff of the bank that contains guidelines for the evaluation of the person that applies for a mortgage, as well as the construction project itself. The information that is stored in MASS during a client consultation is later downloaded to the bank's mainframe for further processing.

While the experience with the system in general has been very positive, the bank observed that only a few of the mortgage advisors followed the company policy for mortgage application assessment. Tracking down these cases, various reasons were found. Often, the mortgage advisors overlooked something or were simply too inexperienced to fully understand the company's policy. Also, although mortgage advisors receive a major part of their salaries as commission on the contracts they close, if the loan goes bad some day in the future, the commission is not taken away. Hence, it is not in the interest of the mortgage advisors to decline credit to dubious applicants.

For these reasons, the Home&Savings bank decided to implement a decision support model in MASS that evaluates the data entered about both the applicant and the building project and that also assesses how well this application fits the definition of the company's policy. As a result, mortgage advisors will get this information interactively at a very early stage of the consultation, thus not wasting time with prospective customers who will not satisfy the criteria for a mortgage anyway.

Extension of Score Card Models by Fuzzy Logic

When the bank started to conceptualize a decision support model, it became obvious that the conventional score card approach, that is, associating scores to properties and adding them together to obtain a single number, will not work accurately for the mortgage loan assessment. The reasons for this have already been thoroughly discussed in Section 1.2.2 of this book, so here I only discuss the specific considerations the Home&Savings Bank had for their application.

Consider the simple score card model of Table 10. The mortgage application is evaluated on both the building project as well as the applicant. The building object is evaluated on the basis of its location and the quality of the workmanship. In this simplified model, ratings from 1 to 5 were given depending on the degree to which the criteria was met by the data in the mortgage application. The rating shown in Table 10 assumes an object in a fair location, a fair quality of workmanship, and an applicant that has pretty low assets but quite a high income.

Object	Location	good	medium	bad
		5	3✓	1
	Workmanship	good	medium	bad
		5	3✓	1
Applicant	Assets	high	medium	low
		5	3	1✓
	Income	high	medium	low
		5✓	3	1

Table 10: Conventional score card model.

Adding all the scores together results a total score of 12. This is exactly in the middle of the maximum result of 20 and the minimum result of 4.

However, such a model cannot represent the bank's policy accurately enough. For example, the bank's policy states that if a building project is in a perfect location, the quality of the workmanship is of minor importance. As discussed in Section 1.2.2, fuzzy logic can easily be used to enhance a score card model to reflect these rules in a far more transparent fashion. Figure 183 shows the example of a fuzzy logic scoring model assessment for the same mortgage application.

With a fair location and a fair quality of workmanship, the building project is rated similar to the conventional score model of Table 10. However, in contrast to the conventional model, the somewhat low assets and pretty high income evaluation do not compensate for each other. Rather, the bank's policy states that in cases where income and assets strongly differ from each other, the applicant is considered "questionable." Thus, the fuzzy logic ranking of the same customer is much less favorable than the conventional ranking of Table 10. What the bank learned from these considerations is that fuzzy-logic-enhanced score card models can better identify discrepancies and react more sensibly to subtle conditions. Also, representing the bank's policy within fuzzy logic rules is much faster and much more transparent compared to score card weights. Furthermore, any change of the company's policy can be implemented quickly and easily and does not require the tedious creation of new parameters for score weights.

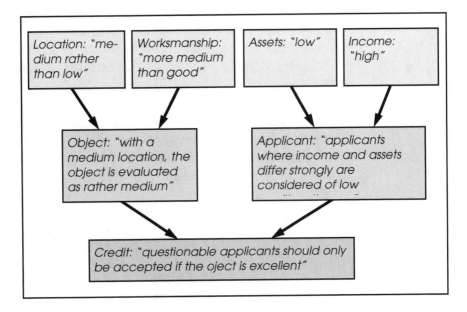

Figure 183: Fuzzy-logic-enhanced score card model.

Another advantage the bank found is that fuzzy logic score models can be set up by translating the policy directly into fuzzy logic rules and membership functions. In contrast, conventional score card models for the most part need tuning through statistical analysis of past data. On other projects, the experience of the bank regarding the use of past data for score card model tuning was:

■ Statistical methods require large amounts of high-quality past data to deliver meaningful results.

■ Past data only represents past policies. Hence, you can only automate what has been done manually before rather than optimizing the decision-making process to represent present desires.

■ Past data is often biased. For example, if the bank uses past data to tune its score card models, the repayment performances of all customers who were declined a mortgage loan are not in the data base. Thus, no information exists on whether these customers would have proven themselves as good risks or whether the decision to reject them was justified. The only true way to get unbiased past data would be to grant everyone a mortgage loan for a period of time and find out later whether the credit went bad or not. Of course, this is a very expensive way to generate past data.

For the same reasons, a neural net solution was not considered for this application. When a neural net performs perfectly, it mimics the past data. Hence, the same problems as with statistically tuned score card models will occur.

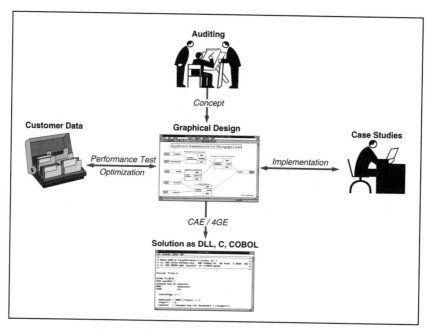

Figure 184: The four-phase system design model used for the development.

Development Approach

After deciding to use a fuzzy-logic-enhanced score card model, the bank used a four-phase approach that covered the design tasks, illustrated in Figure 184. This approach has worked very well for many development projects in which the author has participated, and thus is explained here in more detail.

A preliminary concept of the fuzzy logic score model was developed during design auditing. This design was implemented as a rapid prototype in *fuzzy*TECH. Using hypothetical case studies, the rule base and the membership function definitions were set up. The performance of this system was further optimized and tested with selected past customer cases. The implementation of the fuzzy logic system was simplistic. *fuzzy*TECH then generated the fuzzy logic score model as a Windows DLL that is easily linked to MASS.

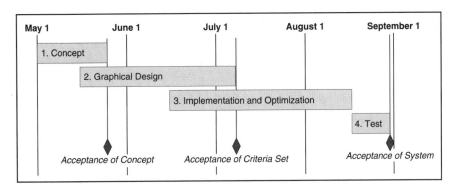

Figure 185: Project plan.

Project Planning

By translating the design tasks illustrated by Figure 184 into a project plan, four distinctive project phases and three milestones were defined (Figure 185). Some of the phases were overlapping, others were not. The entire project was concluded in four months and involved two consulting fuzzy logic experts and two bank experts working full time. In addition to this, the bank established a task force consisting of 15 of the bank's mortgage experts. This task force discussed and verified the design steps, especially during the first and the third phase. In total, the task force met 11 times for an average of half a day each session. The two bank experts involved with the project full-time learned so much about fuzzy logic score model design during the project that they were able to modify and maintain the system without outside assistance after completion of the project.

Milestones

For project management purposes, three milestones were defined. The first one, after only three weeks of the project, was a complete design review. Here, it was verified that the concept would be able to represent all important aspects of the bank's policy. The reason for having such a thorough design review so early in the project was to make sure that the design was in line with the expectations of the project management group, and to establish credibility with upper level management for the project.

After the second phase, part of the rule base and all of the linguistic variable definitions had already been set up. Thus, initial results were already available and a decision regarding the information the fuzzy logic scoring model needed to adequately represent the policy could be made (the input variables of the fuzzy logic system).

At the second milestone, listing of these specific information items finally began. This was important to the MASS programmers, who needed to have a clear definition of which variables they had to provide as inputs to the fuzzy logic scoring model. With this information, they were able to complete the interfaces for the DLL containing the fuzzy logic system in MASS at the same time the fuzzy logic scoring model was completed.

The third milestone was the end of the development project. Since *fuzzy*TECH can output the solution as a DLL without any programming effort, the project was completed immediately after the fuzzy logic scoring model was finished.

Following this brief sketch of the project outline, the work done in each of the four phases will be explained in further detail.

Phase 1: Concept

The first phase involved the auditing of the bank experts by the fuzzy logic experts to develop the concepts for the fuzzy logic scoring model. The bank expert task force consisted of two groups. One comprised experienced mortgage advisors with a great deal of experience with mortgage cases. The others were members of the corporate staff who developed the mortgage granting policy. It was critical to the project to link these two groups because each individual group was not in possession of all the necessary knowledge. The mortgage-granting policy was not covering all practical mortgage cases well and sometimes was even inconsistent. In these cases, the experienced mortgage advisors were able to provide solutions on the basis of their past work experience. However, even the most experienced mortgage advisors did not follow the bank policy completely, so the members of the corporate staff had to detail the reasoning behind the policy.

Phase 2: Graphical Design

As a direct outcome of Phase 1, the fuzzy logic system was designed to represent the information flow structure shown in Figure 186. The mortgage application assessment was based on three types of evaluation:

- The first rule block (Building Project Assessment) evaluates the building project itself (Building), taking into account the building's location (Location) and the quality of its workmanship (Workmanship).

- A second rule block (Applicant's Assessment) evaluates the applicant (Applicant) by their assets (Asset) and their income minus fixed expenditures (Income). These two evaluations are further aggregated by a third rule block (Evaluation of Credit Worthiness), which results in the mortgage assessment (Credit).

- A third type of evaluation occurs in the fourth rule block (Killer Criteria), which evaluates the repayment plan. Evaluating income minus fixed expenditures (Income) and interest charges (Interest) as set forth in the repayment plan, it detects "killer cases" in which a mortgage should not be granted because repayment is endangered. This rule block's output is factored into the mortgage assessment output variable (Credit) as well.

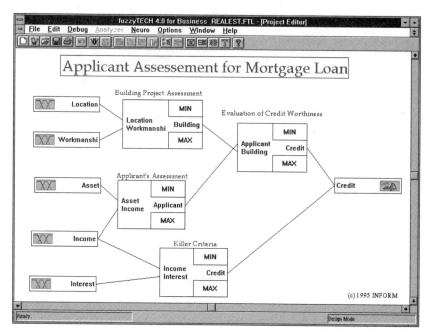

Figure 186: Structure of the fuzzy logic scoring model.

Next was the design of the linguistic variable definitions, that is, the definition of terms and membership functions. Initial rule sets for the four rule blocks were generated as a direct result of the audit. A simplified version of the fuzzy logic system designed is contained in the file REALEST.FTL that is located in the subdirectory \SAMPLES\BUSINESS\REALEST\. You can open this file with *fuzzy*TECH and examine the structure, the linguistic variable definitions, the terms, the membership functions, and the rules defined here.

Phase 3:

The third phase is a refinement phase in which the designers verify the system structure and then modify the membership functions and rules on the basis of hypothetical case studies. Hypothetical case studies are used rather than past data because of the problems inherent to the use of past data discussed previously. Using hypothetical case studies allowed the evaluation of only 50 hypothetical cases that were generated by the experienced mortgage advisors. They took great care that all possible peculiarities and unusual cases they could think of were represented by the 50 hypothetical cases. Because of the relatively low number of cases, discussion of the individual cases with the bank experts was possible in much greater detail, allowing for a much deeper assessment of each expert's reasoning. When forced to defend their decision on distinct, concrete cases, it was much easier for the experts to convey the rules that represented their assessment strategy.

To facilitate this phase, the 50 hypothetical case studies were created as Excel forms. Tables the fuzzy logic system generated in Phase 2 were used to compute the results. Whenever the fuzzy logic system's assessment differed from the expert's rating, the Interactive debug mode of *fuzzy*TECH was used to track down the rules and the membership function definitions that caused the assessment. Then, the fuzzy logic system was modified in order to represent the expert's reasoning. Often, there was a high degree of inconsistency in the way the different experts assessed the cases. Even more frequently, the experts disagreed with the corporate policy. The discussions necessary to come up with compromises took a considerably longer amount of time than the actual design of the entire fuzzy logic system.

Case	Workmanship	Location	Income	Assets	Interest	Fuzzy-Rating	Scoring
1	50	50	50	50	50	38	50
2	50	50	50	50	70	30	42
3	15	30	50	50	50	6	36
4	15	50	50	50	50	6	41
5	50	50	50	50	100	25	30
6	50	50	40	50	90	25	28
7	100	70	60	50	45	64	76
8	30	70	60	50	45	37	59
9	50	1	50	50	50	38	38
10	28	28	28	28	72	7	10

Microsoft Excel - REALEST.XLS — File Edit View Insert Format Tools Data Window fuzzyTECH Help — **Applicant Assessement for Mortgage Loan**

Figure 187: The REALEST.XLS spreadsheet compares the performance of a simple score card model with a fuzzy-logic-enhanced score card model.

You can try this yourself. Install the *fuzzy*TECH Excel Assistant as described in Section 4.1. A simplified set of ten cases is contained in the file REALEST.XLS, which is located in the subdirectory \SAMPLES\-BUSINESS\REALEST\. The spreadsheet contained in this file is shown in Figure 187. Each row represents a hypothetical sample case. The cyan columns are the five input variables of the fuzzy logic system. **Note:** in this simplified version of the fuzzy logic system, all input and output base variable intervals are set to [0; 100]. The magenta column contains the output of the fuzzy logic system, and the green column contains the output of a conventional score card model, as shown by Figure 188.

$$Scoring = \left(\frac{Workmanship + Location + Income + Assets}{4} \right) + \left(\frac{Income - Inte\,rest}{2.5} \right)$$

Figure 188: The conventional score
card model used in the example.

To understand how the fuzzy logic system represents the assessment strategy, compare the different cases. In Case 1, all input parameters are perfectly in the middle, hence, the result of both the fuzzy logic system and the conventional score card model is 50. In Case 2, the Interest input is set higher to 70, which indicates an above-average interest rate for the repayment in contrast to a perfectly average income. In this case, the fuzzy logic system reacts much more strongly than the conventional score card model because of the rules defined in the "killer criteria" rule block. Case 3 is the same as Case 1, however, the building is of a much lower quality. Because the quality of workmanship is of high importance in the rules that define the Building evaluation in the fuzzy logic system, the fuzzy logic system again reacts more strongly. By selecting the other cases or changing the row's values, you can further analyze the fuzzy logic rule base.

Note: when you are in Excel, each time you change values in the spreadsheet, the values of this case are shown in all the editors of *fuzzy*TECH. While connected to Excel, *fuzzy*TECH is set to RCU Debug mode. This debug mode is always active when another software controls *fuzzy*TECH remotely. To ensure consistency, several features of *fuzzy*-TECH are disabled in RCU Debug mode. *fuzzy*TECH is set to RCU Debug mode for the entire time during which the *fuzzy*TECH Assistant is enabled with Excel and Excel is running.

Phase 4:

While hypothetical cases are excellent for implementing a rule base and for defining the membership functions, a final test involved past data. The mortgage experts were asked to each come up with about a dozen past cases that each involved some degree of trickiness. Then the fuzzy logic assessments for these cases were computed and the results discussed with the same group of experts who were involved with the prototype in Phase 1.

First, the cases were presented to the bank experts of the task force, and each of them independently came up with results. These results were recorded for further analysis. Next, the group discussed the cases and recorded the results. Afterwards, the fuzzy logic system assessed the cases, and the results were presented to the group where the fuzzy logic system's result and its reasoning were discussed.

A few cases actually revealed combinations of facts that the fuzzy logic system as implemented by Phase 3 did not cover. This was simply due to the fact that the bank experts did not include such combinations in the hypothetical cases. Reality is sometimes more inventive than the imagination of humans.

After some re-tuning for these cases that the fuzzy logic system did not already cover, the fuzzy logic system consistently became much closer to the task force group decision than the decision of an individual mortgage advisor. The performance of the system as rated by the bank commission met the acceptance criteria of the bank and it was decided to include it in MASS for everyday use. Since *fuzzy*TECH generated the fuzzy logic module directly as a DLL ready for integration in MASS, the end of Phase 4 and the acceptance of the system signified the end of the design project.

Maintenance of the System

Every successful decision-support system is subject to constant modification and update in order to keep track of policy changes. For example, the real estate market changes over time and thus quality of workmanship might become less important than location. Such modifications to the fuzzy logic system are completed by the bank experts themselves. Because they worked closely with the consulting fuzzy logic experts during the four-phase design project, and because fuzzy logic lends itself to easy understanding of the implemented system, they were able to undertake the task of system modifications without outside assistance. The update of a modified fuzzy logic scoring model within MASS is easy: *fuzzy*TECH generates the new policy as a DLL that simply copies over the old one in the MASS installation.

As pointed out at the beginning of this section, the fuzzy logic system in REALEST.FTL is only a very simplified model of the actual application. The real application fuzzy logic system comprises 9 input variables (criteria) and 171 rules in total. It also includes a second output that explains the fuzzy logic decision made so that the mortgage advisor can explain to the customer why he was rejected. Since such an explanatory component is a useful feature in a large number of applications, the principal design of such a component is shown in Section 5.1.1 using the example of MASS.

Benefits of Fuzzy-Logic-Enhanced Scoring Models

Based on the application project discussed above, the bank concluded the following:

*"Fuzzy logic is an enabling technology
for enhancing existing scoring systems"*

■ To achieve better results, no additional criteria are required.

■ The enhanced system ties in seamlessly with the existing database.

■ It is ideal for volume use due to its easy automation.

"Fuzzy logic scoring models are more discriminating"

■ It has stronger reactions to subtle conditions.

■ Consistency checks can be formulated easily.

■ It directly represents bank policy.

*"The accumulated expertise of a bank
can be integrated in the scoring model"*

■ Decision and evaluation flow in the system follows the reasoning of an experienced banker.

■ It includes transparent and understandable decision making.

■ It allows for identification of discrepancies.

*"Fuzzy logic delivers robust
implementation for everyday use"*

■ It does not require statistics or past data for calibration.

■ It can be directly implemented on a PC, workstation, or mainframe.

■ Maintenance and modifications can be made by experienced bank personnel.

5.1.2 Creditworthiness Assessment

In this section, the example used is of ASK, a decision-support system based on fuzzy logic developed by INFORM [19]. This application was first installed in the year 1986, and this probably makes it the first commercially available fuzzy logic decision-support system in the world. ASK is based on psycholinguistic empirical research conducted in the early 1980's [48, 49]. The basic idea has already been introduced in Section 1.2.1. Here, the focus is instead on the results that were achieved with the pilot customer of ASK, a Swiss bank. The bank itself does not publish the fact that it is using fuzzy logic decision-support models nor does it want its name to be referenced in any publication. Hence, we will refer to them as "Alps Credit Bank" for the remainder of the section.

Enforcing Consistent Decision Making

ASK was designed for creditworthiness assessment for consumer credit. Thus, the loan amount typically ranges from SFr. 5,000 to SFr. 25,000. For this "small" type of credit, no thorough credit history analysis is normally conducted and bank clerks in the individual branches assume the decision-making process mainly on the basis of a two-page, internal guideline detailing the acceptance criteria that should be applied.

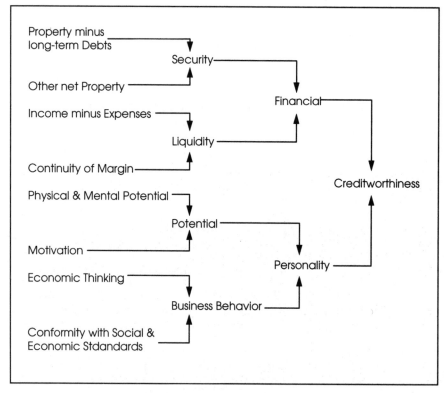

Figure 189: Aggregation hierarchy of a fuzzy logic creditworthiness estimation.

However, experience shows that in the small valleys of the Alps, loan-granting decisions were made more on the basis of family ties than on any evaluation process. Even in larger cities in Switzerland, bank clerks interpret the acceptance criteria in so many different ways that a person who has been declined at one branch of the bank need only visit a different branch of the same bank to get a loan.

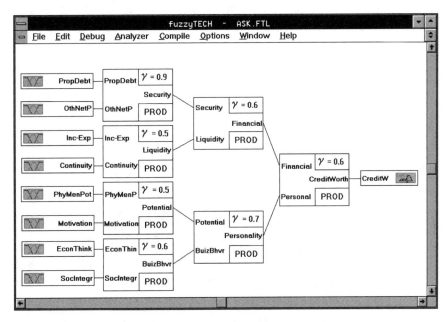

Figure 190: Structure of the fuzzy logic decision support system.

For these reasons, the Alps Credit Bank sought an automated solution that enforced a consistent decision-making procedure in all branches of the bank. In addition, they wanted to be able to modify the credit-granting policy centrally from Zurich, something that can only be achieved using automated decision-making techniques.

The Fuzzy Logic Decision Support System

To evaluate the creditworthiness of the customer, multiple financial and personal factors are used. Figure 189 shows a simplified layout of the system's structure. Figure 190 shows how the structure has been implemented in *fuzzy*TECH. A total of eight input variables are used for the evaluation. **Note:** the upper four input variables denote "hard facts," numbers that stem from inputs that are entered numerically. The lower four input variables denote "soft facts," which are subjective evaluations of the applicant's personality and lifestyle.

The structure of the system is hierarchical: at each node, two elements are aggregated to a new one. This makes three layers of abstraction. The first layer contains the elements Security, Liquidity, Potential, and Business Behavior, which each comprise the information of two input variables. Because information is condensed in each node, we speak of abstraction here. Similar to a human, who takes many input variables into account to come up with one abstract judgment, the aggregation hierarchy proceeds until the output node, Creditworthiness, is reached—the most abstract information in the hierarchy.

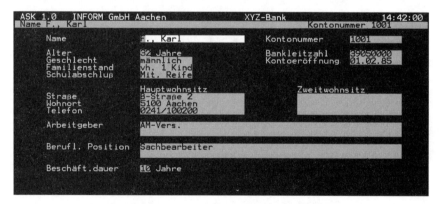

Figure 191: Entering the personal data of the applicant in the user interface of ASK.

Figures 191 to 193 show three screens of the user interface of ASK. ASK runs on mainframes, thus the screens do look different from the Windows screens showed in most other parts of this book. Personal data on the applicant is entered in the screen shown in Figure 191. **Note:** all screens show the German/Swiss version of the user interface. Figure 192 shows the mask where the financial background of the applicant is entered. This screen also contains the computations necessary for the repayment plan.

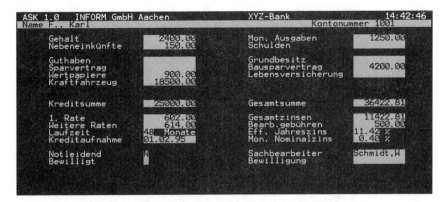

Figure 192: Entering the financial data of
the applicant in the user interface of ASK.

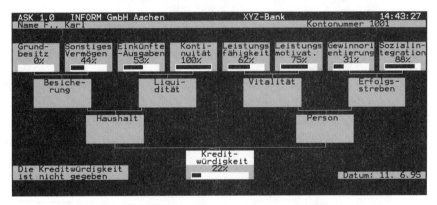

Figure 193: Evaluation tree in the user interface of ASK.

The aggregation of information is shown in Figure 193. The eight input criteria are shown in the top line of nodes. The four left nodes are the "hard facts" that are taken from the financial background input as given in the forms. The four right nodes are the "soft facts," subjective evaluations that are entered by the bank clerk during consultation with the applicant. The final evaluation of creditworthiness is shown by the lowest node. **Note:** the intermediate results are not shown to the bank clerk. This is to avoid clerks learning how to fool the system by making slight misjudgments with the "soft facts." Of course, bank clerks can still fool the system by entering wrong data or making wrong judgments with the "soft facts." However, because these judgments are stored with the credit application, a much better control is achieved compared to the earlier method, in which the bank clerks just entered their decision of "accepted" or "declined" with the application.

Note: to protect the intellectual property contained in ASK, the actual fuzzy logic system is not contained in the *fuzzy*TECH for Business software.

System Design

Very much like the mortgage application assessment system discussed in the previous section, this system design used 75 hypothetical credit applications that were judged by the bank's credit experts. In contrast to the previous example, the results here were directly entered into the ASK system through screens similar to the one shown in Figure 193. The only difference is that the creditworthiness and the other evaluation results from the nodes also had to be entered.

ASK itself used these sample cases to train its aggregation rules. The training algorithm employed is similar in concept to the NeuroFuzzy approach discussed in Section 3 but rather than use neural net techniques to train the fuzzy logic system, ASK uses a proprietary statistical training algorithm [19].

Because the retuning of the credit assessment policy does not require any use of fuzzy logic tools, such as *fuzzy*TECH, even end users can quickly modify a policy without any programming knowledge.

Further Development

Having had such a favorable experience with a fuzzy logic decision model, the Alps Credit Bank plans to extend the degree of automation with the system. The idea is to allow customers of the bank to apply for consumer loans over the BTX system (an Internet-like proprietary computer network of European phone companies) as well as from ATMs (automated teller machines). This will require modifications to the ASK system, as some input criteria of ASK will not be available from the customer records.

Other Risk Analysis Applications

Fuzzy logic is already used in a large number of risk assessment applications. The mortgage application evaluation system described in Section 5.1.1 is one such application. Japanese banks also use fuzzy logic for risk assessment. For example, Nikko Securities of Yokohama uses fuzzy logic for personal loan evaluation in a way similar to the one described in this section [7].

5.1.3 Fuzzy-Enhanced Score Card for Leasing Risk Assessment

To automate the risk assessment evaluation for car leasing contracts, BMW Bank GmbH of Germany and Inform Software GmbH of Germany have developed a fuzzy-enhanced score card system [8].

The primary goal of BMW Bank was to take the decision process away from the bank and give it to the car dealer. This allows the dealer to obtain approval in real-time rather than waiting for BMW Bank to approve a leasing contract.

Decision-Support Systems Streamline Workflow

The fuzzy-enhanced score card system has been integrated with the PC-based software that the dealers use to fill out the contract. These PCs are connected to the German credit history database (SCHUFA) to obtain background data on the applicants.

The implemented system involves three different types of fuzzy logic modules that each are applied to different customer types: private, self-employed, and corporate. For private customers, a score card had previously been developed that covers the parts of the decision process that are considered to be rather static in nature. These include the influence of factors such as age, marital status, length of time at present address, or later insolvencies. Because this score card already existed and BMW Bank considered it to perform well, it was used as part of the fuzzy logic decision model for private customers.

Private Customers

Figure 194 shows the structure of the fuzzy logic risk assessment for private customers. The input variable "ScoreCard" is the result of the score card evaluation. The score card result is used with the other input variables "Unemploy" and "Demographic" in the left rule block to compute a risk profile of the customer himself ("CustProfile"). The input variable "Unemploy" comes from a database that stores the current unemployment rate for the customer's profession. The input variable "Demographic" comes from a database and rates the relative illiquidity risk for the customer's place of residence.

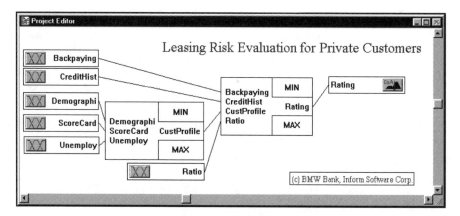

Figure 194: Structure of the fuzzy logic risk assessment for private customers.

The result of this evaluation, "CustProfile," is one input of the right rule block that computes the risk rating for the current leasing contract. In addition to CustProfile, the rule block uses the input variables "Backpaying," "CredHist," and "Ratio." The variable Backpaying describes how timely the customer has paid the rates of his previous leasing contracts, if a past leasing contract with BMW Bank exists. The variable CredHist stems from the German credit history database (SCHUFA) and describes the customer's history of all his past banking history. The variable Ratio is computed as the amount the monthly payment divided by the monthly disposable income of the customer.

Corporate Customers

Figure 195 shows the structure of the fuzzy logic risk assessment for corporate customers. Here, the decision process is more complicated and does involve more input variables.

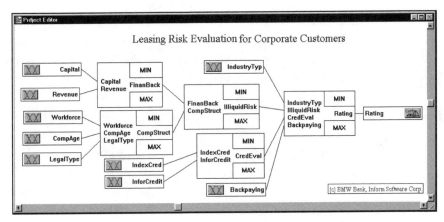

Figure 195: Structure of the fuzzy logic risk assessment for corporate customers.

The rightmost rule block delivers the output variable "Rating" based on the four input variables "IndustryType," "IlliquidRisk," "CredEval," and "Backpaying." IndustryType is an input variable that comes from a database table that maps the type of business to a subjective rating of BMW Bank describing how risky in general a certain type of industry is considered. The variable Backpaying is defined the same way as for private customers.

The other two input variables of the rightmost rule block stem from other rule blocks. CredEval is a combination of the input variables "IndexCred" and "InforCred." Both come from information service providers that maintain credit ratings for each company in Germany. IlliquidRisk is the fuzzy logic system's evaluation of the risk of this company becoming illiquid. A rule block computes this variable from the financial background evaluation ("FinanBack") and the company structure evaluation ("CompStruct"). The financial background evaluation considers the company's capital basis ("Capital") and its annual revenue ("Revenue"). The company structure evaluation considers the number of employees ("Workforce"), the age of the company ("Age"), and the legal status ("LegalType") of the company.

Implementation at BMW Bank

The total fuzzy logic system does involve 413 fuzzy logic rules in three modules. The entire design, test, and verification of the three modules has taken the effort of two person-years. Integrating the DLL modules generated by *fuzzy*TECH in the PC-based software for leasing contract management required another person-month. The system is currently in operation at German BMW dealers, and BMW Bank management considers its performance to be equivalent to an experienced leasing contract expert. Although a detailed cost savings analysis is not published by BMW Bank, a quick estimation on the basis of 50,000 leasing contracts per year and a total evaluation time of 30 minutes for each leasing contract (including obtaining credit history information) results in 25,000 person hours, or 14 persons. Compared to the cost of the fuzzy logic decision support system's implementation and maintenance, this saving is quite substantial.

5.1.4 Fraud Detection

In today's financial world, more and more transactions are carried out electronically and remotely. Thus, the opportunities for criminals to conduct fraudulent transactions rise with the complexity of the system. One of the areas where fraudulent behavior is of great concern to financial institutions is credit cards. Fraud arises through individual criminals who steal credit cards and then use them toward purchases, through criminal groups that steal new credit cards or duplicate credit cards without the knowledge of their holders, and through customer-induced fraud when customers claim that their card was stolen after making some expensive purchases. Even though most credit card purchases today are electronically verified before the actual transaction, various opportunities for fraudulent behavior still exist. Most credit card companies already use sophisticated systems for fraud detection. The common problem of these systems is that they have to work with very little significant data. The only information they have is past customer history and the information about the current transaction. The objective for a fraud detection system is to identify as many cases of fraudulent behavior as possible. On the other hand, if they too easily decline non-fraudulent transactions, customers will become dissatisfied and may switch to another credit card company.

Phone cards are subject to fraud in similar ways. Of course, it is easy to detect fraudulent behavior when a call is made from both New York and San Francisco on the same card within half an hour. But such easy cases are rather rare. More often, one has to evaluate the likelihood that fraud is occurring, like when the phone company computer detects that an Iowa farmer all of a sudden made six very long calls in one week to a small town in Namibia.

Insurance Fraud Detection of a Financial Service Provider

Unfortunately, the willingness of companies to disclose system details about fraud detection systems is very low. Companies are justifiably afraid that a disclosure or even the fact that they use a fuzzy logic fraud detection system may help criminals to circumvent the system. The case study developed in this section stems from a project with a financial service provider who would like to remain anonymous. In the following, any reference to the company will be as "AllFinance" corporation. AllFinance offers its customers both banking and insurance services. The advantage here is that information from both the insurance and banking background of the customer is accessible for detection of insurance fraud.

Organizational Background

AllFinance's application uses a fuzzy logic system to evaluate each insurance claim in the field of home insurance to assess the likelihood of fraudulent behavior. In the field of home insurance, most fraud is not perpetrated by professional criminals but rather by otherwise law-abiding individuals with many different motives for their behavior. Thus, AllFinance wanted to implement a fraud detection system that looks at multiple factors in every insurance claim and selects only those where it assumes a certain degree of likelihood of fraud for manual review.

The output of the fuzzy logic system is twofold. First, a degree of likelihood of fraud (Fraud) is assessed by the fuzzy logic system. A second output variable (Reason) gives an indication why a certain insurance claim was considered to be possibly fraudulent by the fuzzy logic system.

The degree of likelihood of fraud is computed by the fuzzy logic system as a number between zero and one. Zero indicates that an insurance claim was evaluated as totally non-fraudulent, while One indicates a very high likelihood of fraud. After an insurance claim is assessed by the fuzzy logic system, its degree of likelihood of fraud is compared to a threshold value pre-determined by AllFinance. If the result is lower than the threshold, the claim is immediately paid out to the customer. If the result is higher than the threshold, the claim is passed on to a claims auditor together with the Reason result of the fuzzy logic system. The claims auditor will then manually review the claim and make the final decisions on what further steps are to be taken.

Fuzzy-Logic-Supported Fraud Detection

To protect the proprietary information of AllFinance, the fuzzy logic fraud detection system presented in this section is simplified and the rules and membership functions contained within are modified. The fuzzy logic system uses the following seven input variables:

1. Number of claims in the last 12 months (NumClaim)

2. Amount of current claim (Amount)

3. Time with insurance (CustSince)

4. Average balance on all banking accounts over the last 12 months (AvgAmnt)

5. Number of overdrafts over the last 12 months (NumOvr)

6. Annual income of customer (Income)

7. Recent changes in status (StatChng)

These input variables can be divided into three groups. Each group represents a certain aspect of an insurance claim. Input variables 1 to 3 give information about the insurance contract and the claim itself. Input variables 3 and 4 describe the banking background of the customer, and input variables 6 and 7 provide the personal background of the customer.

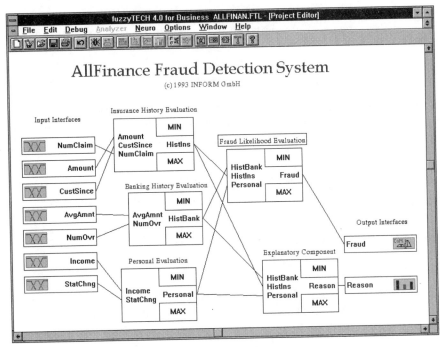

Figure 196: Structure of the AllFinance
fuzzy logic fraud detection system.

The idea behind the structure of the fuzzy logic system as shown by Figure 196 is that no one of these seven input variables alone can significantly identify fraudulent behavior. Only the combination of different facts can provide a good indication of possible fraud. Hence, the fuzzy logic system draws its conclusion from three different sub-assessments of insurance history (HistIns), banking history (HistBank), and personal background (Personal).

Insurance History Evaluation

The linguistic variable HistIns expresses the degree to which the customer uses the insurance contract. To evaluate insurance history, three input variables are used. The first input variable (NumClaim) gives an indication of how often the customer has used the insurance in the past year. The second input variable (Amount) expresses how significant the current claim is. The third input variable (CustSince) takes into account how long the insurance contract has been in existence. This evaluation delivers an indicator of how much the customer has exercised their insurance contract in the past and present.

Banking History Evaluation

The linguistic variable HistBank evaluates the banking history of the customer and its relevance to his or her insurance claim. The two input variables for this evaluation are the average total balance on all banking accounts of the customer (AvgAmnt) and the number of overdrafts on checking accounts (NumOvr). This evaluation can deliver indicators that the customer is in a critical financial situation, and, therefore, suggest a motive for fraudulent behavior.

Personal Evaluation

The linguistic variable Personal assesses the customer's basic situation. The assessment of Personal uses the input variables Income and StatChng. StatChang indicates whether a fundamental change in the customer's life has occurred over the past four months. The possible values (terms) of StatChng are "married," "divorced," "unemployed," and "parent":

married:	Customer married within the last four months
divorced:	Customer divorced within the last four months
unemployed:	Customer was laid off within the last four months and has no new employment yet
parent:	Customer had a child within the last four months

The variable StatChang is entered as a fuzzy variable (see Section 6.2.1), but it is actually a non-fuzzy variable since the possible degrees of truth are only Zero and One. However, more than one term of StatChng may have a degree of truth of One. For example, a customer could have been both divorced and laid off within the last four months. The assessment of the variable Personal detects possible motives within the customer's lifestyle that could motivate fraudulent behavior.

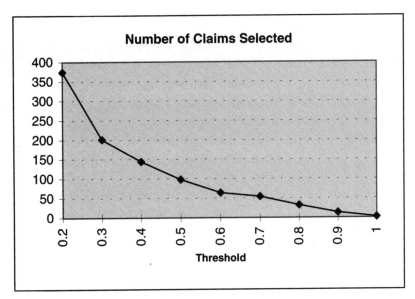

Figure 197: Because the fuzzy logic fraud detection system associates each claim with a number between 0 and 1, the number of claims selected for scrutiny depends on the threshold.

Fraud Evaluation Policy

The determination of the likelihood of fraud is contained in the rules of the four upper rule blocks. The lowest rule block contains the rules that provide the reason for which an insurance claim has been selected for an auditor's review. The fuzzy logic rules contain the actual fraud evaluation policy and analyze whether certain patterns for a possible fraud exist. For example, an insurance claim by a customer that has frequently made claims over the past year and is claiming a large amount would be evaluated as not likely to be fraudulent if he has a stable personal background and no cash problems.

Determination of the Acceptance Threshold by Field Test

A field test involved 1200 arbitrarily selected insurance claims filed with AllFinance. All 1200 cases were reviewed by the fuzzy logic fraud detection system. At the same time, all 1200 cases were also reviewed by experienced auditors. The experienced auditors classified 117 cases as "possibly fraudulent." These cases were the ones selected for further review in the routine operations of AllFinance.

Figure 197 shows the relation between threshold value and the number of claims selected for manual review. For example, if a threshold of 0.477 for the fuzzy logic fraud detection system is selected for the 1200 cases, a total of 117 cases are selected for manual review— the same number as the auditors came up with.

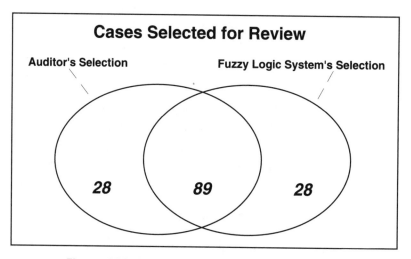

Figure 198: 117 cases were selected by both the auditors and the fuzzy logic system.

The interesting part is that the 117 cases which the fuzzy logic fraud detection system evaluated with Fraud ≥ 0.477 are not the same 117 cases the auditors selected. Only 89 of the cases were the same. Figure 198 illustrates the selections.

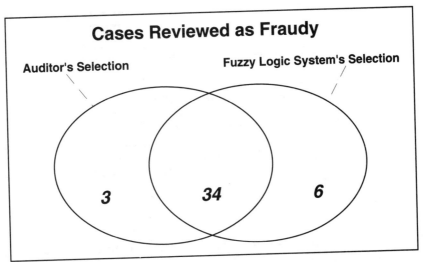

Figure 199: After auditors reviewed all cases selected by either the auditors or the fuzzy logic system, they found 34 actually fraudulent claims of the 89 claims both selected, and 3 and 6, respectively, actually fraudulent claims in the groups selected by only one.

AllFinance then had all 145 cases selected by either the fuzzy logic fraud detection system or by the auditors manually reviewed for fraud. The result is illustrated in Figure 199. Of the 89 cases selected by both the auditors and the fuzzy logic system, fraudulent behavior was found in 34 cases. This corresponds to a 38% hit rate. Of the 28 cases selected by only the auditors, fraudulent behavior was found only in three cases. This corresponds to an 11% hit rate. Of the 28 cases selected by only the fuzzy logic fraud detection system, fraudulent behavior was found in six cases. This corresponds to a 22% hit rate.

Testing Different Threshold Values

AllFinance was quite surprised that the fuzzy logic system was capable of detecting six fraudulent cases that the auditors did not detect. To evaluate how many more fraudulent claims could be found when more claims were selected, the selection threshold of the fuzzy logic system was lowered to 0.4 and to 0.3. Then, the additional claims were reviewed. Table 11 shows the results for both cases in an overview.

	Number Selected	Number Fraudulent	Hit Rate
Auditors	117	37	31.6%
Fuzzy Logic System (Th.: 0.477)	117	40	34.2%
Fuzzy Logic System (Th.: 0.4)	144	46	32.9%
Fuzzy Logic System (Th.: 0.3)	201	48	23.9%

Table 11: Comparison of number of fraudulent claims detected.

Lowering the review threshold for the fuzzy logic system to 0.4 will select 144 cases for review. Of these additional 27 cases, six turned out to be fraudulent. This corresponds to a 22.2% rate of fraudulent claims in the additional claims. This hit rate is much lower than the hit rate for the first 117 selected cases.

In other words, reviewing 27 more cases than the previously selected 117, reveals six more fraudulent cases. Lowering the review threshold even more, down to 0.3, will select 201 cases for review. Of these additional 57 cases, only two were found to be fraudulent. This corresponds to a hit rate of just 3.5%. AllFinance used these results to decide on a threshold value of 0.4 in the final system. Lowering the threshold from 0.477 to 0.4 revealed six more fraudulent claims that cost AllFinance considerably more than the effort of reviewing 27 more cases.

Ultimately, the effort of also reviewing the remaining 999 cases that were neither selected by the fuzzy logic system nor the auditors would have been unwarranted. The actual information on how many fraudulent claims both the auditors and the fuzzy logic system did not select would have been interesting. However, the fact that expanding the selection from 144 cases to 201 cases only revealed two more fraudulent claims provides for the assumption that the remaining fraudulent claims would be in the range of eight cases.

Note: to protect the intellectual property contained in the fuzzy logic fraud detection system, the actual fuzzy logic system is not contained within the *fuzzy*TECH for Business software.

5.1.5 Other Finance Applications

The previous sections gave you in-depth coverage of a number of successful applications of fuzzy logic in finance. Many others do exist, however, not many practical applications have been published. This section contains brief abstracts on other business applications using fuzzy logic. References have been included where applicable in order that you may obtain the full article.

Investor Classification

Many investment houses classify both their customers and their investments into three groups denoting their risk mentality:

- conservative and security-oriented (risk shy),

- growth-oriented and dynamic (risk neutral), and

- chance-oriented and progressive (risk happy).

To analyze how well a customer fits into these three groups, an investment house has designed a questionnaire with about two dozen questions that each have to be answered with values from 1 to 5. The questions range from personal background (age, martial state, number of children, job type, education type, etc.) to what the customer expects from an investment (capital protection, tax shelter, liquid assets, etc.). A fuzzy logic system was designed for the evaluation of the answers to the questions. The application is not published.

Insider Trading Surveillance

A system to automatically detect insider dealing and market manipulation using a combination of fuzzy logic, neural nets, and genetic algorithms has been developed for the London Stock Exchange [13]. The aim of the system is to detect rings of several individuals, or one individual with several accounts. The problem, which is extremely difficult to solve using conventional techniques, involves spotting the "signature" of certain traders from a vast amount of electronic camouflage.

Foreign Exchange Trading

In Japan, fuzzy logic is used in a foreign exchange trading system to predict the Yen-Dollar exchange rate [44]. The system uses fuzzy logic rules to make inferences based on economic news events that may affect the currency market. This news is "translated" into the fuzzy logic system's input format by domain experts.

Cash Supply Optimization

For banks with a large number of local branches and automated teller machines (ATMs), the supply of cash held involves costs. These costs are mostly due to the capital binding in the cash bills. Although it sounds odd at a first glance, cash is bound capital because it is money that cannot be used while it is stored in the form of bills waiting in a branch or ATM to be withdrawn by a customer. Hence, a bank can save a considerable amount of money if the total amount of cash can be reduced in its branches and ATMs. Conventionally, this problem is solved by bankers that assess the minimum amount of cash for each branch and ATM. However, the amount of cash required at the outlets will vary over time. First because of seasonal reasons, the necessary amount of cash will change over the week and the year differently for each branch and ATM. Second, the environment of the individual branches and ATMs changes over time. For example, new shops may open in the vicinity of a branch or a new office of another bank may open nearby. Hence, a one-time definition of a minimum cash amount for each branch and ATM by a banker will become obsolete and, hence, the average minimum amount of cash held in each branch and ATM can become larger than actually required. In a project of a European bank, fuzzy logic was used to re-compute the minimum cash amount of each branch and ATM daily. This fuzzy logic system contained the expertise of the bankers for assessing the required lowest cash amount on the basis of the past cash flow of the branches and ATMs as well as a classification of their neighborhood. The system was able to reduce the average cash supply in the branches and ATMs by 7.1% without increasing the rate of situations where the branch or ATM ran out of cash. For a bank with about 450 branches and 1270 ATMs, this results in an average total of $3.8M less in cash supply.

5.2   Fuzzy Logic in Business Applications

This section presents case studies of successful implementations in various business applications. Sections 5.2.1 to 5.2.4 treat selected applications in more detail. Other business applications, such as the customer profiling system, have already been handled in previous sections of this book.

5.2.1 Supplier Evaluation for Sample Testing

In this section, the commercial software products Invent/W and Invent/R developed by INFORM [21] provide examples. These products use a fuzzy logic supplier evaluation module for sample testing of both incoming goods (Invent/W) and incoming invoices (Invent/R). By reducing complete inspections to sample tests, a significant amount of labor can be saved. The fuzzy logic supplier evaluation analyzes the supplier that delivered the goods to be inspected or that delivered the invoice to be checked. In a way, the fuzzy logic module of Invent searches for the "black sheep" in the herd.

An Incoming Goods Inspection Case Study

One user of Invent/W is the Kaufhof AG corporation of Germany, a leading department store chain. Before the introduction of sample testing, 100% of all incoming goods were tested. Possible supplier errors can be different in nature and gravity. For example, there is a significant difference between a delivery that is supposed to contain 100 pairs of black socks which actually contains only 96 pairs of black socks, and the same delivery that contains 100 pairs of blue socks.

By using the fuzzy logic supplier evaluation system in its storage facilities, Kaufhof was able to significantly reduce the amount of testing required to find the errors. Table 12 shows the results after the first four months of installation. To obtain these results, a 100% test was conducted in parallel.

Month	Sample Size	Differences Found
June	69%	99.90%
August	46%	98.92%
September	40%	95.66%
October	35%	99.49%

Table 12: Sample size and differences found during the first four months of installation.

The first month, June, started with a relatively large sample size of 69%. Because of the very favorable result of 99.9% in differences found, the sample sizes for August and September were significantly reduced. In September, a number of deliveries from new suppliers caused the system performance to drop. After setting new initialization values for the historical trend factors in the fuzzy logic system, the sample size for October was not increased but rather lowered even further. Because even a complete test involves a test error in the order of 1%, the sample testing performance was considered to be excellent, and Kaufhof has now installed the system in all of its storage facilities.

Inspection of Incoming Invoices Using Sample Tests

The other version, Invent/R, uses the same fuzzy logic system for supplier evaluation in the sample checking of invoices. Large corporations have numerous invoices for services for which no delivery of goods is associated. Subsequently, most companies either check all invoices for service or just check every invoice greater than a defined threshold. Companies checking all invoices waste money because of the high labor costs involved in the checking process. Companies that only check invoices beyond a threshold risk that once word of this policy has reached their suppliers, then the invoices under the threshold may not be as carefully prepared as those above. Invent/R is used by large companies receiving a substantial number of service invoices, such as companies in the automotive and the chemical industries. Users of Invent/R include Volkswagen AG and Henkel KG in Germany. The results they achieve are in the same range as those achieved with the Invent/W program discussed earlier. On average, a company can achieve about the same inspection quality with just 50% of the labor costs.

Fuzzy Logic Supplier Evaluation

The remainder of this section describes the fuzzy logic system that performs the supplier evaluation. Figure 200 shows the structure of the system and some membership function definitions. The supplier evaluation LB is derived from two other evaluations: one is the evaluation of the faulty behavior of the supplier in general (Supplier Error Evaluation); the other is the evaluation of the current delivery or invoice.

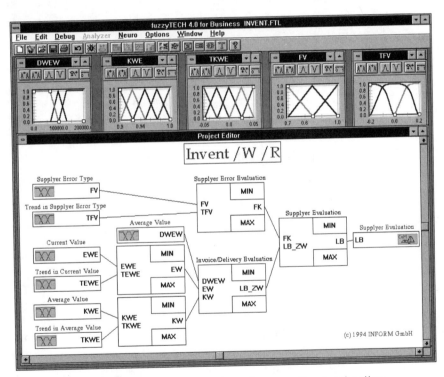

Figure 200: Fuzzy logic system for supplier evaluation.

The supplier error evaluation is based on the error type, which stems from a category listing and its trend. The fuzzy logic system uses trend functions for most input variables in order to automatically adapt to a changing supplier performance.

The invoice or delivery evaluation takes into account:

- the average value of the goods the supplier delivers,

- the value of the current delivery and its trend, and

- the average value of the goods over the last two weeks and its trend.

The output of the fuzzy logic evaluation is a number between 0 and 100, denoting the degree to which the fuzzy logic system classifies the incoming invoice or goods as "questionable." The Invent system uses this information to determine a test probability. By this process, it makes sure that even the most perfect supplier gets checked once in a while. Otherwise, it would be impossible to detect an excellent supplier going bad.

Note: to protect the proprietary intellectual property contained in Invent /W and Invent /R, the actual fuzzy logic system is not contained within the *fuzzy*TECH for Business software.

5.2.2 Customer Targeting

Sections 1.1.1 and 4.3.2 have already introduced a fuzzy logic system for customer profiling. This section introduces other examples of what can be done with fuzzy logic in the field of marketing.

Targeting Different Approaches to Different Customers

A direct extension of the customer profiling application discussed earlier would be to extract the information contained in an existing customer database in order to identify different customer groups and manage them in the best possible way. These selections and management tactics could, for instance, be:

- Predicting the most profitable customers and selecting them for sales promotions.

- Predicting the future business value of customers and cultivating high-income companies.

■ Predicting customers likely to go elsewhere, building their loy-
   alty, and increasing their value.

One benefit of using fuzzy logic for the customer targeting described here is that the results from test campaigns can be used to set
up a fuzzy logic rule base by using NeuroFuzzy techniques.

Defining Target Groups

In the 1960s, when the concept of customer target groups was first
introduced to marketing, clear and easy definitions were possible and
sufficient. Also, the number of different customer target groups for a
company was relatively low and thus easy to manage. This situation
has changed greatly today. More and more, the "traditional" customer
target groups are splitting up into smaller, more fragmented segments
of society. Plus, the speed by which the boundaries of the target groups
change has grown tremendously.

This makes the use of established target group marketing strategies increasingly more difficult. By using fuzzy logic to identify target
groups, those segments and sub-segments that belong together can be
joined by common sense "if-then" rules.

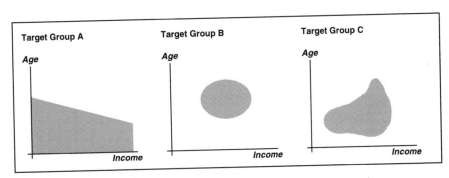

Figure 201: Three customer target group examples.

Expanding Target Group Scoring Models with Fuzzy Logic

In the past, score card models have been widely used for customer
targeting. However, the accuracy of the results achieved depends

mainly on the type of target group to be defined. Figure 201 shows the example of three simplified target groups. For illustration, they define target groups just by age and income. The gray area denotes the target group definition.

In the case of target group A, a score card model will work fine. For example, the simple score model ($\alpha\cdot$Age + $\beta\cdot$Income) < γ can represent the target group A. However, representing a target group such as B or C will require a more complex and thus harder-to-tune and verify score card model, especially if more than just two variables are used. Here, a fuzzy logic expansion of a score card model like the one discussed in Section 5.1.1 will be easier to set up and maintain.

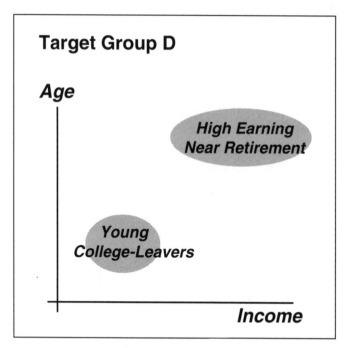

Figure 202: Customer segment sub-markets.

Figure 202 shows an even more complex case. In some cases, the target group may consist of multiple, non-connected customer segments. The transparent definition of such a target group is only possible with expansions of a score card model, such as those that fuzzy logic can provide.

5.2.3 Sequencing and Scheduling

Sequencing and scheduling are both distinct optimization problems that are mostly solved by heuristic optimization techniques. These heuristic optimization techniques are methods used to search for a near-optimal solution and for the most part contain methods for:

1. Generating the initial sequence of a schedule that satisfies all constraints.

2. Moving in the space of possible solutions, that is, modifying the tentative sequence or schedule so that the modified sequence or schedule still satisfies all constraints.

3. Judging the relative merit of each sequence or schedule.

The design of the first two methods depends mainly on the type of sequencing or scheduling problem. They range from simple priority-rule based heuristics for generating the initial solution to complicated node-exchange algorithms for the modification of possible solutions. These methods will not be discussed further here. Rather, the focus is on the third method required for all sequence and schedule optimization processes: the merit judgment of a possible solution.

This judgment is the goal function for the optimization problem. In some applications, there is a clearly defined mathematical model for the goal function, for example, a cost function that the optimization algorithm must minimize. However, in many cases, it is not easy to associate a plausible cost function to a given sequencing or scheduling problem.

Multi-Criteria Optimization

In a production planning system designed by the author for BASF AG in Germany in 1990, the sequence of jobs in a batch processing unit had to be optimized [29]. Job processing time ranged from 0.5 to 20 hours. After each job, the production facility had to be cleaned. The amount of cleaning depended greatly on the sequence of the jobs and ranged from 0.5 hours to 3 complete working days. During cleaning, the production halted.

However, just finding the sequence with the minimum total cleaning time does not deliver a good solution. Such a sequence usually violates delivery deadlines promised to customers and does not take into account the capital tied up in products completed long before their delivery deadline. Thus, a multi-criteria goal function had to be designed that would take all relevant criteria into consideration.

In the cited application, the primary goal for optimization was maximizing overall customer satisfaction. Customer satisfaction is achieved by job completion before or on its due date. In traditional Operations Research, standard approaches to designing such a cost or a goal function include criteria such as:

- number of late jobs

- sum of delays for all late jobs

- delay of the latest job

- weighted sum of late jobs (penalty cost approach)

These criteria aggregate the lateness of a given schedule into a real number. This characterizing number is then used to compare schedules and to direct the optimization algorithm's search. However, these criteria only depict a very rough image of a decision-maker's rating. Therefore, the resulting solution may not actually reflect the decision-maker's concept of an optimal schedule. While discussing the problem with the decision-makers at BASF AG, some observations were made:

- Due dates are not equally important. The importance of satisfying the customer-given due date hinges on the individual customers themselves and on the product.

- Most of the aggregation criteria presented above assume a linear relation between the lateness of a completion date and the associated loss of satisfaction. This implication could not be supported by the actual decision-maker's judgment.

- Rather than something like penalty costs, the decision-maker considers the concept of the latest due date in rating schedules.

The latest due date is an estimate of the utmost, latest delivery date as decided by the decision-maker or the marketing department.

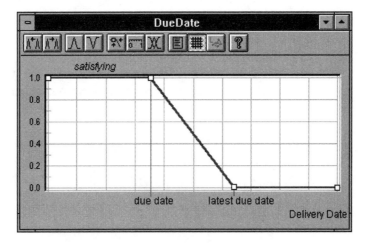

Figure 203: Membership function expressing how satisfactory the current delivery date is.

Those observations led to the formulation of a fuzzy logic decision-making model. Figure 203 shows the membership function for customer satisfaction of a single delivery. To compute the degree of customer satisfaction, the degree to which each delivery deadline satisfies the customer must be aggregated to a single value.

Multiple Objective Optimization

While the previously cited application basically only considers maximizing overall customer satisfaction, other production planning systems take multiple objectives into account. FELIS, the production optimizing system developed by INFORM GmbH [20], provides the next example. FELIS contains both a visualization and an optimization component. It draws its data from an underlying production planning system. The optimization component uses fuzzy logic in two ways:

- To judge the quality of a production plan with respect to all the relevant criteria. Criteria include average tardiness of completion dates, average total processing time of all jobs in the shop, capacity usage fluctuations, and capacity usage.

■ Often, the constraints given such as shift duration or capacity are not precisely definable. If a production scheduler does not fill in a job that requires 110 minutes operation time in a shift that has 115 minutes left, then it does not exploit the tolerance for imprecision like humans do. Also, operation times are often not precisely definable. Only a vague idea of operation time exists, especially with jobs that have never before been processed on the machine.

Because FELIS can exploit the inherent tolerances in production scheduling by using fuzzy logic, the generated production plans are better and more robust when handling minor changes in the constraints.

Servicing and Maintenance Scheduling

A typical example of a scheduling problem where many criteria must be taken into account is the scheduling of servicing and maintenance. As an illustration, the example of a help desk for computer users within Moody's Investors Service of New York is used [5].

Moody's is primarily a financial services firm, which internally runs multiple local and wide area networks between computer workstations, mainframe database servers, and PCs. Like many large organizations with large computer bases, Moody's has an in-house support group to aid in resolving technical problems.

In addition, they have a help desk where users can report problems or in some cases they can get help in resolving those problems over the phone. The scheduling problem in this case involves the assignment of specialists to the list of problems reported in order to minimize the total loss for the company because of computer downtime. For this, many different factors have to be considered. How severe is the reported problem? Can the user live with an inconvenience for some time? How long might it take to solve a reported problem? Which of the service personnel would be most suited for the job?

To solve this scheduling problem, Moody's used a genetic algorithm to generate an initial valid schedule and to create new candidates for a solution from this schedule. Genetic algorithms mimic nature's way of creating new species from existing ones and of adapting existing species to different environments. In short, they consider a job within a schedule to be a gene in a chromosome. The start is a set of different possible schedules resulting from various job combinations (chromosomes). Next, they divide the job combinations or chromosomes into pieces and re-combine them (fertilization) into new schedules (offspring). By crossover, (sexual reproduction) or mutation (minor modifications in the chromosome) they generate variations of the offspring, i.e., new schedule possibilities. The offspring are then evaluated by the fitness function which decides which offspring will survive into the next generation and propagate further.

The fitness function is the cost or goal function that judges the relative merit of the current solution. As in many scheduling problems, this goal function needs to consider multiple criteria and objectives. Often, a mathematical model for such a goal function does not exist. Here, fuzzy logic can help by allowing the goal function to be defined linguistically.

In the case of Moody's help desk scheduling application, the goal function was primarily the minimization of total computer downtime. The computer downtimes were weighted by how much computer users rely on their computers for work and/or whose time is expensive relative to that of the average user. This goal function was then modified by a "goodwill" function, which estimates how dissatisfied each user would be if forced to wait the amount of time prescribed by the schedule. This "goodwill" function was designed using fuzzy logic.

Priority Rules Using Fuzzy Logic

Often, much simpler methods are used for sequencing and scheduling, i.e., priority rules. Such rules determine only the next job to be processed from a queue of waiting jobs. For example, in production scheduling rules are used that:

- take the job with the closest due date,

■ take the job that requires the least amount of time to be processed, or

■ take the job where the due date minus the total processing time it requires before completion is minimal.

Most priority rules employed in industrial applications use only one or two of these criteria. Hence, if a machine is short on capacity, then some jobs may not be processed for a long time. This can result in problems with the overall production plan. Also, the scope of such rules is very narrow. They do not consider the total situation on the shop floor. For example, if the number of orders in the entire shop is relatively low, then priority rules that maximize capacity usage are not useful. Also, at times when there are large order quantities, priority rules that minimize the capital tied up in production are not useful.

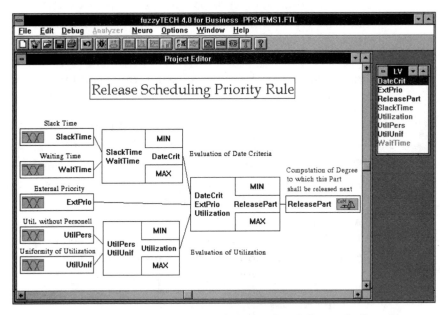

Figure 204: Structure of the release scheduling priority rule.

In these cases, fuzzy logic can help to design more meaningful priority rules for production scheduling. Because fuzzy logic allows the design of cost functions that involve many input parameters based on human experience, it was used in the application discussed in [11]. Two fuzzy logic systems have also been used to schedule production in a flexible manufacturing system (FMS). In the remainder of this section, this case study illustrates the design of fuzzy logic priority rules.

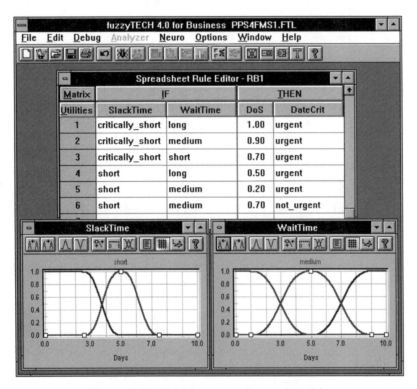

Figure 205: Rule base and membership functions of the release scheduling priority rule.

The fuzzy logic priority rules are used for two decisions: release scheduling and machine scheduling. Release scheduling decides when and what job shall start to be processed by the different stations of the FMS. For each machine, machine scheduling decides which of the waiting jobs should be processed next.

Figure 204 shows the structure of the release scheduling priority rule used in *fuzzy*TECH. For each job, the priority rule computes a degree to which this job belongs to the set of jobs that should be started. The jobs with the highest ranking are to be started in the FMS. The degree to which a job should be released next is computed from the following criteria: date, utilization, and the external priority assigned to the job. The criteria data itself is computed from the slack time and the waiting time. Slack time is the time left before the job is due to be completed minus all remaining operation times for the completion of this job. The waiting time is the time the job has already been waiting to be processed by the FMS.

Figure 205 shows the two linguistic variable definitions for the input variables SlackTime and WaitTime and the rules contained in the rule block for the DateCriteria evaluation. **Note:** this application uses S-Shaped membership functions (see Section 6.1.3) and weighted rules.

Once a job is released into the FMS, it is processed by a number of the FMS stations in a certain sequence. When a job is due to be processed next on a machine that is already busy processing another job, a queue develops. The machine scheduling priority rule then decides which of the waiting jobs for the machine is to be taken next. Hence, the machine scheduling priority rule is applied individually at each machine that has a queue. **Note:** in an FMS, a job can usually be processed by more than one machine in the FMS.

Figure 206 shows the structure of the fuzzy logic machine scheduling priority rule. For each part waiting to be processed on the machine in consideration, a degree to which this part should be the one processed next is computed (ProcessPart). This evaluation stems from two criteria:

- A part-related criterion (PartCrit) which considers how long the job has already waited (WaitTime) and how close the due date is getting (SlackTime).

- Machine-related criterion (MachCrit), which considers how quickly this job can be processed on the machine (OperatTime) and also how well another machine could process this job (AltMach). AltMach is assessed by the relation of the queue length of this machine relative to the average queue length of all other machines capable of processing this job (QueueLengt) and by the operating time the job requires on this machine relative to the average operation time the job requires on all other machines capable of processing this job (rOpTime).

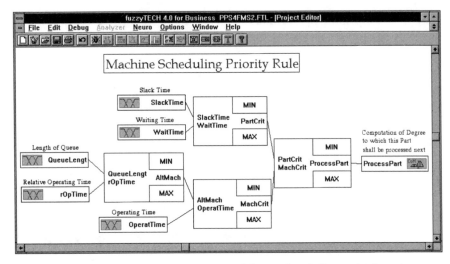

Figure 206: Structure of the machine scheduling priority rule.

5.2.4 Optimizing Research and Development Projects

This section covers the application of fuzzy logic in a development maturity evaluation system at Mercedes Benz Corporation of Germany [39]. The objective of the project was to optimize the design process of truck components, such as gear boxes, axles, or steering. For this optimization, it was necessary to measure the "maturity" of the design process with a single parameter. Fuzzy logic was used to assess this single parameter from the numerous sources of information that describe various aspects of the design process.

Using Different Types of Information

The information sources contain both quantitative data (objective criteria) describing aspects such as the number of design changes last month, as well as qualitative data (subjective criteria) such as maturity of the parts of the component.

After the single parameter describing the design maturity has been derived by the fuzzy logic system, its value is used to determine the optimal amount of design effort to be put into the project until completion.

Optimal is defined by minimizing the total cost, the major parts of which are:

- ■ development costs (increases with increasing design effort),

- ■ warranty costs (decreases with increasing design effort), and

- ■ opportunity costs (due to non-delivery and loss of image when delivering too late).

The remainder of this section covers only the design of the fuzzy logic system that evaluates the maturity of a development project.

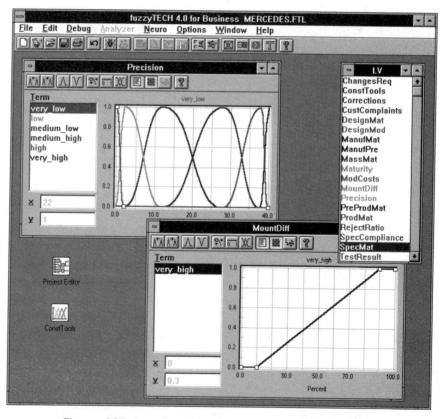

Figure 207: Two linguistic input variable definitions.
The variables describing qualitative information sources
each have six terms; the ones describing
quantitative information sources each have one term.

Representing Qualitative and Quantitative Inputs

The fuzzy logic system uses a total of ten input variables. Since the input variables for the qualitative criteria already denote the fulfillment of the criteria, only one linguistic term per variable is defined. For the quantitative criteria, each linguistic variable contains six terms using S-shaped membership function definitions like those discussed in Section 6.1.3. Figure 207 shows two sample definitions.

Figure 208 shows the hierarchical structure of the fuzzy logic system. To enable comprehensive design of the fuzzy logic rules, no more than three variables are connected in each rule block. With its hierarchical structure, the system "concentrates" the information contained in the ten input variables into a single parameter, the development project maturity.

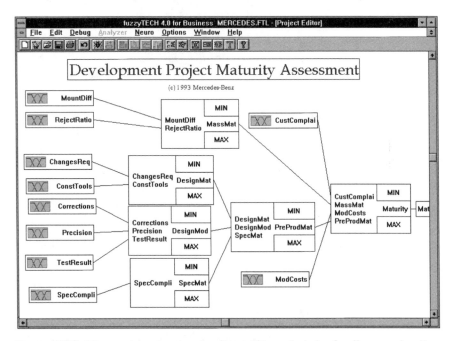

Figure 208: Hierarchical aggregation of input data for the evaluation of the design maturity.

In total, the system uses 19 linguistic variables, where eight linguistic variables are used to express intermediate results in the aggregation hierarchy. In the rule blocks of the system, a total of 78 rules are defined. **Note:** to protect the intellectual property of Mercedes-Benz, the actual fuzzy logic system is not contained within the *fuzzy*TECH for Business software.

5.2.5 Knowledge-Based Prognosis

A prognosis is the "black art" of predicting the future. It is used in many different areas. Basically, a prognosis works on a defined system. A system is something that has input conditions (influenced from outside the system) and state conditions, which describe the state of the system. Prognosis means that you can predict the behavior of the output variables for some time in the future when just the input variables of the system are known. In order to make the prognosis, you need to first assemble knowledge of the system behavior in a mathematical model of the system. For example, if you want to predict the water level of a rain barrel and you know just the water flow in and out of the barrel, then you can predict the future water level as the integral over the difference between the in- and out-flow. The mathematical model in this case is the integral. Yet, in most business applications, the model is rarely this simple. Often, the system can at best be only partially described by a mathematical model. In these cases, human expertise about the system behavior or simply the experience of observing the system's behavior over time must also be considered. Such knowledge about the system's behavior cannot be expressed by a mathematical model in an easy and transparent fashion. Here, fuzzy logic has shown to be a useful tool to expand and complement a mathematical prediction model.

Sales Prognosis of a Mail-Order House

Often, a combination of statistical techniques and fuzzy logic can be successfully employed for prognosis. In a recent application, a European mail-order house used a combination of fuzzy logic and statistical techniques to forecast sales. The mail order house wishes to remain anonymous, so they are referred to here by the alias "La Source." The problem that La Source needed to solve was the following: each Fall, La Source sends out their new catalog to three million households. At the same time, La Source will have already stocked large quantities of the goods offered in the catalog. The stock quantity was estimated by the purchasers at La Source when the product was included in the product portfolio. For most products, the initial stock quantity is about 25% of what La Source estimates it will sell during the entire year that the catalog is valid.

To avoid late deliveries or expensive subsequent deliveries due to lack of inventory, La Source starts to analyze purchase orders ten days after the catalog is sent out. This analysis uses a statistical model to estimate the total sales volume of the product. While this statistical model works adequately with many products, it does not with other products. This is due to a number of reasons. For example, some articles are seasonal. If an article is something typically bought as a Christmas gift, it will not follow the assumptions upon which the statistical model is based. The order frequency for clothing also tends to be seasonal. If a product fits more than one of these categories, it can get even more complex.

Previously the purchasing managers used "rules of thumb" to estimate the demand for these products from the initial demand figures. Because not all purchasing managers are experienced enough, La-Source implemented the "rules of thumb" fuzzy logic system. As a result, the number of articles out of stock in the first year of the systems implementation dropped by 73% compared to the previous year. The total value of products in the warehouse over the year remained the same. LaSource has not published the results nor the structure of this fuzzy logic system design and wishes to remain anonymous.

5.3 Fuzzy Logic in Data Analysis Applications

Data analysis deals with the extraction of information from raw data. Information is defined as a piece of knowledge that can be used to evaluate and optimize processes in business and finance, as well as in engineering [41]. The technologies used most often for these types of applications, such as regression analysis and clustering, stem from conventional statistics. Most of these techniques try to identify a mathematical model behind the data they analyze. For example, linear regression tries to identify the mathematical model of data in the form $y = mx + a$. However, data can frequently be interpreted much more easily linguistically than by means of a mathematical model. This section provides examples as to how conventional data analysis techniques can be enhanced through fuzzy logic.

5.3.1 Fuzzy Data Analysis in Cosmetics

The development of cosmetics products is often achieved through extensive lab testing. These tests deliver large amounts of data that need to be interpreted to get useful information on how well the product satisfies a set of objectives. In this section, the example is of shampoo development at Henkel KGaA [17]. Henkel is one of the major European manufacturers of cosmetics and its labs are located in Dusseldorf, Germany.

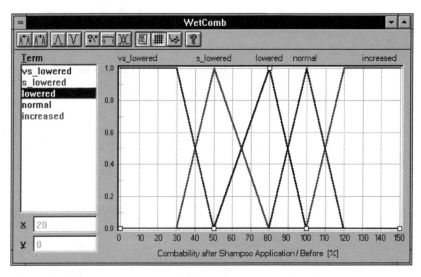

Figure 209: The linguistic variable WetComb evaluates the relation between combing forces after and before shampoo application.

Positioning of Shampoos

Today, most manufacturers offer a range of different shampoos that are positioned for different customer needs. For instance, there are simple shampoos to provide basic cleaning, special shampoos for conditioning, and others for extra care applications. The primary factors that determine what type of purpose a shampoo can be positioned toward are dry combing ability and wet combing ability after shampoo application. These and other factors determine in which segment the shampoo can be successfully positioned.

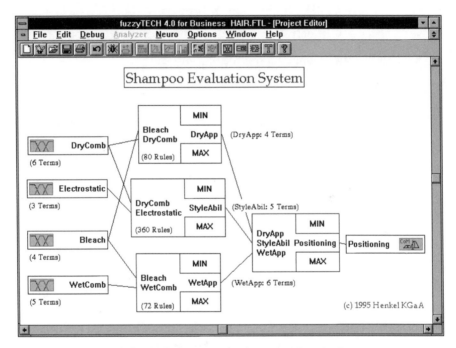

Figure 210: Structure of evaluation in the Henkel shampoo evaluation system.

The combing ability is measured by a special comb that measures force while combing. To measure wet combing ability, the shampoo is applied to only one side of the scalp. Then, wet combing ability is measured as the force on the side where the shampoo was applied divided by the force on the side where the shampoo was not applied. Dry combing ability is measured the same way after the hair is dry. Figure 209 shows the definition of WetComb, the linguistic variable that assesses the wet combing ability. A wet combing ability of 50% denotes that application of the shampoo reduced the combing force by half, and a wet combing ability of 200% denotes that application of the shampoo doubled combing forces.

In total, four input variables are used for the evaluation of the best positioning for each shampoo tested (Figure 210):

- dry combing ability,

- electrostatic charge build-up during combing,

- bleaching degree of hair, and

- wet combing ability.

The degree to which the hair of the test person is bleached is an input variable because bleaching strongly changes the combing properties of hair. In an expansion of the system currently under development, additional input variables such as lather build-up, lather response, shininess of hair, skin tolerance, and hair repair factors are considered.

Fuzzy Cluster Analysis

The fuzzy logic system generated for positioning shampoos in the market is also used to cluster the product portfolio of all Henkel's shampoos. The fuzzy clustering of different market positions shown in Figure 211 is a result of the intermediate variables of the fuzzy logic system shown in Figure 210.

Fuzzy cluster analysis shows how basic shampoos with primary cleaning objectives can be differentiated from shampoos that contain additives for conditioning. In addition, the cluster analysis differentiates target groups such as long/short hair. The benefit of such an analysis is that the product designers can obtain information on how a new shampoo can best be positioned on the market. This results in more accurate product placement.

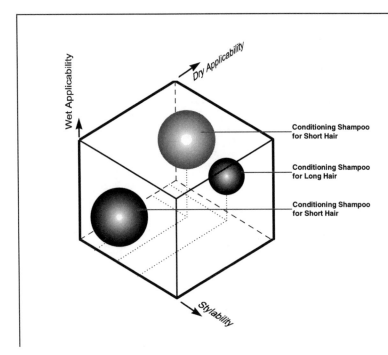

Figure 211: Fuzzy cluster analysis for shampoos.

Using NeuroFuzzy

While for the product positioning evaluation just described, such expertise is not available, human expertise was available to design the membership functions and the rule base. In this situation, the NeuroFuzzy technique can be used if representative data sets are available.

One example is the fuzzy logic module that assesses the hair damage during bleaching. Figure 212 shows the experimental results for three cases. The curves show the hair damage (given as wet combability) depending on the pH value for different cases. Experimental data like this was used to train a fuzzy logic rule base (as shown in Figure 213) using NeuroFuzzy training.

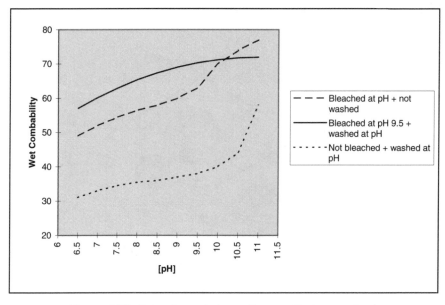

Figure 212: Experimental results on pH-dependent
hair damage during bleaching.

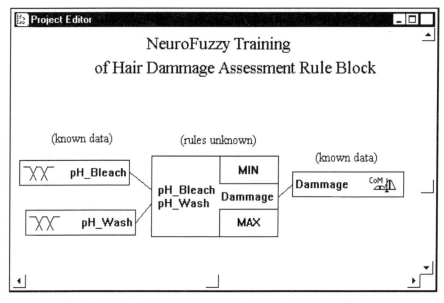

Figure 213: Generation of rules from sample
data for hair damage assessment.

5.3.2 Other Fuzzy Data Analysis Applications

The previous sections gave you in-depth coverage of a number of successful applications of fuzzy logic in finance. Many others do exist, however not many practical applications have been published. This section contains brief abstracts on other business applications using fuzzy logic. If they are reported in literature, I have included the reference so that you can obtain the full article.

Address Matching in Databases

In a number of applications, the decision has to be made whether two people in a database are the same. The applications range from de-duplication to merging of databases. This decision problem is harder than it appears at first glance because there are many means by which the same person can be input into a database in slightly different ways. This includes minor differences in spelling, concatenation of words, and typos. While most humans, based on their experience comparing addresses, can come up with a pretty good guess whether two addresses in a database belong to the same person, a mathematical model for the similarity of two addresses is hard to define. Humans use pieces of experience such as: "if the zip codes are different but the city name is very similar or the same and the names are very similar or the same, then the two records point to the same person," or, "if the last names are identical and the address is very similar or the same, then different first names probably point to different members of the same family." With fuzzy logic it is possible to use these "rules-of-thumb" to create a decision model that assesses a likelihood that two addresses are the same based on the differences between the fields in the records of the two addresses. To compute the differences between words in the records, algorithms such as Soundex are used.

Recently, a German bank used a fuzzy logic system to determine the likelihood that two addresses in a database point to the same person. The problem arose because of a recent change in tax law: all banks are now obligated to withhold 30 percent of any interest paid to a customer in excess of the annual amount of DM 6000. To determine how much interest a customer has accumulated on all his accounts, the bank has to establish a link between the customer and all his accounts. The cited bank, however, does not store the customer data in records that point to all his accounts. Rather, a different record exists for each account, and this record contains all the information on the customer. Hence, a separate record exists for each account that each contains the entire address of the customer. To link all the accounts of each customer, the addresses had to be compared and the likelihood that two addresses referring to the same customer had to be evaluated by the fuzzy logic system. Unfortunately, neither performance results nor system details have been made public.

Hospital Stay Prediction

Hospitals all over the world strive toward increased efficiency by optimizing their capacity usage. Restricted capacities in a hospital include hospital beds, intensive care unit beds, and the number of patients the different teams can handle. In times where only a small fraction of the hospital beds is used, the hospital's policy is to select and schedule patients in a way that at least makes best use of the staff. However, if empty hospital beds become in short supply, the policy becomes to select and organize work schedules in a way that optimizes the staff's limited time. In other words, if the hospital is short on beds, they would prefer to plan for outpatients and those patients that only require a short stay.

In order to conduct such capacity usage optimization, however, a good estimation of how long a patient will stay in the hospital right from the moment when the patient enters the hospital is required. In a pilot study, a U.S. hospital, which wants to remain anonymous, uses fuzzy logic to estimate the length of hospital stay of patients accepted to the hospital. The system uses the information that is provided by the doctor that accepts the patient to the hospital in his first check. The fuzzy logic system takes into account the diagnosed disease, the patient's general condition, the likelihood of complications, the patient's previous medical history (if available), and other information. The system is still under development, hence, no detailed results are currently available.

Evaluation of Slots for TV Commercials

In the European TV commercials market, so-called media-buying agencies (MBAs) purchase TV commercial slots wholesale from TV stations for subsequent distribution. When purchasing TV slots, MBAs can select time slots from different TV stations. A single MBA purchases up to 5000 TV slots a year. To make a good buy decision, a number of different factors need to be considered:

- The expected number of viewers for the commercial,

- Normalized price per viewer (price of the commercial*(length/30sec) / total number of viewers),

- Viewer structure (distributions by age, demographic, profession, or income group),

- Program type that contains the commercial (show, soap opera, news, sports, etc.),

- Distribution of the MBA's clientele.

One European MBA, which wants to remain anonymous, uses fuzzy logic to evaluate the attractiveness of each TV commercial slot. The design was carried out by contracted fuzzy logic consultants that had prior experience in this area and took just 8 weeks. This prototype was tested and optimized, using the buyer team's decisions for the prior three months, until the management of the MBA was convinced that the performance of the fuzzy logic system was as good as the buyer team's decisions. Now the system is in continuous use and is capable of restructuring all buy decisions in only five minutes. This allows rapid adaptation of the portfolio of commercial slots offered by the MBA in case of policy changes, new clients, or any other changes in the TV media market.

6

Advanced
Fuzzy Logic Design Techniques

This chapter contains sections on advanced fuzzy logic design techniques. You will find the discussions contained herein useful when you start your own fuzzy logic design work and when you design more complex systems than those handled in the case studies of Chapter 2. Section 6.1 shows you how to design linguistic variables and their membership functions for a given application. Section 6.3 discusses advanced fuzzy logic inference methods that have proven to be useful in complex applications, and Section 6.4 compares different defuzzification methods.

6.1 Linguistic Variables and Their Membership Functions

Linguistic variables are the "vocabulary" of a fuzzy logic system. The rules that express a certain decision-making policy draw conclusions from this vocabulary. Hence, they must closely represent the way humans evaluate numerical figures. This section guides you through the basic development methodology of linguistic variables and their membership functions.

6.1.1 Design Methodology of Linguistic Variables

In scientific literature, many approaches have been suggested for the design of linguistic variables and their membership functions. In Section 6.1.3, a few of these techniques are discussed in further detail. Here, the layout for a simple design methodology is described that has proven to work well in most applications.

Basic Terminology

The possible values of a linguistic variable are called "linguistic terms" or simply "terms." These terms are possible linguistic interpretations of technical figures. For example, the technical figure "distance," which can be measured in yards, can also have linguistic interpretations {far, medium, close, zero, too_far}. The technical figure that a linguistic variable describes is called the "base variable" in fuzzy logic design.

How Many Terms for a Linguistic Variable?

Most applications use between three and seven terms for each linguistic variable. Less than three terms are rarely used, because most concepts in human language consider at least two extremes and a middle point in between them. On the other hand, one rarely uses more than seven terms because humans interpret technical figures by using their short-term memory, which can only compute up to approximately seven symbols at a time.

Additionally, most linguistic variables have an odd number of terms. This is due to the fact that most linguistic variables are defined symmetrically and that one term describes the middle between the extremes. Thus, most fuzzy logic systems use either three, five, or seven terms.

In determining whether to use three, five, or seven terms, there are a couple different approaches to consider:

- ■ Try formulating a few typical fuzzy logic rules. By doing so, you get an idea which terms and how many terms you need to define in the complete rule base.

- ■ If the advance formulation of the rule is difficult, you can start your design by defining three terms for each linguistic input variable and five terms for each linguistic output variable. Experience shows that these are the minimum number of terms for most applications. Later, during actual formulation of the rule base, you can add new terms as you need them.

Membership Functions

The degree to which a numerical value satisfies the linguistic concept of a linguistic variable is called the degree of membership. For a continuous variable, this degree is expressed by a function called a membership function (MBF). The membership functions map each value of the numerical figure (base variable) to the membership degree to which it satisfies the linguistic concept of the linguistic terms. Usually, the membership functions for all terms are drawn in the same diagram (Figure 214).

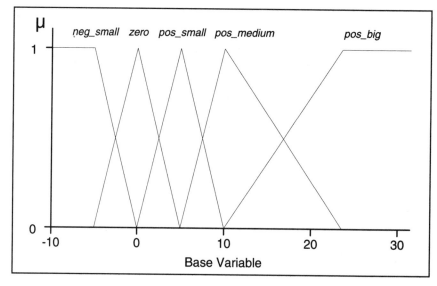

Figure 214: Membership functions of all terms of a linguistic variable.

6.1.2 Linear Standard Membership Functions

A great variety of membership functions have been proposed in the scientific literature. However, most practical implementations use only "Standard Membership Functions" (Standard-MBF) of linear or spline shape. Four different types of Standard-MBFs exist: Z-type, Λ-type (lambda), Π-Type (pi), and S-type. Figure 215 shows these four types. Standard-MBFs are also normalized, that is, their maximum is always $\mu=1$, their minimum $\mu=0$.

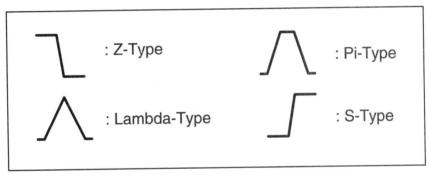

Figure 215: Standard membership functions.

The linguistic variable plotted in Figure 214 uses three types of Standard-MBFs (Z-, Λ-, and S-Type). Standard-MBFs have a number of advantages. First, they are the simplest functions accurate enough to represent most decision systems. Second, they always remain easy to interpret. Third, the implementation of Standard-MBFs is computationally very efficient on most target hardware platforms. To define Standard-MBFs, follow these four easy steps:

Definition of Standard Linear Membership Functions

Step 1:
For each term, define the value that best fits the linguistic meaning of the term. This most typical value for each term gets the membership degree $\mu=1$.

Step 2:

For each term where the terms adjacent to it have their most typical value, set the membership degree to μ=0.

Step 3:

Connect the point μ=1 with the points μ=0 by straight lines. This results in membership functions of Λ-type for the inner terms.

Step 4:

For the terms adjacent to the linguistic variable boundaries, the left-most and rightmost terms on the right side, no outer adjacent terms exist. Hence, every value beyond the point where the term defines μ=1 is considered to also fully belong (μ=1) to the term. For the left-most term, this results in a Z-type membership function. Do the same for the rightmost term in an S-type membership function.

Figure 216 illustrates the four steps for the term "zero." Three values define the Λ-type membership function: the typical value for "zero" defines the point μ=1 and the typical values for "neg_small" and "pos_small" define the points μ=0.

In some applications, the typical value of a term is an interval rather than a value. For example, if you consider any value of the base variable in the interval [-2; +2] to be completely "zero," define it as a Π-type membership function as shown in Figure 217.

Linear Standard-MBFs have been used as the basis for the vast majority of practical fuzzy logic applications in the past. Also, they have been used in most of the simpler examples in this book so far. However, Spline Standard-MBFs, as introduced in the next section, provide more accurate models of human linguistic concepts for more complex data analysis and decision support applications.

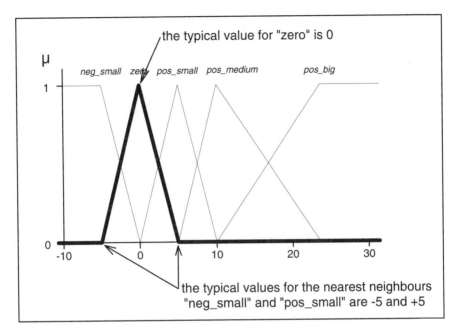

Figure 216: Definition of a Λ-type membership
function for the term "zero."

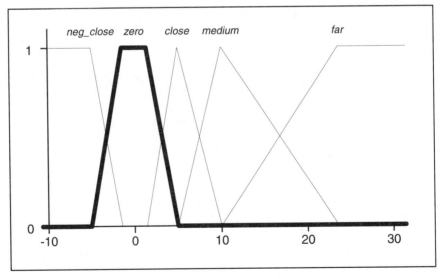

Figure 217: Definition of a Π-type membership
function for the term "zero."

6.1.3 Membership Function Shapes

A variant of the membership function definition discussed in the previous section is to use spline functions to connect the points $\mu = 0$ and $\mu = 1$. Spline functions have proven to be useful because of the results from psycholinguistic studies showing that membership functions should follow this set of axioms:

1. $\mu(x)$ is continuous over X
   A small change of the base variable value cannot result in a step in its evaluation.

2. $d(\mu(x)) / dx$ is continuous over X
   A small change of the base variable value cannot result in a step in its evaluation rate.

3. $d^2 (\mu(x)) / dx^2$ is continuous over X
   Necessary for 4.

4. $\mu(x): \min_\mu (\max_x (d^2(\mu(x)) / dx^2))$
   The change of slope is minimal.

where μ is the membership degree, $\mu(x)$ is the membership function, and X is the universe of the base variable.

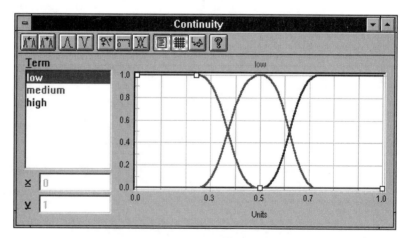

Figure 218: Linguistic variable "Continuity" from Figure 37 with S-shaped membership functions.

These axioms are satisfied by the interpolative cubic spline function. To use them for membership function definitions, you follow the same steps as with Standard MBFs. The only difference is that you use the cubic spline function (S-shaped) to connect the µ=0 and µ=1 points rather than straight lines. Figure 218 shows such a definition for the variable Continuity from Figure 37.

To switch a membership function shape from L-shape to S-shape, open the Term Dialog box for the respective term with a double-click on the term name in the Term list box. In the Shape group

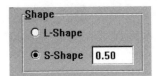

you can select between the different shapes. For S-shaped membership functions, you can define an asymmetry factor in the edit field.

Other Membership Function Definitions

Quite a few other types of membership functions have been proposed in the scientific literature. Some examples are:

- Analytical functions, such as $1/(x_0-x)^2$. These functions have been proposed because of certain mathematical properties. However, membership functions should represent intuition, not mathematics.

- Stochastic functions, such as the Gaussian distribution. Proposed by those who want to link statistics and fuzzy logic. However even then, membership functions still represent linguistic fuzziness, not stochastic uncertainty.

- Piecewise linear functions. During optimization, it is sometimes useful to approximate an empirical function with a piecewise linear function.

- Empirical functions. These are membership functions that have been defined using an empirical approach to derive a membership function for a certain term out of a simulated decision process [50]. This approach is of prohibitive effort for most applications.

None of these types of membership functions play any role in current practical applications. For more details on membership functions refer to [51, pp. 344].

Membership Functions for Output Variables

Everything presented thus far deals only with membership function definitions for input variables of a fuzzy logic system. For output variables, most applications use only Λ-type membership functions.

6.2   Fuzzy Interfaces

All of the fuzzy logic systems discussed thus far translate numerical values into fuzzy logic values (fuzzification), compute fuzzy logic "if-then" rules (inference), and then re-translate the results back into numerical values (defuzzification), as illustrated in Figure 22. Sometimes one or both of the translation steps is not necessary because you have input or output variables that are linguistic in nature. These variables are already "fuzzified" and no fuzzification or defuzzification needs to occur. Section 6.2.1 shows the definition of fuzzy interfaces and debugging techniques. Section 6.2.2 shows the design of explanatory components as an application of fuzzy interfaces.

6.2.1 Defining Fuzzy Interfaces

In some applications, the inputs of a fuzzy logic system are linguistic rather than numerical. In these instances, fuzzification is not necessary. Also, in some cases output variables are linguistic in nature and thus defuzzification is not necessary.

Fuzzy Inputs

Open the file CREDIT3.FTL located in the subdirectory \SAMPLES\BUSINESS\CREDIT\. Next, double-click on the interface box for Continuity

in the Project Editor window to open the Interface Options dialog box. Enable Fuzzy Input

in the Interface type group and click on [OK] to close the dialog box. The interface box for Continuity will now display the icon for a fuzzy input/output:

Next, enable the Interactive Debug mode and open the Debug: Interactive window as shown in Figure 219. For Continuity, there are three rows for data input, one for each term. You can now select the three terms for Continuity individually and modify their input value from zero to one, representing the membership degree directly. **Note:** the question mark that appears in the "Outputs:" list box to the right of the output value of Liquidity indicates that no rules fired for the given combination of input values. No rules fired because all terms for Continuity have the membership degree of zero. If no rules fired, the output value is the "Default" value, which you enter in the "Range" group of the Base Variable dialog box.

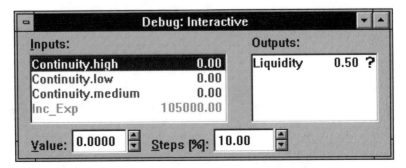

Figure 219: Debug:Interactive window with fuzzy interface.

Set "Continuity.high" to "0.3" and "Continuity.medium" to "0.7." Now, rules do fire and the question mark disappears. Open a linguistic variable editor for Continuity by double-clicking on the name "Continuity" in the Variables window. The Linguistic Variable Editor now shows a bar for each term in the plot area (Figure 220). The height of the color bar in each black bar shows the degree of membership for each term; intermediate variables are represented in the same way.

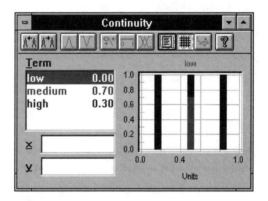

Figure 220: Linguistic Variable Editor for Continuity in Interactive Debug Mode.

The remainder of the fuzzy logic inference remains the same. **Note:** a linguistic variable can now express values that were not possible before. For example, setting all membership degrees to one results in a linguistic value that could not be expressed with the earlier membership function definition.

Fuzzy Outputs

If you do not want to defuzzify an output variable—for example, if you want to use the "fuzzy" value to form a linguistic output or if you want to use you own defuzzification method—you can select Fuzzy Output as the defuzzification method. Leave the Interactive debug mode and double-click on the Liquidity interface box. Next, select "Fuzzy Output"

⊙ Fuzzy Output

as the defuzzification method and click [OK] to close the dialog box. The Liquidity interface box now displays the icon for fuzzy input/output:

Enable the Interactive debug mode, and open a linguistic variable editor for Liquidity and Inc_Exp. Next, apply different input values to the system to see how fuzzy input/output variables are visualized in *fuzzy*-TECH. **Note:** the MS-Excel *fuzzy*TECH Assistant cannot support fuzzy interfaces due to some restrictions of Excel. Also, the fT-Link and the Serial Link debug modes of *fuzzy*TECH do not support fuzzy interfaces. However, you can use the File Recorder and the Batch debug mode with fuzzy interfaces. For detailed information, refer to [22] or the on-line help system.

6.2.2 Building Explanatory Components

Often, it is useful not only to get an evaluation result from a fuzzy logic system but also to obtain an explanation for a decision. Designers of fuzzy logic systems get the complete explanation of why a decision has been made from analysis of the fuzzy logic inference in all the editors and analyzers of *fuzzy*TECH. While this approach never leaves anything in a fuzzy logic system unexplained, it is overwhelmingly complex to most end users.

An Explanatory Component for the Mortgage Assessment System

For example, the mortgage assessment support software MASS, featured in Section 5.1.1, requires a concise explanation for each decision denying the mortgage application. Hence, a sentence generator has been included that translates the value of a fuzzy output variable into a natural language sentence. This fuzzy output variable, named "Declination," contains the three terms "building_project," "interest-_rate," and "applicant."

Thus, each term denotes a possible reason for declination. The sentence generator in MASS uses the fuzzy output value to create sentences like: "Mortgage declined because repayment plan is risky," "Mortgage declined primarily because of poor building project, also the mortgagee is evaluated below average." The sentence generator uses the degrees of membership to identify which of the three possible declination reasons has been the major and which the minor factor.

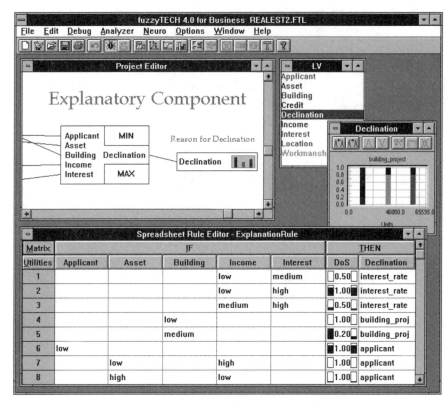

Figure 221: Explanatory component for the mortgage assessment case study of Section 5.1.1.

The algorithm of the sentence generator is simple. No more than two reasons shall be given in a sentence in order to make it easy to comprehend. Also, if two reasons are given, one shall be pointed out as major and the other one as minor.

REALEST2.FTL from \SAMPLES\BUSINESS\REALEST\ contains the mortgage assessment system with an added explanatory component. Figure 221 shows the structure of the explanatory component.

It consists of an added rule block, the new linguistic variable Declination, and a fuzzy output interface.

Note: the current version of the Excel *fuzzy*TECH Assistant cannot access fuzzy interfaces because this data type is not supported by release 5.0 of Excel.

6.3 Fuzzy Inference Methods

Fuzzy inference is the method through which the rules of a fuzzy logic system are processed. The inference comprises two components: Premise Aggregation and Result Aggregation. The Premise Aggregation step (dubbed just "Aggregation") is the combination of all input variables into a rule to formulate the degree to which the rule is considered appropriate for the given situation. Then, this degree is weighted by the degree of support (DoS) and all results with the same conclusion are combined by the Result Aggregation component. Section 6.3.1 discusses the operators used for Premise Aggregation, and Section 6.3.2 explains the methods used for Result Aggregation.

6.3.1 Premise Aggregation with Fuzzy Logic Operators

In the first seminal paper on fuzzy logic, Lotfi Zadeh already introduced fuzzy logic operators for the logical operations AND, OR, and NOT as extensions of their Boolean origins [47]. These operators were Minimum, Maximum, and 1-μ.

Basic Fuzzy Logic Operators

You can use *fuzzy*TECH for Business to plot the transfer characteristics of a fuzzy logic operator. Double-click on the MIN box [MIN] of a rule block box in the Project Editor to open the Aggregation dialog box, as shown in Figure 222. Alternatively, you can use the [Aggregation...] button in the Rule Block Configuration dialog box or the [IF] button in the Spreadsheet Rule Editor. The Operator Plot always shows an example of the aggregation of two membership degrees on the horizontal axes into a result plotted on the vertical axis.

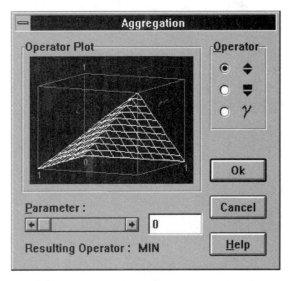

Figure 222: The aggregation dialog box plots the transfer characteristic of every fuzzy logic operator.

Figure 223: Transfer characteristic of the maximum operator.

As the plot shows, the points (0; 0), (0; 1), (1; 0), and (1; 1) that are located at the corners of the horizontal base square result in the same aggregation result value as the Boolean AND, that is, only if both membership degrees are 1 will the result be 1. Between the corners of the horizontal square, the Minimum operator yields a continuous approximation. This is the proof that fuzzy logic is a true generalization of Boolean logic. Boolean logic is the result of limiting fuzzy logic to membership degrees of 0 and 1.

Move the scroll bar "Parameter:" to the right until the value in the edit field becomes 1. This changes the transfer characteristic of the operator to Maximum (Figure 223). Just as the Minimum operator is a continuous extension of the Boolean AND, the Maximum operator is a continuous extension of the logical OR, that is, the result is 0 only when both inputs are 0.

Limits of the Min/Max Operator Models

The Minimum and Maximum operators were not only the first ones proposed they also became the ones most often used in practical applications. This is due to a number of reasons. First of all, the Minimum and Maximum operators are plausible at first glance. If you combine two evaluations through a linguistic "AND," the meaning behind this is that both need to be valid for the output to be valid. Hence, the output is true at least to the degree that the least valid one is fulfilled, i.e. the Minimum of the two membership degrees. The same is true for the OR. If you combine two evaluations through a linguistic "OR," what you mean is that only one or the other needs to be valid for the output to be valid. Hence, the output is true at least to the degree that the most valid one is fulfilled, i.e. the Maximum of the two membership degrees.

There are also other reasons why the Minimum and Maximum were chosen in many applications. For example, in control engineering applications, the area where most past applications have been completed, computing time is critical. The computation of Minimum and Maximum is very fast even on low-performance microcontrollers. Other developers have chosen the Min/Max operators for certain mathematical properties. Many others chose them just because these operators have been so widely publicized or because many fuzzy logic software tools targeted specifically for control engineering have not supported other operators.

Even though the Min/Max operators have been so widely used, they suffer from some limitations in the accuracy level to which they can mimic human evaluation processes. For example, assume the following rule for a system that evaluates cars bought for driving on the autobahn (autobahn := the place in Germany where speed limits are unknown but gas is expensive):

IF TopSpeed = high AND Mileage = good THEN Car = attractive

Three cars are to be evaluated and fuzzification has resulted in the membership degrees shown in Table 13. Table 14 shows the Premise Aggregation results using the Minimum operator.

	TopSpeed	"high"	Mileage	"good"
Car A	112 mph	$\mu_{high}=0.3$	20 mpg	$\mu_{good}=0.4$
Car B	112 mph	$\mu_{high}=0.3$	30 mpg	$\mu_{good}=0.8$
Car C	108 mph	$\mu_{high}=0.25$	35 mpg	$\mu_{good}=1.0$

Table 13: Evaluation of "TopSpeed = high" and "Mileage = good" for 3 Different Cars.

Assuming all rules have DoS = 1, the Premise Aggregation result of Table 14 becomes the degree to which the "Then-part" of the rule, "Car = attractive," is valid. Car A is thus considered attractive to the degree 0.3. Just by looking at Car A, this result seems plausible at first glance. However, comparing it to the evaluation of Car B reveals the problem. While Car B is just as fast as Car A, it delivers much better mileage. However, the Minimum operator evaluates them as both equally attractive. The evaluation of Car C makes this even clearer. Car C has a slightly lower top speed, yet a much better mileage than the others. This makes Car C the most attractive car for most people. By contrast, Car C is evaluated as the least attractive car by the Minimum operator.

Car A	$\text{Min}\{\mu_{high}=0.3; \quad \mu_{good}=0.4\} = 0.3$
Car B	$\text{Min}\{\mu_{high}=0.3; \quad \mu_{good}=0.8\} = 0.3$
Car C	$\text{Min}\{\mu_{high}=0.25; \quad \mu_{good}=1.0\} = 0.25$

Table 14: Premise aggregation results using a minimum operator.

Expanding the Rule Base

There are two solutions to the problem presented above: expansion of the rule base or use of a different fuzzy logic operator. For instance, you could define new terms for each linguistic variable to expand the rule base:

- ■ for TopSpeed, also define "very_high" and "mildly_high,"

- ■ for Mileage, also define "excellent" and "somewhat_good," and

- ■ for Car, also define "very_attractive" and "slightly_attractive."

Using these additional terms, you can now combine 27 rules that express the same thing as the one rule from above:

$$
\textbf{IF } \text{TopSpeed} = \left\{ \begin{array}{l} \text{very\_high} \\ \text{high} \\ \text{mildly\_high} \end{array} \right. \textbf{AND } \text{Mileage} = \left\{ \begin{array}{l} \text{excellent} \\ \text{good} \\ \text{somewhat\_good} \end{array} \right. \textbf{THEN } \text{Car} = \left\{ \begin{array}{l} \text{very\_attractive} \\ \text{attractive} \\ \text{slightly\_attractive} \end{array} \right.
$$

With these 27 possible rules, you can now express the original meaning behind the evaluation much more accurately and conform more to human intuition. However, if there is not just one rule in the fuzzy logic system but many, this technique can cause your rule base to explode and thus make the system non-transparent and hard to maintain.

Other Fuzzy Operators

To expand the rule base, a better approach may be to use a different fuzzy logic operator that does not suffer from this problem. When a human aggregates two criteria with the linguistic AND, in most cases what he means is that both criteria need to be fulfilled. However, the more both are fulfilled, then the better overall. In the example of the car comparison, the customer is looking for speed and fuel efficiency, but furthermore a car that satisfies these two criteria to the greatest extent is best. In other words, a slightly lower top speed can be compensated by a much better fuel efficiency. The amount of increased fuel efficiency required to compensate for a certain amount of lower top speed is called "degree of compensation." Alas, the degree of compensation is not a constant in human decision making, but instead depends on context. If the evaluation is to be made whether a certain car can be used for a ride, then it needs to have four wheels AND fuel in the tank. Here, no compensation is considered, eight wheels do not compensate for no gas in the tank and no amount of fuel can compensate for the lack of wheels.

Compensatory Operators

The degree of compensation through which humans aggregate criteria is not expressed by the Minimum operator, and that is the cause of the problem discussed above. For OR, the situation is similar. By using the Maximum as the aggregational operator, only the more fulfilled criteria is considered ("winner takes all") [47]. Human evaluation is different: if you compare lunch alternatives and your goal is that it should be either very fast OR very good, then you would be most pleased if it is both fast and good.

If you consider more examples of real-world human evaluation processes, you discover that an entire spectrum of aggregations exists. However, our everyday language only provides two words for these aggregations: "and" and "or." Figure 224 illustrates the spectrum of possible aggregations between the extremes of the Minimum and Maximum operators. The Minimum represents the "extreme AND" as it only considers the lesser fulfilled criteria, and the Maximum represents the "extreme OR" as it only considers the more fulfilled criteria. In our everyday language, the aggregations we use are located within the entire spectrum between these two extremes. The aggregations more to the left are called "and" and the ones more to the right are called "or."

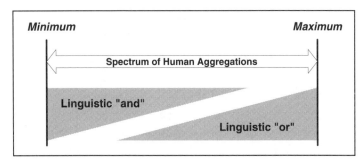

Figure 224: Aggregational operators in human evaluations range from the extreme AND represented by the minimum operator to the extreme OR represented by the maximum operator.

Sometimes, the aggregation you use is almost exactly between the extremes, and it becomes hard to decide whether the word "and" or "or" should be used. In such a situation, reword the sentence so that what you want to say is expressed more clearly.

Even though our everyday language provides us with only two words for an entire spectrum of aggregations, we are quite successful in communicating what we mean when we talk to others. The reason for this is that we can guess the degree of compensation implied by a statement from its context. Look at the car example: with the attractiveness evaluation, it is clear to everyone that one criteria compensates for the other to a certain extent. But with the wheels/gas example, it is also clear to everyone that one criteria by no means compensates for the other. If something remains unclear in human communication, we can always ask. A fuzzy logic system does not have this choice. A fuzzy logic system neither understands what we imply with our statements nor can it abstractly ask for more information based on its intuition. Thus, if you want to use aggregations other than the extremes AND and OR, you also need to define the degree of compensation underlying the statement.

Gamma Operator

You still need a fuzzy logic operator that lets you use a degree of compensation and as such more accurately represents human decision making. In the 1980s, such an operator was been developed by a multidisciplinary research group [48]. In later empirical studies it was shown that this aggregator concept represents the human decision process much more accurately than the Min/Max operators [49]. A short treatise of the theoretical background of this work is also contained in [50]. The mathematical formula of this operator is shown in Figure 225. The parameter γ denotes the degree of compensation. It can be set from 0 to 1, representing no compensation at all or complete compensation. Thus, this operator covers the entire range of human aggregations. Because of the use of γ as a parameter, the name "Gamma operator" was coined.

$$\mu = \left(\prod_{i=1}^{m} \mu_i \right)^{(1-\gamma)} \cdot \left(1 - \prod_{i=1}^{m} \left(1 - \mu_i \right) \right)^{\gamma}$$

Figure 225: Mathematical model of the Gamma operator (aggregation of m criteria).

The mathematical model of the Gamma operator is much more complex than the Min/Max operator. Hence, it is easier to understand the function of the Gamma operator by analyzing its transfer curve. Open the Aggregation dialog box and select "Gamma"

in the operator group. Figure 226 shows the Operator Plot for the Gamma operator with a degree of compensation of 0.3. As with the Minimum operator, the points (0; 0), (0; 1), (1; 0), and (1; 1) located at the corners of the horizontal base square result in the same aggregation result value as the Boolean AND. Hence, both the Minimum and Gamma operators are true generalizations of the Boolean AND.

However, the operators do differ in the way they approximate the continuum between the values of the Boolean AND. The Minimum operator follows the concept "the shortest path between two points is the straight line." Thus, a "little less of the one" cannot be compensated by "much more of the other." For the Gamma operator, this is not the case.

Figure 227 illustrates how compensation is reflected in the transfer curve.

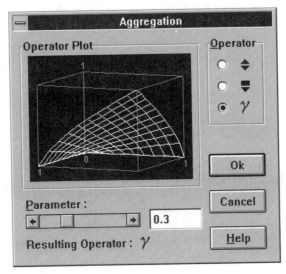

Figure 226: Transfer characteristic of
the Gamma operator with γ = 0.3.

If you use the Gamma operator with a small degree of compensation (γ = 0.3) for the car evaluation example, you obtain the results shown in Table 15. These results represent a human evaluation much more accurately than those obtained by the Minimum operator.

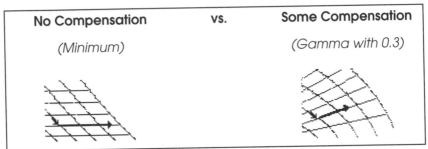

Figure 227: Compensation is reflected in the transfer curve of the operators. With No Compensation (Minimum), a "little less of one" cannot be compensated by "much more of the other." With Some Compensation (Gamma of 0.3), such compensation is provided.

Car A	Gamma{μ_{high}=0.3; μ_{good}=0.4} = 0.19
Car B	Gamma{μ_{high}=0.3; μ_{good} =0.8} = 0.35
Car C	Gamma{μ_{high}=0.25; μ_{good} =1.0} = 0.38

Table 15: Premise Aggregation results
using a Gamma operator of $\gamma = 0.3$.

Operator Families

To provide all fuzzy logic operators relevant for practical applications in a consistent manner, *fuzzy*TECH includes three operator families:

■ MinMax (✦),

■ MinAvg (✦), and

■ Gamma (γ)

in parametric form. For the MinMax operator shown in Figure 228, the parametric form is a linear combination of the Minimum and the Maximum operators. The parameter λ determines the linear combination.

$$\mu = \lambda \cdot \max_{i=1}^{m}\{\mu_i\} + (1-\lambda) \cdot \min_{i=1}^{m}\{\mu_i\}$$

Figure 228: Mathematical model of the MinMax operator.

MinAvg Operator

Another operator that has not only been suggested in research papers but has also been applied in some practical applications is the MinAvg operator. It consists of a linear combination between the Minimum operator and the average, combined with a parameter λ. Figure 229 shows the mathematical formula of the MinAvg operator.

$$\mu = \frac{\lambda}{n} \cdot \sum_{i=1}^{m} \mu_i + (1-\lambda) \cdot \min_{i=1}^{m}\{\mu_i\}$$

Figure 229: Mathematical model of the MinAvg operator.

Because of the use of the average, the MinAvg operator also involves a degree of compensation. However, this operator does not represent the human evaluation process as well as the Gamma operator [50]. Also, the four points (0; 0), (0; 1), (1; 0), and (1; 1), which are located at the corners of the horizontal base square, do not give the same aggregation result values as the Boolean AND. Hence, the MinAvg Operator is not a true extension of the Boolean AND.

The practical value of the MinAvg operator stems mostly from the fact that a degree of compensation can be expressed and that at the same time the MinAvg operator is much faster to compute compared to the Gamma operator. Hence, for applications that need to crunch massive amounts of data in short time periods, the MinAvg operator provides an interesting alternative.

Note: the operator plot visualizes the operator transfer curve as you parameterize it. Simply select an Operator family and drag the scroll bar.

Many more fuzzy logic operators have been proposed in the literature and their mathematical implications have been widely studied. Refer to [51] for details.

Determining the Degree of Compensation

The issue yet to be discussed here is, how does one determine the appropriate degree of compensation when using the Gamma operator. Humans determine the degree of compensation intuitively from context, and there is no direct method of extraction. While there are many ways to determine the degree of compensation through empirical analysis [49], a simple approach that has worked quite well in many real-world projects is presented below.

Determination of the Degree of Compensation

Step 1:
To determine the degree of compensation, γ, for the "If-part" of the rule "IF LV1 = term1 AND LV2 = term2," first determine for each linguistic variable the base variable value corresponding to the following membership degrees: {0.2, 0.25, ..., 0.8}.

Step 2:
Compute the results of the Gamma aggregation for all combinations of the base variable values from Step 1. Start with $\gamma = 0.1$, then repeat for $\gamma \in$ {0.15, 0.2, ... 0.4}.

Step 3:
For all γ values from Step 2, find the pairs of base variable values that deliver a result from the Gamma aggregation in the interval: (0.45; 0.55). This results in a set of base value pairs for each γ considered.

Step 4:
Select the one list where the base variable pairs inserted in the "If-part" of a rule best match the rule equally. The γ of the selected list is the one that should be chosen as the degree of compensation.

In Steps 1 and 2 you create an equally distributed set of possible input variable combinations. Because values that have a membership degree close to zero and one are harder to interpret, you restrict this to the membership degree interval [0.2; 0.8]. You may lower the interval to increase the resolution of the approach. In Step 3, you filter the base variable pairs located near the value $\mu = 0.5$. By determining the set in which the base variable pairs are considered most equal, you find the best value for γ.

Using this approach for each rule in a fuzzy logic system is tedious. However, experience has shown that there are some shortcuts to this approach:

- Rules that have the same input and output variables usually have the same degree of compensation. Thus, you only need to determine the appropriate γ once for each rule block.

- In most practical implementations, the value of γ lies between 0.1 and 0.4.

- A simplified approach to determine the value of γ is to first set γ = 0.25 as the default. Then, if you find the degree of compensation inappropriate during the debugging process, start to increase/decrease the value by intervals of 0.05.

6.3.2 Result Aggregation

In order to change the result aggregation, click on the [THEN] button in the Spreadsheet Rule Editor. *fuzzy*TECH supports two methods for result aggregation, the maximum method and the BSUM method. If more than one rule has the same result, the first method takes the maximum of the two as the final result, the second one takes the bounded sum. **Note:** BSUM result aggregation is different from BSUM MoM and BSUM CoA. The boundaries are zero and one. This section illustrates the difference between the two methods using the CREDIT3 case study.

Comparison of MAX and BSUM Result Aggregation

To follow the example developed in this section, you have to start *fuzzy*TECH and open the file CRANE3.FTL, which is located in the \SAMPLES\BUSINESS\CREDIT\ subdirectory. Enable Interactive debugging mode, open the Debug:Interactive window, open Linguistic Variable editors for all three variables, and open the Spreadsheet Rule Editor for the rule block. Minimize the Project Editor and the Variables window. Set the input variables Continuity and Inc_Exp to 0.55 and 155000 in the Debug:Interactive window. These input variables result in a Liquidity assessment of 0.78 as shown in Figure 230, and the rules fire as shown in Figure 231.

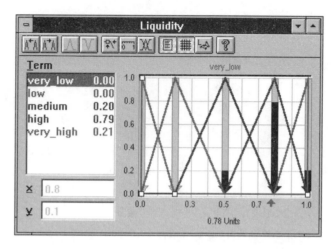

Figure 230: Defuzzification of the rule inference results in Liquidity = 0.78.

For this combination of input variables, the four rules #3, #5, #6, and #7 fire. However, only three terms of the output variable Liquidity have non-zero truth degrees, that is:

Liquidity = {very_low = 0.0, low = 0.0, medium = 0.2, high = 0.79, very_high = 0.21}

While only rule #3 fires for the output term "medium" and only rule #7 fires for the term "very_high," two rules, #5 and #6, fire for the term "high." Thus, the results of both need to be aggregated into a single result before defuzzification can take place.

This aggregation is called the "Result Aggregation." Two different mathematical models of the Result Aggregation have been used in practical applications: the Maximum operation (MAX) and the Bounded Sum (BSUM). The use of the Maximum operation stems from the consideration that in a fuzzy logic system, all rules are formulated alternately: either rule *A* is true, OR rule *B* is true, OR rule *C* is true, OR.... In fuzzy logic, the logical OR is often represented as the Maximum (cf. Section 1.3.2). This is why most applications use the MAX for Result Aggregation. In the example involving CREDIT3, in which Rule #5 asserts that Liquidity is high with a firing degree of 0.2 and Rule #6 asserts that Liquidity is high with a firing degree of 0.79, the result of Rule #5 is completely masked by the result of Rule #6. This is the same effect as discussed for Premise Aggregation in Section 6.3.1.

Matrix	IF		THEN	
Utilities	Continuity	Inc_Exp	DoS	Liquidity
1		low	☐1.00☐	very_low
2	low	medium	☐1.00☐	low
3	medium	medium	☐1.00☐	medium
4	low	high	☐1.00☐	medium
5	high	medium	☐1.00☐	high
6	medium	high	■1.00■	high
7	high	high	☐1.00☐	very_high
8				

Figure 231: Rule firing display for the example.

"Winner Takes All"

In a way, using the MAX operator for Result Aggregation is like saying "the winner takes it all": only the strongest rule makes it to defuzzification. If, for example, one rule asserts that Liquidity is low with a firing degree of 0.5 and then 20 other rules assert that Liquidity shall be high with a firing degree of 0.5, then low and high would both be valid to the same degree in the defuzzification step. This type of aggregation is what is necessary in most applications. The fact that many rules indicate a certain result only indicates that many rules have been formulated for this context. And the fact that many rules indicate a certain result does not mean that the result is more true.

"One Man, One Vote"

However, in some applications it can be useful if not just the highest firing degree for a certain term of an output variable is considered, but rather all firing degrees of all rules which fire for the term. For these types of applications, you can use the Bounded Sum operator because all firing degrees are summed up before the defuzzification in this operation. For example, open the Project Editor window and double-click on the MAX box at the bottom right of the rule block box. This opens the Result Aggregation dialog box as shown in Figure 232.

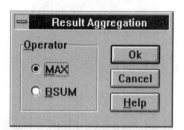

Figure 232: Result Aggregation dialog box.

Select BSUM in this dialog box and then click the [OK] button. Now, the results of Rule #5 and Rule #6 are added before defuzzification. The term "high" of Liquidity now is valid to the degree 0.99 (Figure). If the sum of the rule firing degrees for a term exceeds 1, it is bounded at 1. Thus, this term is considered to be totally true.

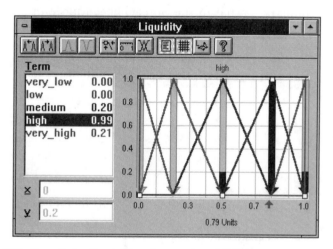

Figure 233: Result for liquidity when using BSUM result aggregation.

Here is where you need to be careful when using the BSUM method. For example, four rules that each result in the same output variable term with a firing degree of 0.25 will make this term 100% true. **Note:** even though no single rule was 100% appropriate for the input variable value combination, the output term is considered 100% true.

For more details on aggregation and result aggregation methods, refer to [22] or [41].

6.3.3 Matrix Rule Representation

The Matrix Rule Editor can be used as an alternative to the Spreadsheet Rule Editor. For large rule bases and rule bases that involve many input variables, experienced fuzzy logic designers prefer to use the Matrix Rule Editor rather than the Spreadsheet Rule Editor. To follow the example in this section, open the file CREDIT5.FTL located in the \SAMPLES\BUSINESS\CREDIT\ subdirectory.

Matrix Rule Editor

In order to activate the Matrix Rule Editor, either click the [Matrix] button in the Spreadsheet Rule Editor or open the properties menu of the rule block by clicking right on the rule block. Figure 234 shows the window of the Matrix Rule Editor. This editor is only available for rule blocks that do not contain rules with "don't care" conditions.

The lower part of the window has a list box for each input and output variable of the rule block. Each list box shows all the terms that are defined for the respective variable. By highlighting a term in each list box, a single rule is addressed. The weight of this rule is shown by the scroll bar and the edit field in the group "Degree-of-Support." Rules that are not defined are identical to zero-weighted rules in the Matrix Rule Editor. To add a rule in the Matrix Editor, address the rule by highlighting the respective terms in the list boxes and set the DoS to a non-zero value. To erase a rule in the Matrix Editor, address it and set its DoS to zero.

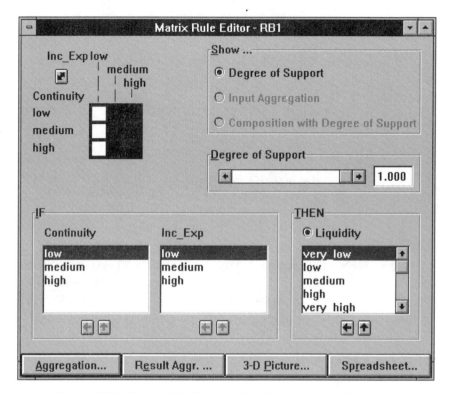

Figure 234: The Matrix Rule Editor shows a slice through
the multi-dimensional rule space as a matrix.

To visualize the rule base, you may select two of the variables for the matrix display in the upper left part of the window. Use the two arrow buttons underneath each list box to select variables for the matrix. The arrow buttons of the two variables currently displayed in the matrix are disabled. Use the left arrow button to select the variable as the vertical matrix variable and use the up arrow button to select the variable as the horizontal matrix variable. To flip the two variables displayed in the matrix, use the double-arrow button in the upper left corner.

Browsing the Matrix

Next, highlight different terms in the list box "Liquidity." For each of the terms selected, the matrix shows which input variable combinations yield the selected output term. In the matrix, rules with a DoS of

1 are shown as white squares and rules with a DoS of 0 as well as non-existing rules as black squares. Rules with a DoS between 0 and 1 are shown with respective shades of gray. The matrix field that corresponds to the addressed rule is identified by a red outline. You may also address rules by clicking their respective matrix field. To toggle the DoS of a rule between 0 and 1, you may double-click the respective matrix field. This is faster than using the scroll bar.

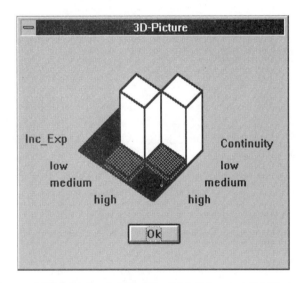

Figure 235: Display of the DoS Matrix as a 3D Picture.

You may also visualize the DoS matrix three-dimensionally. Highlight the term "medium" in the "Liquidity" list box and click the [3-D Picture] button to display the DoS matrix for the current selection, as shown in Figure 235.

The group "Show…" lets you select what the matrix should display in any debug mode. The options are:

- Degree of Support, which shows the weight of the rules,

- Input Aggregation, which shows to what degree the condition for the rules is true, and

- Composition with Degree of Support, which shows to what degree the output of the rule fires.

The button [Spreadsheet] lets you go back to the Spreadsheet Rule Editor. Next, close the Matrix Rule Editor by double-clicking on the system icon.

If you have more than one rule block in your project, you may simultaneously open any type of rule block editor for each block. To differentiate between different rule block editors, the name of the rule block is shown in the title bar.

6.4   Defuzzification Methods

The defuzzification step translates a linguistic result from the rule inference back into a numerical value. Most fuzzy logic systems require this step because the desired output value often needs to be numerical rather than linguistic. Section 1.3.3 introduced the "Center-of-Maximum" defuzzification method that is used in most practical fuzzy logic applications. However, other defuzzification methods deliver more accurate results for some applications. This section presents some of these defuzzification methods and discusses their differences.

6.4.1 Best Compromise vs. Most Plausible Result

The objective of a defuzzification method is to derive a non-fuzzy (crisp) value, which best represents the fuzzy value of the linguistic output variable. Similar to the different membership function types, different methods for defuzzification exist. To select the proper defuzzification method, you need to understand the linguistic meaning that underlies the defuzzification process. Experience shows that two different linguistic meanings of defuzzification are of practical importance:

- Determine the "best compromise."

- Determine the "most plausible result."

One defuzzification method is the Center-of-Maximum (CoM) method already described in Section 1.3.3. CoM first determines the most typical value for each term and then computes the best compromise of the fuzzy logic inference result.

Car Steering Example

To illustrate the differences between the different defuzzification methods, let's use the example of steering a car. The output variable of this car is the steering angle as defined in Example 6.

Example 6:

Let the most typical values for Steering be:

strong_right	-30°
right	-15°
straight	0°
left	15°
strong_left	30°

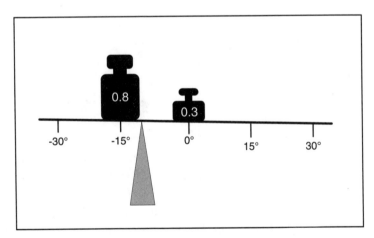

Figure 236: The Center-of-Maximum defuzzification method balances out the fuzzy logic inference result.

Let the fuzzy logic inference result for a certain situation be: {0, 0, 0.3, 0.8, 0}. To obtain the best compromise value for the result of the fuzzy logic inference (right with 0.8, straight with 0.3) as a real number, the inference results are considered "weights" at the positions of the most typical values of the terms. The best compromise is where the defuzzified (crisp) value balances the weights. In Figure 236 the value (result of defuzzification) is –12°. This result is a compromise between the two rule firings.

In some cases, this defuzzification approach does not work. Consider the example shown in Figure 237. The straight direction is blocked, while the paths to the right and left are open.

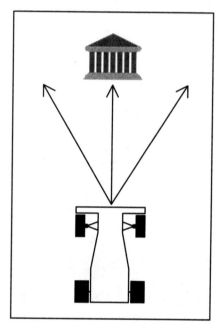

Figure 237: Drive situation in which the pathway is blocked straight ahead, but open to the left and right.

In such a situation, the result of the fuzzy logic inference is that no evidence exists suggesting that the car should go straight, while equal amounts of non-zero evidence call for both a right and a left turn. Figure 238 shows this result. If you would use the Center-of-Maximum method for defuzzification, the "best compromise" is to go straight. Why does the defuzzification fail so drastically here? To find out why, consider Example 7, which demonstrates how humans handle such decisions.

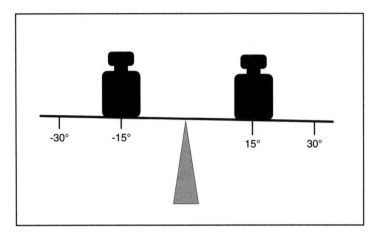

Figure 238: Possible inference result for the situation in Figure 237.

Example 7:

You are driving a car with your spouse and your mother-in-law. You do not know the neighborhood, and both your spouse and your mother-in-law give you directions. Suddenly the road on which you are driving is comes to a T.

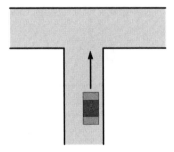

What if your spouse says you should turn right while your mother-in-law wants you to turn left? The compromise, to go straight, is not a good solution here.

Here, the best compromise as illustrated in Figure 238 is clearly not the method of choice. In Example 7 you want the "most plausible result." One defuzzification method that delivers the "most plausible result" is the "Mean-of-Maximum" method (MoM). Rather than balancing out the different inference results, MoM selects the typical value of the term that is most valid. For the situation shown in Figures 237 and 238, the defuzzification result would only be either -15° or +15°, whichever term is more valid.

Center-of-Area Defuzzification Method

The first applications of fuzzy logic used the so-called Center-of-Area (CoA) method, sometimes called Center-of-Gravity. This method first cuts the membership function at the degree of validity of the respective term. The areas under the resulting functions of all terms are then superimposed. Balancing the resulting area gives the compromising value. For the example shown in Figure 27, Figure 239 shows the defuzzification of the same result using Center-of-Area defuzzification. Note how the results differ.

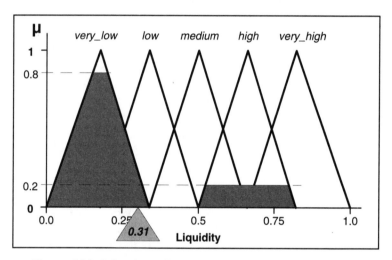

Figure 239: "Center-of-Area" defuzzification method.

There are some implausible conditions possible in the Center-of-Area method. Consider the linguistic variable defined in Figure 240a. If an inference result of $\mu_{LN} = \mu_Z = 1$ should be defuzzified as shown in Figure 240b, the term LN has a much greater impact than the term Z due to the larger area under the membership function of the term LN. However, the only reason the area under LN is larger is that the best-fit values of the neighboring terms are further apart than those for Z.

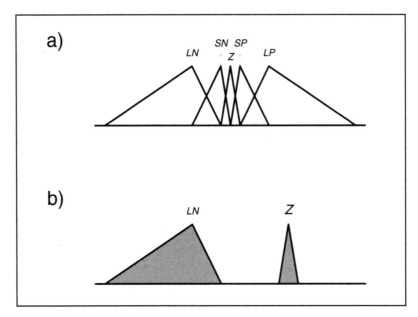

Figure 240: Implausibilities with Center-of-Area defuzzification. With a linguistic variable defined as in a), the term LN would have a much greater impact in a defuzzification than term Z.

Another disadvantage of the Center-of-Area defuzzification method is its high computational effort. The center of area is computed by numerical integration that can take up to 1000 times longer than the computation of the center of maximum, depending on the resolution and type of processor. For these reasons, most software development tools and fuzzy logic processors use an approximation of CoA, the so-called fast-CoA. Fast-CoA computes the individual areas under the membership functions during compilation to avoid numerical integration during runtime. This approach neglects the overlapping of the areas; hence, it is only an approximation of the "real" CoA.

There are also variants of the Mean-of-Maximum defuzzification method. They differ from MoM by the computation of the most typical value of a membership function. For Λ-type membership functions, the most typical value is uniquely defined. For Π-type membership functions, variants are possible (Figure 241). They have gained very little practical relevance because one can achieve the same result by shifting the membership function.

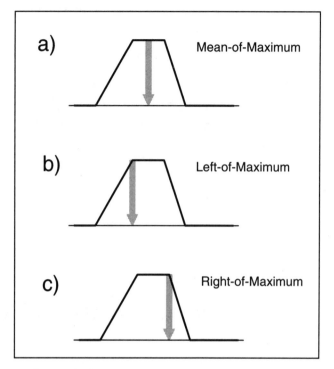

Figure 241: Variants of MoM: LoM and RoM.

6.4.2 Comparison of Defuzzification Methods

An important property of defuzzification methods is continuity. The definition of continuity is as follows:

Consider a fuzzy logic system with a complete set of rules (for each combination of input variables, at least one rule fires) and overlapping membership functions. A defuzzification method is continuous if an infinitesimally small change of an input variable can never cause an abrupt change in any output variable.

CoM and CoA/CoG methods are continuous, while MoM/LoM/RoM are discontinuous. This is due to the fact that the "best compromise" can never jump to a different value because of a small change in the inputs. On the other hand, there is always a point at which the "most plausible solution" jumps to a different value. In the example shown in Figures 237 and 238 this means there will be a point at which an infinitesimally small change in the inputs will cause the decision to abruptly shift to the other value.

Table 16 compares the three defuzzification methods presented: CoA/CoG, CoM, and MoM.

	Center-of-Area (CoA, CoG)	Center-of-Maximum (CoM)	Mean-of-Maximum (MoM)
Linguistic Characteristic	"Best Compromise"	"Best Compromise"	"Most Plausible Solution"
Fit with Intuition	Implausible with varying MBF shapes and strong overlap of MBFs	Good	Good
Continuity	Yes	Yes	No
Computational Efficiency	Very Low	High	Very High
Applications	Control, Decision Support, Data Analysis	Control, Decision Support, Data Analysis	Pattern Recognition, Decision Support, Data Analysis

Table 16: Comparison of different defuzzification methods.

Which Defuzzification for What Application?

In decision support systems, the choice of defuzzification method depends on the context of the decision. Use CoM for quantitative decisions, such as budget allocation, credit worthiness evaluation, or project prioritization. Use MoM for qualitative decisions, such as credit card fraud detection or customer segmentation.

Pattern recognition applications mostly use MoM defuzzification. If you want to identify objects by classification of a sensor signal, you are interested in the most plausible result. Some applications do not even use any defuzzification at all. The vector of membership degrees for the output linguistic variable is the result of the classification as it defines the similarity of the signal to the objects.

6.4.3 Information Reduction by Defuzzification

Mathematically, defuzzification is the mapping of a vector (the value of the linguistic variable) to a real number (crisp value). This mapping is not unique, that is, different values of a linguistic variable can map to the same defuzzified crisp value (Example 8). In cases #1 through #3 below, the result of the defuzzification is the same even though they are drawn from different linguistic values.

Example 8

Let OUT be a linguistic variable with the terms {LN; SN; Z; SP; LP}. Consider the following three values of OUT:

#1:   { 0; 0; 0.7; 0; 0}

#2:   { 0; 0.3; 0; 0.3; 0}

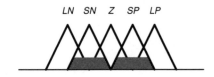

#3:   { 0.8; 0; 0; 0; 0.8}

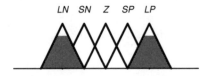

All three values of the linguistic variable would be defuzzified to the same crisp value by CoA/CoM defuzzification methods.

Example 8 shows that the defuzzification step involves a reduction of information. Although the "best compromise" is the same for all three linguistic variable values, the three cases are in fact not the same. In case #1 the best compromise was very clear, while case #3 was much more in conflict.

For most technical fuzzy logic applications, this is no problem and information about the unequivocal nature of the defuzzified result is not useful. In decision support applications, this is different. Here, advanced defuzzification methods exist, especially to rank membership functions [27, 50].

Practical Experience with Defuzzification Methods

- In practical applications, the only difference between defuzzification methods is whether they deliver the best compromise (CoM, CoA, CoG) or the most plausible result (MoM, LoM, RoM).

- Within these groups, no relevant differences exist that cannot be equalized by modifying membership functions or rules.

- Complex membership function shapes do not deliver better results for output variables. Use only Λ-type membership functions. CoM and MoM defuzzification methods only use the maximum of the membership functions anyway.

- The widespread use of CoA/CoG defuzzification has historical reasons. Depending on overlap and area under the membership functions, CoA/CoG can deliver implausible results. Use CoM instead.

- Some applications use CoA defuzzification with singleton membership functions. This is exactly the same as CoM defuzzification with any other membership function type.

- Fast-CoA, which is used in most software tools and fuzzy logic processors, is equal to a weighted CoM defuzzification.

Bibliography

[1]   Aihara, K., "Philosophic Aspects of Uncertainty—Deterministic Dynamics and Predictability in Chaotic Systems", Joint Japanese-European Symposium on Fuzzy Systems in Berlin, Publications of the Japanese-German Center Berlin, Volume 8 (1994), ISSN 0937-3799.

[2]   Anderson, J.A. and Rosenfeld, E. (Eds.), *Neurocomputing*, Boston/London (1988).

[3]   Bezdek, J. C., Tsao, E. C.-K., and Pal, N. R., "Fuzzy Kohonen Clustering Networks," FUZZ-IEEE Conference (1992), p. 1035-1043.

[4]   Capon, N., "Credit Scoring Systems: A Critical Analysis," *Journal of Marketing*, Vol. 46 (1982), p. 82–91.

[5]   Dhar, V. and Stein, R., "Raising Organizational IQ: Strategies for Knowledge Intensive Decision Support," Prentice Hall (1996).

[6]   Ehlers, F., "The Bandpass Indicator," Technical analysis of stocks & commodities, 9/94, (1994).

[7]   Feldman, K., "Intelligent Systems in Finance," *Applied Mathematical Finance* (1994), Vol. 1(1), p. 195–207.

[8]   Güllich, H.-P., "Fuzzy Logic Decision Support System for Credit Risk Evaluation," EUFIT Fourth European Congress on Intelligent Techniques and Soft Computing (1996), p. 2219-2223.

[9]   Hebb, D., *The Organization of Behavior*, New York (1947).

[10] Hecht-Nielsen, R., *Neurocomputing*, Boston (1989).

[11] Hintz, G.W. and Zimmermann, H.-J., "A Method to Control Flexible Manufacturing Systems," *European Journal of Operations Research* (1989), p. 321–334.

[12] Houlder, V., "New Tools for Routine Jobs," *Financial Times*, September 29 (1994), p. 16.

[13] Houlder, V., "Tackling Insider Dealing with Fuzzy Logic," *Financial Times*, September 29 (1994), p. 16.

[14] Kosko, B., *Neural Networks and Fuzzy Systems*, Englewood Cliffs, NJ: Prentice Hall (1992).

[15] Lippmann, R.P., "An Introduction to Computing with Neural Nets," *IEEE ASSP Magazine* 4 (1987), p. 4–22.

[16] Mamdani, E.H., "Twenty Years of Fuzzy Control: Experiences Gained and Lessons Learnt", *Second IEEE International Conference on Fuzzy Systems* (1993), ISBN 0-7803-0615-5, p. 339–344.

[17] Müller-Kirschbaum, Th. *et al.*, "Using Fuzzy Logic in Cosmetics Design," *Fifth fuzzyTECH User's Conference* (1995), p. 43–47.

[18] McNeill, D. and Freiberger, P., *Fuzzy Logic*, New York: Simon & Schuster (1993), ISBN 0-671-73843-7.

[19] ———, "CreditExpert—ASK," INFORM GmbH Aachen and Inform Software Corporation Chicago (1986).

[20] ———, *FELIS User Manual,* INFORM GmbH Aachen and Inform Software Corporation Chicago (1989).

[21] ———, "Invent /W and Invent /R," Brochure, INFORM GmbH Aachen and Inform Software Corporation Chicago (1994).

[22] ———, *fuzzyTECH for Business Reference Manual*, INFORM GmbH Aachen and Inform Software Corporation Chicago (1996).

[23] Rummelhart, D.E., Hinton, G.E., and Williams, R.J., "Learning Representations by Back-Propagating Errors," *Nature* 323 (1986) p. 533–536.

[24] Schwartz, Th., "Fuzzy Systems Come to Life in Japan," *IEEE Expert*, Vol. 5(1), p. 77–78.

[25] Stumpf, H. and Lux, F.H., "Extraction of Subjective Assessments of Tires for Handling, Comfort, and Noise Based on Laboratory Tests by Use of Fuzzy Logic," *Proceedings of the ISATA 26th International Symposium on Automotive Technology and Automation* (1993), p. 415–424.

[26] Sugeno, M., "Philosophic Aspects of Uncertainty—Categories of Uncertainty and Their Modalities," Japanese-European Symposium on Fuzzy Systems (1992).

[27]   Tong, R.M. and Bonissone, P.P., "Linguistic Solutions to Fuzzy Decision Problems," in Zimmermann, H.-J., Zadeh, L.A., and Gaines, B.R. (Eds.), *Fuzzy Sets and Decision Analysis*, Amsterdam (1984), p. 323–334.

[28]   Wassermann, P.D., *Neuro Computing: Theory and Practice*, New York (1989).

[29]   von Altrock, C., "A Fuzzy Set Decision Model as Optimization Criterion," EURO—European Conference on Operations Research, Aachen (1991).

[30]   von Altrock, C., Krause, B., and Zimmermann, H.-J. "Advanced Fuzzy Logic Control of a Model Car in Extreme Situations," *Fuzzy Sets and Systems*, Vol. 48, 1 (1992), p. 41–52.

[31]   von Altrock, C. and Krause, B., "On-Line-Development Tools for Fuzzy Knowledge-Base Systems of Higher Order," *2nd International Conference on Fuzzy Logic and Neural Networks Proceedings*, Iizuka, Japan (1992). ISBN 4-938717-01-8.

[32]   von Altrock, C., Krause, B. and Zimmermann, H.-J., "Advanced Fuzzy Logic Control Technologies in Automotive Applications," *IEEE Conference on Fuzzy Systems* (1992). ISBN 0-7803-0237-0, p. 831–842.

[33]   von Altrock, C. and D'Souza, S., "Fuzzy Logic and NeuroFuzzy Technologies in Appliances," *Proceedings of the Embedded Systems Conference* (1994), Vol. 2. ISBN 0-87930-356-5, p. 423–444.

[34]   von Altrock, C., Franke, S., and Froese, Th., "Optimization of a Water-Treatment System with Fuzzy Logic Control," Computer Design Fuzzy Logic '94 Conference in San Diego (1994).

[35]   von Altrock, C., "NeuroFuzzy Technologies," *Computer Design Magazine* 6/94 (1994), p. 82–83.

[36]   von Altrock, C., Krause, B., Limper, K., and Schäfers, W., "Optimization of a Waste Incineration Plant Using Fuzzy Logic," EUFIT '94 Conference in Aachen (1994).

[37]   von Altrock, C., Arend, H.-O., Krause, B., Steffens, C., and Behrens-Rommler, E., "Customer-Adaptive Fuzzy Control of Home Heating System," IEEE Conference on Fuzzy Systems in Orlando (1994).

[38] von Altrock, C., "Enhanced Fuzzy Systems Using Data Analysis Techniques and Neural Networks," Computer Design Fuzzy Logic Conference, San Diego (1994).

[39] von Altrock, C. and Krause, B., "Multi-Criteria Decision Making in German Automotive Industry Using Fuzzy Logic," *Fuzzy Sets and Systems* 63 (1994), p. 375–380.

[40] von Altrock, C., "Fuzzy Logic Applications in Europe," in Yen, Langari, and Zadeh (Eds.), *Industrial Applications of Fuzzy Logic and Intelligent Systems*, Piscataway, NJ: IEEE Press (1995).

[41] von Altrock, C., *Fuzzy Logic and NeuroFuzzy Applications Explained*, Upper Saddle River, NJ: Prentice Hall (1995). ISBN 0-13-368465-2.

[42] Wilder, W., *New Concepts in Technical Trading Systems*, Greensboro, NC: Trend Research, 1978.

[43] Yager, R., "Implementing Fuzzy Logic Controllers Using a Neural Network Framework," *Fuzzy Sets and Systems* 48 (1992), p. 53–64.

[44] Yuize, H. *et al.*, "Decision Support System for Foreign Exchange Trading," International Fuzzy Engineering Symposium (1991), p. 971–982.

[45] Zadeh, L. A., "Fuzzy Sets," *Information and Control*, Vol. 8 (1965), p. 338–353.

[46] Zadeh, L.A., "Outline of a New Approach to the Analysis of Complex Systems and Decision Processes," *IEEE Trans. Systems Man Cybernet.*, Vol. 3, Num. 1 (1973), p. 8–44.

[47] Zimmermann, H.-J. and Thole, U., "On the Suitability of Minimum and Product Operators for the Intersection of Fuzzy Sets," *Fuzzy Sets and Systems*, Vol. 2, p. 173–186.

[48] Zimmermann, H.-J. and Zysno, P., "Latent Connectives in Human Decision Making," *Fuzzy Sets and Systems*, Vol. 4 (1980), p. 37–51.

[49] Zimmermann, H.-J. and Zysno, "Decision Analysis and Evaluations by Hierarchical Aggregation of Information," *Fuzzy Sets and Systems*, Vol. 10 (1983), p. 243–266.

[50]   Zimmermann, H.-J., *Fuzzy Sets, Decision Making, and Expert Systems,* Boston: Kluver Academic Publisher (1987). ISBN 0-89838-149-5.

[51]   Zimmermann, H.-J., *Fuzzy Set Theory—and Its Applications,* Second Revised Edition, Boston: Kluver Academic Publisher (1991). ISBN 0-7923-9075-X.

[52]   Zimmermann, H.-J. and von Altrock, C. (Eds.), *Fuzzy Logic— Band 2: Die Anwendungen,* Munich: Oldenbourg (1993). ISBN 3-486-22677-0.

Index

MINIMUM TERMS OF END USER LICENSES

NOTICE TO END USER: CAREFULLY READ THE FOLLOWING LEGAL AGREEMENT. USE OF THE SOFTWARE PROVIDED WITH THIS AGREEMENT (THE "SOFTWARE") CONSTITUTES YOUR ACCEPTANCE OF THESE TERMS.

1. *License Grant.*   PH grants to you (either as an individual or entity) a personal, non-transferable, and non-exclusive right to use the copy of the object code version of the SOFTWARE provided with this license. The term of this agreement will be for the duration of the owner's copyright in the SOFTWARE. You agree you will not copy the SOFT-WARE except as necessary to use it on a single computer system. You agree that you may not copy the written materials accompanying the SOFTWARE. If you transfer the single computer system, you may assign your rights under this Agreement to a third party who agrees to be bound by this Agreement prior to the assignment and provided that you transfer all copies of the SOFTWARE and related documentation to the third party or destroy any copies not transferred. Except as set forth above, you may not assign your rights under this Agreement.

2. *Copyright.*   You acknowledge that no title to the intellectual property in the SOFTWARE is transferred to you. You further acknowledge that title and full ownership rights to the SOFTWARE will remain the exclusive property of PH or its suppliers, and you will not acquire any rights to the SOFTWARE except as expressly set forth above. You agree that any copies of the SOFTWARE will contain the same proprietary notices which appear on and in the SOFTWARE.

3. *Reverse Engineering.*   You agree that you will not attempt, and if you are a corporation, you will use your best efforts to prevent your employees and contractors from attempting, to reverse compile, modify, translate, or disassemble the SOFTWARE in whole or in part.

4. *No Warranty.*   You acknowledge that the SOFTWARE provided to you under this agreement is demonstration software provided on an "AS IS" basis. PH DISCLAIMS ANY AND ALL EXPRESS OR IMPLIED WARRANTIES TO THE EXTENT PERMITTED BY LAW AND SPECIFICALLY DISCLAIMS THE WARRANTIES OF NON-INFRINGE-MENT OF THIRD PARTY RIGHTS, MERCHANTABILITY AND FITNESS FOR A PARTICULAR PURPOSE. IF SUCH DISCLAIMER IS NOT PERMITTED BY LAW, THE DURATION OF ANY SUCH IMPLIED WARRANTIES IS LIMITED TO 90 DAYS FROM THE DATE OF DELIVERY. SOME JURISDICTIONS DO NOT ALLOW THE EXCLU-SION OF IMPLIED WARRANTIES OR LIMITATIONS ON HOW LONG AN IMPLIED WARRANTY MAY LAST, OR THE EXCLUSION OR LIMITATION OF INCIDENTAL OR CONSEQUENTIAL DAMAGES, SO SUCH LIMITATIONS OR EXCLUSIONS MAY NOT APPLY TO YOU. THIS WARRANTY GIVES YOU SPECIFIC LEGAL RIGHTS AND YOU MAY ALSO HAVE OTHER RIGHTS WHICH VARY FROM JURISDICTION TO JURISDICTION. This limitation shall apply notwithstanding any failure of essential purpose of any limited remedy.

5. *Severability.*   Invalidity of any provisions of this Agreement shall not affect the validation of the remaining provi-sions of this Agreement.

6. *No Liability for Consequential Damages.*   IN NO EVENT SHALL PH BE LIABLE FOR ANY LOSS OF USE, INTERRUPTION OF BUSINESS, OR INDIRECT, SPECIAL, INCIDENTAL OR CONSEQUENTIAL DAMAGES OF ANY KIND (INCLUDING LOST PROFITS) ARISING OUT OF THE USE OF THE SOFTWARE REGARDLESS OF THE FORM OF ACTION, WHETHER IN CONTRACT, TORT (INCLUDING NEGLIGENCE), STRTICT PRODUCT LIABILITY OR OTHERWISE, EVEN IF PH HAS BEEN ADVISED OF THE POSSIBILITY OF SUCH DAMAGES. IN NO EVENT WILL PH'S AGGREGATE LIABILITY FOR ANY CLAIM, EXCEED THE LICENSE FEE PAID BY YOU.

7. *Export.*   You acknowledge that the laws and regulations of the United States may restrict the export and re-export of certain commodities and technical data of United States origin, including the SOFTWARE. You agree that you will not export or re-export the SOFTWARE without the appropriate United States or foreign government licenses.

8. *Governing Law.*   This Agreement will be governed by the laws of the State of New York. The United Nations Convention on Contracts for the International Sale of Goods (1980) is specifically excluded from application to this Agree-ment.

9. *Entire Agreement.*   This Agreement represents the entire agreement between you and PH relating to its subject matter and supersedes all prior representations, discussions, negotiations and agreements, whether written or oral, relating to the subject matter of this Agreement. This Agreement may be amended or supplemented only by a writing that refers explic-itly to this Agreement.

10. *Information.*   If you have any questions regarding performance of the SOFTWARE and/or the availability of full-featured versions of the SOFTWARE, you should contact the SOFTWARE owner at the following addresses:

USA/Canada: Inform Software Corporation, 2001 Midwest Rd., Oak Brook, IL 60521, USA
Phone: 630-268-7550
Sales: 1–800–929–2815, Fax: 630-268-7554, fuzzy@informusa.com

Japan: TOYO/Inform, 26-9, Yushima 3-chome, Bukyo-ku, Tokyo 113, JAPAN
Phone: 03-5688-6800, Fax: 03–5688–6900.

Europe and elsewhere: INFORM GmbH, Pascalstrasse 23, D–52076 Aachen, GERMANY
Phone: +49–240–894–5680, Fax: +49–240–894–5685, hotline@inform-ac.com

If the media containing the SOFTWARE is defective or damaged, PH will replace the damaged or defective CD-ROM or refund the money, or if you desire to contact PH for any reason, please write to Robin Short, Prentice Hall PTR, One Lake Street, Upper Saddle River, New Jersey 07458.

PLEASE NOTE:

During the installation process of *fuzzy*TECH for Business you will be prompted for the installation code. The code is
123456